CHAUTAUQUA MOVEMENT.

BY

JOHN H. VINCENT.

WITH AN INTRODUCTION

BY

PRESIDENT LEWIS MILLER.

BOSTON:

CHAUTAUQUA PRESS,

117 FRANKLIN STREET.

1886.

PREFACE.

THIS book has been prepared in the midst of arduous official labors, and nothing but the writer's interest in the cause it represents could have induced him to attempt the task now completed

The author has of necessity made use of some material already published in "The Chautauquan," and presented in lectures and addresses in all parts of the country To such reproductions much new matter has been added; and it is hoped that the book will give to many persons who know little or nothing about Chautauqua, and to those who may have been prejudiced against it, the true view of its aims and plans, and thus secure to the cause new and firm friends, and increase its power for good.

It is the author's purpose (or at least his hope), at some future time to publish a volume of "Chautauqua Memorials," with detailed programmes of what was done at every Assembly, and with the memoranda of things proposed from time to time, never yet accomplished. Such a compilation will make a souvenir for Chautauquans.

Concerning the author's personal relations to the beginning and to the development of the Chautauqua enterprise, he has said but little in this volume content and grateful to have been permitted, by a gracious Providence, to engage in the good cause with the worthy workers who have helped to found and to build it up. Some kind words on this subject by Mr. Miller, in his Introduction, the author has taken the liberty to suppress.

The book is now committed to the "hosts of Chautauqua" and to "the outside world," in the humble hope that it may help to advance the noble cause which aims to lift and broaden and in manifold ways to bless humanity.

J. H. VINCENT.

PLAINFIELD, N J., March 3, 1886.

TABLE OF CONTENTS.

INTRODUCTION.

By LEWIS MILLER, Esq.

CHAUTAUQUA was founded for an enlarged recognition of the Word. What more appropriate than to find some beautiful plateau of nature's own building for its rostrum, with the sky for its frescoed ceiling, the continents for its floor, the camp-meeting spirit of prayer and praise for its rostrum exercises, the church-school for thought and development? It was, at the start, made catholic as to creeds; not undenominational, but all-denominational, — a place where each denomination or organization, as at the great feasts, brings its best contribution which the particular order would develop as a consecrated offering for magnifying God's word and work; and, when gathered, each to bring its strongest light, and with the lights blending and the rays strengthened and focussed, with square and plumb, with compass and sun-dial, with telescope and microscope, with steam-engine and telegraph, with laboratory and blackboard, with hammer and spade, search out the deep and hidden mysteries of the Book.

The original intention was to make Chautauqua an international centre, — a place where the highest officials in all spheres of life should come to give the Book that recognition which would magnify it in the eyes of all the people, so that every citizen throughout the land should have a higher appreciation of the church and church-school in their midst. The visit of that greatest of generals and statesmen, U. S. Grant, while president of the United States, had a significance beyond a mere general and pleasure-seeking purpose. When the presentation of the Bible, by the chancellor of Chautauqua, was made, the true purpose became apparent. The acceptance of the Book by that great man, in silence, had the appearance of indifference in interest; but that great heart being too full of gratitude for utterance, silence became a higher tribute than words, and may it ever stand as a seal of humble and highest recognition.

It was the purpose that the scientist and statesman, the artisan and tradesman, should bring their latest and best to this altar of consecration and praise; that the tourist and pleasure-seeker should here stop and find their best place for reveries; when thus strengthened, to return to their respective fields, and there, through the year, weave into the fibre of the home-work the newly gathered inspiration and strength.

My past experience brings the conviction that the great want of humanity is recognition. The men of trade, factory, or field, need the association of the theorist and the professions; the theorist and the professions need contact with the arts and artisan. This thought has not in it equality of ability, equality of wealth, equality of social power, but equality of consideration, of privileges, and of rights. The One who gave us, and is, the model of our Christian religion, could dispute with the lawyers and doctors at twelve years of age, but went on strengthening until he was thirty, before associating himself with the fishermen of Galilee; and not until the second year of his ministry was the multitude gathered on the mount for the great inaugural for common humanity. The national spirit, as it gathers strength and greatness, should be, to come nearer and to care more for the common citizen.

As the arts multiply, and the facility for producing with rapidity increases, the wants for all become greater. There must come to the common citizen, if justice is done, more leisure, more pay, more knowledge, more pleasure. The beloved Garfield, in his short, well-timed speech at Chautauqua, said, " It has been the struggle of the world to get more leisure, but it was left for Chautauqua to show how to use it."

Not the least of Chautauqua's mission is to develop and make more practical the teaching of the Book as condensed in the great second commandment, " Love thy neighbor as thyself." All our schemes and steps of development must, if founded in a true spirit, have in them a common good for all. Three thoughts of the Bible are : Know the Lord ; Love the Lord ; Love thy neighbor as thyself. How pleasing now the thought, as the world is asked to take a survey of the foundations of Chautauqua, that the public platform and private tent were first consecrated by praise and adoration to God, that the first school for increased knowledge was the church school, and that the gathered people sat and ate at one common table ! May that spirit ever remain. This principle is fundamental in our Republic. The Declaration of Independence was an inspiration from a heart that saw clearly this need of human recognition. In this spirit the right of representation through the ballot is given to all our citizens. The right of the ballot brings with it the need of general intelligence . our national and public schools are already a model for the Old World. The church school must mould and guide the conscience and heart of the ever-rising generation, and keep guiding principles constantly impressed.

We are in the midst of great problems and struggles, — the right of the people to deal with the commonly accepted national questions, such as temperance, and sabbath observance, the rights of property, the rights of labor, the rights of trade, the rights of money, the rights of woman. These problems the present and near future must solve. Lovers of our common religion, lovers of our great Republic, lovers of common humanity, must make one common cause, must recognize the situation, and raise themselves up to the magnitude of the occasion, and carry all through to the brightness beyond.

Chautauqua must perform her part. The churchman, the statesman, the humanitarian, must be brought on her platform, and there, free from caste and party spirit, discuss questions, solve problems, and inaugurate measures that will mould and inspire for the right.

Those whose love and self-sacrificing efforts helped so much to make Chautauqua, are too numerous to receive special mention.

The Chautauqua Camp-meeting Managers gave the Assembly movement a most hearty welcome, and, when permanence was assured, deeded over their charter with its privileges and all their property to the Managers of the Sunday-school Assembly.

The Board of Trustees selected from the different States of the Union and Canada, and as far as possible from all the denominations, are men of wisdom and business integrity. They gather as often as called, and give their most hearty and full support to all its interests. It will be permitted to mention the names of FRANCIS H. ROOT of Buffalo, N.Y., and JACOB MILLER of Canton, O , who, beside giving their wise counsel through all the years, gave special financial support. The Secretaries in their order, as elected, cannot be passed over without special mention being made of them. Brother LESLIE, who was Secretary of the first Sunday-school Assembly, performed his work faithfully and well. He was one of the first to pass away, and make it necessary that another should take up the work where he left off. Dr. W. W WYTHE, then of Erie, Penn., succeeded Mr. Leslie. Many are the places of special interest that are the work of his hands, and not a few his contribution of original design. A. K. WARREN was Dr. Wythe's successor. He was a man of sterling integrity, was a good accountant, had most excellent taste, and a man of great ability.

Many of the finer buildings now on Chautauqua grounds are of his design. He served the Association faithfully to the time of his death. W. A. DUNCAN of Syracuse, N.Y., is Mr. Warren's successor, and is the present Secretary, and Superintendent of Grounds. He has always taken great interest in the Y. M. C. A. throughout the State of New York, and did much to build up throughout the State that institution. The finances under his management are in most excellent condition. The cottage-holders, as a body, have done their part by providing for bodily comforts, which did much to induce guests to return from year to year.

Much credit should be given to the editors and managers of the Chautauqua "Herald," and "Chautauquan," for their perseverance during days of trial and doubts. The final success of these papers is largely due the present editor and publisher, Dr. T. L. FLOOD, who gave up the pulpit to make these two publications his only work.

The thoughtful and entertaining exercises on the platform and in the hall brought the life and spirit which is felt in thousands of churches, circles, and homes.

AKRON, O., February, 1886.

THE CHAUTAUQUA MOVEMENT.

CHAPTER I.

THE IDEA.

" If a man write a book, let him set down only what he knows." — GOETHE.

THE task I have taken upon myself is to tell, in a simple way, the story of Chautauqua, — a story of to-day; without romantic, heroic, or tragic element; a story of the people, a story in which the scholars will be interested, because the scholars are a part of the people; a story in which the rich and the refined will be interested, — the rich who are truly refined, and the refined whether rich or poor, — because they believe in the brotherhood of the race and in its high destiny, and are proud to account themselves a part of it.

I shall make no effort to excite the pity of the wealthy and the learned for the poor and the illiterate, — class for class, upper for lower. Chautauqua is not one of the "associated charities," nor is it a department of "home missions." It comes alike to the door of want and of wealth, with proffered blessings for both, and is as likely to gain entrance at one door as at the other. It deals with matters which, by the order of an impartial Providence, belong to "all classes and conditions of men." The full-orbed "Chautauqua idea" must awaken in all genuine souls a fresh enthusiasm in true living, and bring rich and poor, learned and unlearned, into neighborship and comradeship, helpful and honorable to both.

Education, once the peculiar privilege of the few, must in our best earthly estate become the valued possession of the many. It is a natural and inalienable right of human souls. The gift of imagination, of memory, of reason, of invention, of constructive and executive power, carries with it both prerogative and obligation. No man dare with impunity surrender, as to himself, this endowment, nor deny to his neighbor the right and obligation which it involves. Given, intellectual potentiality; required, intellectual discipline and power. The law holds among leaders of thought, teachers and law-makers; among nobles and the favorites of fortune. It holds no less among the lowly, — the plebeians and the peasants of society.

Diversity in the direction of talent, and difference in degree, together with inequalities of social condition, may modify the demand upon the individual for culture and service; but the utter neglect of intellectual capacity is criminal, whether it be by menial or millionnaire. It involves a wrong to self, to the family, to the state: to self, since it leaves him blind whom God created to enjoy the light; to the family since it turns him into a physical or commercial machine whom God appointed to be companion and comforter; to the state, since it makes him a mere figure-head — whether of clay or gold — whom God intended to be a counsellor and helper, and to "have dominion" according to the measure of his power. No man has a right to neglect his personal education, whether he be prince or ploughboy, broker or hod-carrier. He needs knowledge, and the wisdom which makes knowledge available. Where the power lies, there rests responsibility for its use. Circumstances seem to favor the prince, and to be against the ploughboy; but, after all, the latter, overcoming adverse conditions, may acquire an education worth a great deal more to the world than that of the prince with his opportunities. Struggle against what men call fate brings power. One hour of study every day, with heroic purpose, may prove more valuable to the student than five hours a day of easy memorizing and reciting. The prince may complete his course in a few years, and, having "finished," graduate. The ploughboy, moving slowly, may require four times the number of years to cover the same ground; but that length of time may be an advantage to the humble student. It may require greater concentration when he does study; and the long hours of manual labor may be enriched by thought, and thus may knowledge gain a firmer hold, and its vitalizing power be increased.

Chautauqua has a work to do for college graduates. It enters protest against the suspension of intellectual effort when the compulsory *régime* of the recitation-room has been remitted, — a fault so common and so pernicious that college men themselves frequently bring into disrepute the college system. Intellectual activity must be continuous in order to promote intellectual health and efficiency. College life is the vestibule to a great temple. He who crosses its pavement, and reads the inscriptions on its doors, but goes no farther, might as well never have entered the campus at all. Too many suspend literary pursuit when the diploma is won, and the world of business opens before them. Chautauqua provides, for such as these, incentives to a personal review of the entire college curriculum in a series of English readings. It urges them to prosecute advanced courses of study, and suggests a plan by which college prestige and power may be used in helping less favored neighbors who desire education. This last class is large. It is made up of eager minds who need direction and encouragement. They would ask questions, and gratefully accept assistance, if college graduates would simply place themselves within reach.

Chautauqua has therefore a message and a mission for the times. It exalts education, — the mental, social, moral, and religious culture of all who have mental, social, moral, and religious faculties ; of all, everywhere, without exception. It aims to promote a combination of the old domestic, religious, educational, and industrial agencies ; to take people on all sides of their natures, and cultivate them symmetrically, making men, women, and children everywhere more affectionate and sympathetic as members of a family ; more conscientious and reverent, as worshippers together of the true God ; more intelligent and thoughtful as students in a universe of ideas ; and more industrious, economical, just, and generous, as members of society in a work-a-day world. The theory of Chautauqua is that life is one, and that religion belongs everywhere. Our people, young and old, should consider educational advantages as so many religious opportunities. Every day should be sacred. The schoolhouse should be God's house. There should be no break between sabbaths. The cable of divine motive should stretch through seven days, touching with its sanctifying power every hour of every day.

Kitchen work, farm work, shop work, as well as school work, are divine They hide rare pearls in their rough shells. They are means of discipline in the highest qualities of character, and through them come some of the greatest and mightiest energies from the heavens People should be guarded against that baleful heresy, that, when they leave the hour of song, prayer, and revival power, and go to homely service in shop or field, they are imperilling spiritual life, as though only so-called sacred services could conserve it.

We need an alliance and a hearty co-operation of Home, Pulpit, School, and Shop, — an alliance conse crated to universal culture for young and old ; for all the days and weeks of all the years ; for all the varied faculties of the soul, and in all the possible relations of life.

Chautauqua teaches that each of these institutions embodies and represents an idea, and that every man needs in his own life these representative ideas, — the home idea of mutual love and tenderness ; the church idea of reverence and conscientiousness ; the school idea of personal culture ; and the shop idea of diligence, economy, and mutual help. The young and the old need these things. The rich and the poor need them. Capital and labor need them The educated and the illiterate need them. Chautauqua says therefore : Give them to the people. Hold up high standards of attainment. Show the learned their limitations, and the illiterate their possibilities. Chautauqua pleads for a universal education ; for plans of reading and study , for all legitimate enticements and incitements to ambition ; for all necessary adaptations as to time and topics ; for ideal associations which shall at once excite the imagination, and set the heart aglow. Chautauqua stretches over the land a magnificent temple, broad as the continent, lofty as the heavens, into which homes, churches, schools, and shops may build themselves as parts of a splendid university in which people of all ages and conditions may be enrolled as students. It says : Unify such eager and various multitudes. Let them read the same books, think along the same lines, sing the same songs, observe the same sacred days, — days consecrated to the delights of a lofty intellectual and spiritual life. Let the course of prescribed reading be broad and comprehensive; limited in its first general survey of the wide world of knowledge ; opening out into special courses, according to the reader's development, taste, and opportunity. Show people out of school what wonders people out of school may accomplish. Show people no longer young, that the mind reaches its maturity long after the school-days end, and that some of the best intellectual and literary labor is performed in and beyond middle life. College halls are not the only places for prosecuting courses of study. College facilities are not the only opportunities for securing an education. A college is possible in everyday life if one choose to use it , a college in house, shop, street, farm, market, for rich and poor, the curriculum of which runs through the whole of life; a college that trains men and women everywhere to read and think and talk and do; and to read, think, talk, and do, with a purpose; and that purpose, that they may *be:* a college that trains indolent people to work with their own hands; that trains people who work with their hands, to work also with their brains, — to think in their work, to think for their work, and to make other people work and think.

A plan of this kind, simple in its provisions, limited in its requirements, accepted by adults, prosecuted with firm purpose, appealing to the imagination and to the conscience, must work miracles, intellectual, social, and religious, in household, neighborhood, and nation. And this is the "Chautauqua Idea;" and the idea in active operation is the CHAUTAUQUA of which I write

Its benefits are manifold and obvious. It brings parents into fuller sympathy with their children, at the time when sympathy is most needed, — sympathy with them in their educational aims, sympathy with them in lines of reading and study.

It helps parents to help the teachers of their children, preparing infants under school age to make a good beginning ; inciting and assisting the children who have entered school, to do good work in preparation and recitation ; protecting them against the peculiar temptations of playground and class-room ; holding them to the end of the high-school course ; inspiring them to seek the higher education of the college, or to pursue after-school courses of reading and study at home.

So general a scheme of education must increase the refining and ennobling influence of home life, promoting self-control and dignity of deportment, mutual respect and affection, a laudable family pride, and true social ambition; giving the whole house an air of refinement; touching with artistic skill floors, walls, and windows, finding the right place and the right light for the right picture, putting the right book on shelf and table, furnishing a wider range of topics for home conversation; crowding out frivolity and gossip, removing sources of unrest and discontent at home; making evenings there more agreeable than life on the street, creating a real independence of the outside world, and making one's own house the centre of the whole world of science, literature, art, and society. Windows open out through every wall; and beyond vines, trees, and garden, the inmates see the old world of history, the new world of science, the rich world of literature, the royal world of art. And through skylights they look up and see the world of God, — his love and holiness, and the boundless life to which he invites us. And thus they all in that household learn, that, seen aright, all realms of knowledge, both past and present, are flooded with the light of God.

Popular education through the Chautauqua scheme increases the value of the pulpit by putting more knowledge, thoughtfulness, and appreciation into the pew, and encouraging the preacher to give his best thought in his best way.

It must put more good sense into popular religious utterances, so that the talk of the prayer-meeting will be sobered by wisdom and directed by tact, thus gaining in its influence over cultivated people, and especially over the young people of high-school and lecture-hall.

It must enable everybody more accurately to measure the worth and the limitations of science, and must cause them to fear far less the dogmatism of pseudo-scientists concerning religious facts and doctrines.

Such popular education must increase the power of the people in politics, augmenting the independent vote which makes party leaders cautious where lack of conscience would make them careless concerning truth and honesty.

It must tend to a better understanding between the classes of society, causing the poor to honor wealth won by honest ways of work, by skill and economy; to despise wealth and winners of wealth, when greed and trickery gather the gold, to honor knowledge and a taste for knowledge, whether it be found clad in fine linen or in linsey-woolsey; to hate with resolute and righteous hatred all sham and shoddy, all arrogance and pretentiousness; to avoid struggles between capital and labor, and to promote, in all possible ways, the glorious brotherhood of honesty, sympathy and culture, — a culture that addresses itself to all sides of a man's nature.

Under the auspices of this great Chautauqua "every-day college," you may imagine the soliloquy of a woman more than forty-five years of age. She says, —

"I am busy with many duties, — household cares or shop work. I have something to do all the time. There seems no end to calls, toils, worry, and weariness. In kitchen, parlor, farm, or factory, something is to be done.

"I am old, — that is, older than I once was. Don't let us talk about that. Gray hairs? No, you cannot find any gray hairs in my head — or, can you ? Never mind. The heart's young, and it's nobody's business how old the bones are.

"I am going to college ! Never mind about thirty years, or fifty, or seventy : I am going to college. Harvard ? No, nor Yale, nor Boston, nor Middletown, nor Evanston, nor Wellesley I don't want to mix with a lot of reckless boys, or ambitious girls, just now. I have enough of them at home or in the neighborhood. I am going to college, my own college, in my own house, taking my own time ; turning the years into a college term ; turning my kitchen, sitting-room, and parlor into college-halls, recitation-rooms, and laboratory. What a *campus* I have ! green fields and forests, streams and mountain ranges, stretching out to the sunset. What a dome surmounts my college ! vast space, blue background, billowy clouds, resplendent stars ! What professors I have, in books ! immortal books of history and science and art, books of poetry, fiction, and fact.

"In my college are enrolled the names of glorious men and women who never enjoyed any other college, — Shakspere, Benjamin Franklin, Washington Irving, John G. Whittier, Horace Greeley, Abraham Lincoln, and hosts of others who went to their own college, and wrought out their own education, as I will do in 'my college' I can never be what they were ; but I can be something, and can make the world better, and children happier, and life nobler, because of the feeble efforts I put forth to get a better education.

"I am going to college ! I want to improve all my talents. I have intellect I intend to develop and enrich it. I must know more. I must love to know.

I must know more, for the sake of larger influence over others for their good, — children, servants, neighbors, church associates God has given me at least one talent I ought to improve it I will improve it.

"I am going to college! I am a 'child of a King,' and have a right to my inheritance. 'All things are yours.' Well, I want to take up my property in stars and flowers, and in the knowledge men have gathered about my royal Father's kingdom Astronomers, bring me what you have discovered in the outlying domains of my Father's universe! Geologists, tell me the story you have learned from the rocky pages of the earth, concerning the beginnings and the development of the planet I live on. Thus I intend to lay hold of all the treasure-seekers and teachers and high priests of nature and literature and art, and bid them bring the truth they hold, my Father's truth, *my* truth, and place the goodly inheritance at my feet 'Whatsoever things are true, . . . think on these things.' I am going to college!

"'Where am I going?' I shall stay at home, and construct a college there. My house — small, poorly furnished (never mind) — is my college centre My neighbors, the richest of them and the poorest, the most humble and ignorant, and the most scholarly, shall be my professors. I will ask questions about every thing, and of everybody, till I find out what I want to know. Some of the stupidest people can tell me something, and when I draw them out I do them good. Getting, I can give.

"And don't talk to me about age. Let the poet answer your raven cry : —

'But why, you ask me, shall this tale be told
To men grown old or who are growing old?
It is too late! Ah! nothing is too late
Till the tired heart shall cease to palpitate.
Cato learned Greek at eighty; Sophocles
Wrote his grand "Œdipus," and Simonides
Bore off the prize of verse from his compeers,
When each had numbered more than fourscore years;
And Theophrastus at fourscore and ten
Had but begun his "Characters of Men,"
Chaucer, at Woodstock with the nightingales,
At sixty wrote the "Canterbury Tales;"
Goethe at Weimar, toiling to the last,
Completed "Faust" when eighty years were past.
These are, indeed, exceptions, but they show
How far the gulf-stream of our youth may flow
Into the arctic regions of our lives,
When little else than life itself survives.
Shall we, then idly sit us down and say —
The night hath come it is no longer day?
The night hath not yet come we are not quite
Cut off from labor by the failing light
Something remains for us to do or dare;
Even the oldest tree some fruit may bear;
For age is opportunity no less
Than youth, though in another dress;
And as the evening twilight fades away,
The sky is filled with stars invisible by day.' "

The entire Chautauqua movement is based upon the following propositions —

1 The whole of life is a school, with educating agencies and influences all the while at work, from the earliest moment to the day of death These agencies and influences should be wisely and continuously applied by and in behalf of each individual, through life, according to circumstances, capacities, and conditions.

2 The true basis of education is religious. The fear of the Lord is the beginning of wisdom, — the recognition of the Divine existence, and of his claims upon us as moral beings; the unity and brotherhood of the race, with all that brotherhood involves; harmony with the Divine character as the ideal of life for time and eternity; and the pursuit and use of all science in personal culture, the increase of reverent love for God, and of affectionate self-sacrifice and labor for the well-being of man.

3. All knowledge, religious or secular, is sacred to him who reverently surrenders himself to God, that he may become like God, according to the divinely appointed processes for building character. And he has a right to all attainments and enjoyments in the realm of knowledge, for the possession of which he has capacity and opportunity. Science, travel, literature, the works of art, the glories of nature, — all things are his who is one with God. This law applies to the poor and lowly, as well as to the rich and so-called "favored classes" of society. It gives lofty ideals to lowly life, and transforms humble homes into places of aspiration and blessedness.

4. In mature life, beyond the limits of the usual school period, the intellect is at its best for purposes of reading, reflection, and production. While the training of the schools may discipline the juvenile mind, and thus give it an advantage as its powers mature, the discipline of every-day life, in solving problems of existence, support, and business, gives a certain advantage to the so-called uneducated mind during the middle period of life. Between the ages of twenty and eighty

lie a person's best intellectual and educational opportunities ; and he needs direction, encouragement, and assistance, in order to use them most effectively.

5. Early lack of culture, felt by full-grown people, begets a certain exaltation of its value and desirability, and a craving for its possession. This craving creates intellectual susceptibility and receptivity, and renders the more easy the acquisition of knowledge. Mere verbal memory may be less efficient in these adult years; but the power of reasoning, and of utilizing knowledge for practical results, is much greater than in the early years

6 The necessity for wise direction, assistance, and encouragement of this mature intellectual power and desire is as great as in the period of youth and of school life Therefore grown people need courses of study outlined, books for reading indicated, questions answered, associations formed, and all the conditions guaranteed which tend to promote hope, confidence, ambition, and strong purpose

7. Where a mature mind desires to use its energies and opportunities to the maximum of its possibility, and to do thorough intellectual work of the most exacting sort, the influence of the best teachers may be brought to bear upon him by frequent correspondence, including questions, answers, praxes, theses, and final written examinations of the most exhaustive and crucial character. To such persistent purpose and faithful effort, after rigid testing, there should come the testimonials and honors in diploma and degree, to which any student anywhere else, or at any other period of his life, would be entitled.

8. The advantage of mental attrition by personal recitation and conversation is a large factor in the schools. This advantage may be enjoyed by voluntary associations, local circles, contact with resident scholars, occasional attendance upon special lectures, and class recitations in local high-schools, seminaries and colleges, and at summer schools and assemblies.

These are some of the fundamental thoughts on which the Chautauqua movement is based. It is a school for people out of school who can no longer attend school, — a college for one's own home ; and leads to the dedication of every-day life to educational purposes.

The Chautauqua movement embraces : —

1. Work done at Chautauqua and similar assemblies, in lectures and by class instruction, for a few weeks every summer.

2. Work done away from Chautauqua, in voluntary *reading* through the year, which reading is under direction, and is reported to headquarters at Plainfield, N J.

3. Work done away from Chautauqua during the entire year, in *study* under faithful teachers, by correspondence ; such work being tested by final examinations of a rigid character, and rewarded by certificates, diplomas, and the usual scholastic degrees.

How the movement began, and how it has grown to its present state of achievement and promise, from its very beginning, it is the mission of the following chapters to tell.

CHAPTER II.

THE BEGINNING.

" The groves were God's first temples." — W. C BRYANT.

THE Chautauqua Assembly opened as a Sunday-school institute, — a two-weeks' session of lectures, normal lessons, sermons, devotional meetings, conferences, and illustrative exercises, with recreative features in concerts, fireworks, and one or two humorous lectures It was called by some a "camp-meeting." But a "camp-meeting" it was not, in any sense, except that the most of us lived in tents There were few sermons preached, and no so-called " evangelistic " services held. It was simply a Sunday-school institute, a protracted institute held in the woods We called it at the first "The Chautauqua Sunday-school Assembly."

There had been before the Assembly a camp-meeting at "Fair Point," the old name of the present "Chautauqua" It was organized under a charter granted by the Legislature of the State of New York, in 1871. There lies on my table, as I write, a copy of " The Chautauqua Lake Journal, published for the Chautauqua Lake Camp-Meeting Association " No 1 of Vol. I. bears date "Fair Point, N.Y., July, 1873." The first column is filled with an announcement of the " Fourth Erie Conference Camp-Meeting of the Methodist-Episcopal Church," to be held at " Fair Point, Chautauqua

County, N.Y., commencing Tuesday, Aug. 12, and closing Friday, Aug. 22, 1873." It was during the session of the camp-meeting of 1873, that Mr. Miller and the writer visited "Fair Point," and selected it as the place for our "Assembly." And the Assembly was totally unlike the camp-meeting. We did our best to make it so.

The first programme was comprehensive, and thoroughly prepared. The lecturers and teachers were widely known as men and women of superior ability and large experience Every thing centred in the Sunday school. Never were so many representative Sunday-school people so long together, and so long at institute or normal work in Sunday-school lines. Never had Sunday-school work been more carefully canvassed, or its methods more fully or admirably illustrated Large classes were daily drilled in the one text-book of the Sunday-school, the Holy Bible, and in the institution itself, its relations to other departments of church work, its organization and officers, and the duties of teachers. The most radical questions pertaining to pedagogy were considered. Foundations were laid First principles were discussed by the leaders in educational science. Plans of teaching were shown in actual operation by most gifted instructors. Criticism, favorable and adverse, was freely encouraged The details of Sunday-school work at Chautauqua during the first few years of its existence will be described later on It is enough for our present purpose, to observe that the basis of the Chautauqua work was in the line of *normal training, with the purpose of improving methods of biblical instruction in the Sunday school*

and the family.   The opening words on the first evening in 1874 were words from the Holy Bible   Thus
the first vocal utterance at Chautauqua was divine.
The mission of Chautauqua has been to "study the
Word . . . of God."   Later attention to His manifold
"works" in nature, in history, in mind, has diminished
neither the confidence of Chautauqua leaders in the
Word, nor their use of its sacred contents.   They have
not taken less interest in the personal religious life.
Indeed, while true Chautauquans study the Word and
the works of God, so firm is their faith in the Spirit who
wrought the works and inspired the Word, and in the
spirit of man for whom the Word was inspired, that
they deem it not strange that God the Father should
"dwell in the midst of them," folding his own children
to his heart, and breathing of his own Spirit into their
spirits, enlightening, regenerating, comforting, witnessing.   And as trust grows, and desire increases, this
access becomes less and less interrupted ; and they hope
one of these days, in all wisdom, to trust in God continually, and every day to feel his presence and rejoice
in his grace.   They do, however, discriminate between
this Divine possession which captures and sways intellect and will, weekdays and Sundays, in business and
in church life, steadily and effectively, — and the mere
spasms of resolution under pressure of occasion, the
selfish efforts over fancied personal security, the studied outward conformity to religious duties, according to
the ebb and flow of religious emotion.   They believe
so firmly in the kingdom and patience of our Lord, that
obedience is worth more than comfort and faith, a firmer
foundation than sight or feeling.

Chautauqua opened as a school, a Bible school, a normal school, a Sunday-school institute in which the highest standards were sought and the best teachers employed. The work of that first year was every way deserving of commendation; and so far as its ideals, provisions, and methods are concerned, the first assembly has not been excelled.

The success of Chautauqua must be especially gratifying to LEWIS MILLER, Esq. The Chautauqua Assembly is one of the fruits of his thoughtful, active, and earnest life. He has always taken great interest in educational matters. Circumstances changed his early purposes from literary to mechanical lines, but he never lost his interest in education, both in and out of the Church. He was successful as a manufacturer, making many inventions; the one most prominent was that of "The Buckeye Mower," which revolutionized farm-machinery. This gave him, and those with whom he was associated, great prominence. He early became connected with educational institutions; in 1866 was made president of a college board of trustees; in 1867 was appointed by the Governor of his State a member of a Board to prepare and report to the Legislature a scheme for a State school, to carry out a Congressional enactment, and appropriate the funds donated to the State for an educational institution intended for the greater development of the mechanical and agricultural arts. Mr. Miller was also a friend of the camp-meeting, but believed that the institution could be improved by changing the evangelistic phase, to which was always given great prominence, to one that should enlarge the outlook of the

already consecrated church-member.   He believed that
at the encampment advanced thought should be discussed, new methods of church-work developed by representatives of the several denominations, and that the
various antagonizing schools of thought should be fairly
and thoroughly met.   He believed in science and literature being brought to the support of Christianity.   It
was therefore a privilege, and a rare opportunity, on
the part of the author of this volume, with such a man
of breadth, inventiveness, administrative and financial
ability, to go into the grove at Chautauqua, where our
combined and long-cherished educational, ecclesiastical,
and catholic schemes might be fully developed.   Mr.
Miller's devotion to education, his inventive genius,
business capacity, and well-known liberality, promised
from the beginning large success to Chautauqua.

In "The Sunday-School Journal" for April, 1870,
Silas Farmer, Esq., of Detroit, Mich., writes as follows :

"Shall we not have them?   Every one concedes
that camp-meetings have been a *power* for good in
the past history of the Church.   The grand old forest
trees have often re-echoed the glad thanksgivings of
God's people, and many a weary soul has received
the gospel of 'rest,' while beneath the leafy arches
of 'God's temple.'   On many camp-grounds for years
special services have been held for the children.
Why not have district and State gatherings for a
week at a time, especially for the teachers and children with their parents?   Our institute work is often
imperfectly done for want of time, and our children's
meetings accomplish but little of what they might if

there was more of continuity of thought and purpose. What great things might be done for the Master if we 'gathered together the people, men, women, and children,' and '*taught* them the fear of the Lord,' combining in one meeting the idea of a camp-meeting and an institute, with talks on home religion, religious culture, children's work, methods of teaching, and practical Bible lessons, interpersed with prayer and experience meetings both for children and teachers! Surely, with such a meeting, seed-time, growth, and fruit-gathering would come together. What state or district will have the first 'camp-meeting institute'?"

The scheme of Mr. Miller was a larger scheme than that proposed by Mr. Farmer, although both embraced the thought of utilizing the camp-meeting.

While the exercises of the first season (1874) were devoted to the Sunday school, the wide range given to the topics bearing upon this theme, and the varied talent brought to the platform, furnished much that was interesting to all classes of minds. There was no narrowness in the first programme at Chautauqua. With God's word as the text-book, there could be no limitation as to topics. In our private conversations, Mr. Miller and I had anticipated much that followed. In the original suggestion of Mr. Miller concerning the improvement of the camp-meeting by the presentation on the platform of scientific as well as theological subjects, the wide relations of biblical and Sunday-school work to general culture were recognized ; and in the pleas which the writer had made for so many years for the increase of "week-day power" in connection with Sunday-school work, one may easily discover the germs from which developed in process of time the varied departments of Chautauqua. The programme of 1885 would have been impossible in 1874; but with the programme of 1874, the programme of 1885 was a necessity.

Chautauqua began on a broad and catholic basis. It was of necessity Methodist Episcopal in origin, because the suggestion of a protracted normal institute came from a Methodist-Episcopal Sunday-school worker who occupied a responsible official position in that church, and because also Methodist-Episcopal people have been especially active in camp-meeting work; although it is claimed that the Presbyterians had at least as much to do with the origin of this out-door movement in America as did the Methodists It is said that the "first camp-meeting in the United States was held in 1799 on the banks of Red River in Kentucky. Two brothers by the name of M'Gee, one a Presbyterian and one a Methodist, being on a religious tour from Tennessee, where the former was settled, to a place called 'The Barrens,' near Ohio, stopped at a settlement on the river to attend a sacramental occasion with the Rev. Mr M'Greedy, a Presbyterian." A marvellous manifestation of religious energy was the result. The meetings continued for several days. The church was so crowded that it became necessary to erect an altar in the forest. "This gave a new impulse to public interest; and many came from every direction, with provisions and other necessaries for encampment, and remained for several days, dwelling in tents. It was a wonderful occasion. Sectarian divisions seem to have been forgotten in the general concern for the prevalence of spiritual religion. The services were conducted by Presbyterians, Baptists, and Methodists. The result was unparalleled. Another meeting of the kind was held on Muddy River, and still another on what was called 'The Reach,' both of which were attended by immense throngs." Presbyterians and Methodists united in the conduct of these meetings. "Because of this union of sects in their support, they were called 'general camp-meetings.' It is said that the roads leading to the groves where they were held were literally crowded, and that entire neighborhoods were forsaken of their inhabitants. A Presbyterian minister calculated that there were at least twenty thousand persons present at one time at a meeting held in Kentucky." Thus it appears that they had at least the denominational unity and the enthusiasm of Chautauqua, in 1799.

The Chautauqua Sunday-school Assembly proposed, as has already been indicated, was formally instituted by the board of managers of the Sunday-school Union of the Methodist-Episcopal Church at their regular meeting in October, 1873, when the following resolution was adopted : "*Resolved*, That we approve the project of a Sunday-school teachers' assembly in August, 1874, on the Chautauqua Lake camp-ground, and that we refer the whole matter, with full power to order and arrange, to the committee of this board in charge of the normal department." This action was in response to a request from the executive committee of the Chautauqua Lake Camp-ground Association.

Immediately after the adjournment of the board in October, a meeting of the normal committee was held

It consisted of J. H Vincent, superintendent of instruction, Rev. H M. Simpson, secretary, Rev. J. C. Thomas,
J Bentley, and A. G. Newman.   This was Oct. 22, 1873
All the members were present.   The design of the
proposed assembly was stated by the superintendent,
substantially as follows : To hold a prolonged institute,
or normal class, occupying from ten to fifteen days, for
the completion of the course of normal study prescribed
by the department (see Hand-book, 1872, pp. 48–53) ; to
secure the presence of as many pastors, superintendents, and other officers and teachers, as possible, that a
new and general interest may be awakened throughout
the Church on the subject of normal training for Sunday-school workers ; to command as far as practicable
the best talent in the country to assist in the conduct
of this assembly ; to utilize the general demand for summer rest by uniting daily study with healthful recreation, and thus render the occasion one of pleasure and
instruction combined.   The name " The Sunday-school
. Teachers' Assembly " was adopted.   Lewis Miller, Esq ,
of Akron, O., was elected president, Rev. Dr. J. H
Vincent superintendent of instruction, Rev. Henry M.
Simpson secretary.   The committee issued an announcement urging all pastors and superintendents to
organize normal classes at once in their several churches,
that before Aug. 1, 1874, there might be a large number
of teachers ready to begin with the second or junior
course of normal study   The committee at the same
meeting passed the following resolution : " Whereas
this course of study is in substantial agreement with
that adopted by the normal departments of the Baptist, Presbyterian, and American Sunday-school Union

boards, and as the leading workers in these and other branches of the Christian Church will be at the assembly to assist by their experience and counsels, and as it is our purpose to make the occasion one of the largest catholicity, the committee cordially invite workers of all denominations to attend, and to participate in the services of the assembly."

It will thus be seen that the Chautauqua movement began, as of necessity it must have done, with the Methodist-Episcopal Church; and that at the very outset the denominational lines were almost entirely obliterated, people of all the churches invited to participate, and a course of study selected which had already been virtually agreed upon by the several churches Later on, with the local incorporation of the Chautauqua Sunday-school Assembly, the unfolding of the various departments of the Chautauqua work, the identification with the movement of representative men from all branches of the Church, it became necessary to lift the entire institution to a pan-denominational and catholic platform.

People coming to Chautauqua are not expected to abandon their church relations. They come, without compromising conviction, to join in a broad movement for the increase of power in every branch of the Church, and throughout our American society. True denominationalism is catholic, and he who loves his own wisely is likely to love others generously. At Chautauqua all churches have opportunity to meet in their several centres for prayer and conference. Every Wednesday evening at seven o'clock, prayer-meetings are held by the several denominations in their respective headquarters :

Baptist, Congregational, Disciples, Lutheran, Methodist-Episcopal, Presbyterian, United Brethren, United Presbyterian, Protestant Episcopal, Reformed Episcopal, Cumberland Presbyterian, and many others. On one day every season, a denominational congress is held, to discuss some phase of the question, "How can we make Chautauqua helpful to our branch of the Church?" The utmost good feeling has always prevailed. There have never been manifested uncomfortable rivalries. Men of the several denominations have appeared on the platform, giving the people of each church a chance to hear and enjoy the talent of their sister churches; thus creating a sense of mutual obligation for benefits received, and increasing, also, the appreciation by each church of the ability, scholarship, and power of the other churches Mutual respect has thus been promoted, and co-operation of the most radical and effective kind secured

The highest form of catholicity is that in which points of divergence are brought before the several schools of thought, without diminishing the feeling of Christian affection. On one morning, in the Hall of Philosophy at Chautauqua, Dr. Daniel Curry of the Methodist-Episcopal Church discussed the Arminian theology On the next morning, Dr Archibald Alexander Hodge of the Presbyterian Church considered the Augustinian theology. The kindest feeling prevailed. Every man saw how his brother could fortify himself with arguments in the maintenance of his view of church creed and usage.

On one occasion, in the temple on the hill, a meeting of Baptists, Congregationalists, Methodists, and Pres-

byterians was held, twenty minutes each being given to
representatives of the four denominations for the statement in a positive way of the doctrines and usages
of their respective churches   The Rev. Mr. Seymour
of Boston, Baptist ; the Rev. Mr. Williston, then of
Jamestown, N.Y., Congregationalist ; the Rev Dr. Hatfield of Chicago, Ill., Methodist-Episcopal ; and the Rev.
J. A Worden, then of Steubenville, O., Presbyterian,
—occupied altogether one hour and twenty minutes.
Each man gave, in a plain, straightforward way, a statement of the views of his own church, with no allusion
whatever to other interpretations or forms of faith.
The utmost attention was given by all.   The best of
good feeling prevailed.   At the close of the last address,
the entire audience arose, and joined in singing, —

" Blest be the tie that binds
Our hearts in Christian love."

This occasion was thoroughly characteristic of Chautauqua, the president of which, Lewis Miller, Esq.,
represents the Methodist-Episcopal Church ; the secretary, and superintendent of grounds, the versatile
and indefatigable W. A Duncan, Esq., being a Congregationalist ; and the solid and trustworthy treasurer,
E. A. Skinner, Esq, and Miss K. F. Kimball, our wise
and efficient C. L. S. C. secretary, being Presbyterians.
On the Chautauqua faculty, nearly all the leading denominations are represented.

CHAPTER III.

THE DEVELOPMENT.

" O mother Ida, many-fountained Ida." — TENNYSON.

FROM the seed sown in Chautauqua soil in 1874, there has come up a remarkable growth. It has been a surprise to its friends. Out of one we have many. The little one has become a thousand. Yet the herb has yielded seed after his kind, and the tree yielded fruit whose seed was in itself. The numerous and various features of the present Chautauqua work are natural outgrowths of the original basal ideas, — biblical study, Sunday-school normal work, and the necessity of utilizing and regulating in the interest of true living, the "week-day power." What we have must of necessity have come from what we had.

Sunday-school workers could not content themselves, year after year, with the discussion of the same old practical questions of organization, administration, and method ; questions of accumulation, classification, and communication ; questions about infant-classes, teachers, and superintendents. The theory of Sunday-school work is very simple ; and its methods are to be mastered by practice at home, not by reiterations in professional meetings. People who are enterprising and energetic enough to do effective work in the sphere of religious

teaching are limited and belittled by mere routine.
They detest ruts. They want radical ideas, and new
adaptations of them to every-day service. But the
compass of pedagogical and governmental philosophy as
applied to the Sunday schools is not wide ; and thoughtful, earnest souls loathe husks and platitudes and repe-
titions. Therefore the subsequent programmes of our
Assembly must differ from the first, or there must be
such modifications and enlargements of the old programme as to make its scope broader and its contents
more attractive.

The Bible indeed never grows old. Nor can Bible-
study prove a weariness to spiritual and enthusiastic
souls. Its pages throb with life, and shine with beauty ,
ever old, ever new, never dull. One never exhausts any
of its most familiar passages. The oldest and the com-
monest text may flash out some new beauty while one
puts his devout thought upon it. Chautauqua exalts
the Bible. It may not trouble itself about the *modus*,
the *quantum*, and the *qualitas* of inspiration. It simply
takes the book in its entirety, as the book given to be
studied, trusted, loved, and obeyed, as individual conscience and judgment respond to its contents after
calm, devout, and diligent study of them ; and not to
be quarrelled over, or quibbled about, or forced to sustain preconceived or pre-accepted notions by a string
of separated texts, on the cord of a curious fancy or an
antiquated dogma. Chautauqua believes in the Bible
as the revealed word of God. It therefore puts book
and soul together, and trusts both thoroughly for fair
treatment. It encourages Bible study.

But it is possible to insist upon too many hours of

Bible study each day. Even a good thing may be carried to excess. Busy brains need variety of occupation. There is increase of power in recreation. Good sense is a good balance-wheel for religious zeal.

People who for summer rest settled for the season in the grove by the lake, could not all be interested in Sunday-school discussion or in biblical studies. The large population within easy reach of the Chautauqua gates and dock needed some other attraction to bring them to our Assembly. And we required for our more radical work their financial support ; while they needed, more than they desired, the quickening and awakening which come from great ideas. To bring them up to an appreciation of our best, we must give them what would be to them their best, and, without catering to weakness or wrong, gradually improve their tastes and ideas by making Chautauqua a place of rest and delight to them. This policy has brought tens of thousands every season to the sessions of the Chautauqua Assembly.

There was a multiplying power back of these popular demands in the Chautauqua work. The proper study of the Divine WORD leads to and requires the more careful study of the Divine works. The Author of the Book is the Creator of the universe, and the Ruler of the race. He who examines the writing will turn with new interest to the wonderful facts and laws which are set forth in the vast fields of science and history. He will discover a kinship and sweet harmony where he fancied division and antagonism. The word "secular" gains new significance. It loses its hard, metallic ring. It begins, like Aaron's rod, to blossom with spiritual beauty. Things secular are under God's governance, and are full of divine meanings. If God created all things, if he governs all things, if the channels of history have been furrowed out by his own hand, if the beating life of the physical universe is from Him who is Life before life, Life of all life, then nothing is secular in any such sense as to make it foreign or unattractive to the saints of God. If "the heavens declare the glory of God," he who knows most of the stellar spaces may know most of the glory of God as set forth in the heavens. He may as a scientist "consider the lilies," and note the "fall of a sparrow," and "go to the ant ;" and, other things being equal, learn more of the wisdom and care and ethical standards of his heavenly Father than he can who looks casually upon disconnected phenomena of the material world. To Chautauquans, therefore, all things hold a measure of God's infinite wisdom. All things are precious; for in all things one may find traces of his grace. All things are sublime; for all things are connected with a glorious unity, which fills heaven and earth, eternity past and eternity to come. Flowers, fossils, microscopic dust, foul soil, things that crawl and things that soar, ooze from the sea-depths, lofty heights that salute the stars, — all are divine in origin and nature.

Nor were the benefits of this new combination experienced wholly by one class. Secular teachers found great advantage in this introduction to the atmosphere of Chautauqua, and to fellowship with Sunday-school workers. For, while the former gave to Sunday-school people better instruction in the philosophy and plans of teaching, they themselves received a large measure of healthful influence from these more sympathetic, evangelical, practical, and humanitarian church people. They gave ideas, and received impulses There was a mutual interchange of light and heat And both were blessed.

Thus the normal work as applied to the work of all schools, especially to that first and best school, — the family, — became the distinguishing feature of Chautauqua. It began as a Sunday-school normal institute. It became a universal normal institute, and has been a guide and an inspiration to teachers of all grades, in Sunday school, grammar school, high school, college, and pulpit.

Beyond the specific normal plan there came into existence — it was a necessity — other and broader departments of Chautauqua work The Sunday-school teacher needed a measure of secular knowledge in order to his greatest efficiency as a teacher of sacred things. When one has a devout spirit, the more he knows of the works of God in nature and in providence, the larger and fuller must be his conceptions of truth in revelation, and the more ample his resources. Our Sunday-school scholars come to us from a world full of knowledge of this kind, and rife with the spirit of inquiry and research. They live in that world seven days a week. The Sunday-school teacher ought himself to be familiar with it, that he may understand the difficulties which his scholars encounter, the objections to Christianity which they hear, the social, æsthetic, and literary allurements, good and evil, by which they are helped or hindered between Sundays ; and that he may pre-occupy them with right ambitions, legitimate social and intellectual pursuits, and thus make the activities of the world a help in the kingdom of Jesus Christ.

There is this additional advantage in familiarity with general knowledge, that the religious teacher is thereby furnished with illustrations by which he may set forth the mysteries of the spiritual kingdom. There is a marvellous harmony between the two realms. The God of the one is the God of the other. He is in both. Both are of him. He said, " Let there be light." The sun to this day obeys him. He caused other light to shine out of darkness, and in the spiritual heavens is the " Sun of righteousness." Blessed are they who "walk in the light" Thus the world is full of harmonies ; whether analogies merely, or " correspondences " according to the thought of Swedenborg, or " unities " as claimed by Professor Drummond Jesus in his day filled his talk with these resemblances. Would he not do the same were he to live to-day, in this age of steam and telescope, of telegraph and electric light ? Well for the Sunday-school teacher if he can employ even to a moderate degree the marvellous and exquisite illustrations which are furnished in our times through the new unfoldings of science and the discoveries of travel ! He should be able to make use of the material supplied by history, by literature, by art, by science, and thus apply lessons of spiritual truth with freshness, variety, wisdom, and effectiveness

I have spoken of the manner in which the biblical and Sunday-school normal work of the beginning expanded into work in behalf of the people who could not be drawn or held by merely Sunday-school studies ; into work in which science was exalted ; into work by which day-school and Sunday-school teachers might give mutual help ; into work by which the Sunday-school teacher might enter into fullest sympathy with his most cultivated pupils, who are most familiar with the busy and brainy world, and be able to employ, in teaching them spiritual things, the rich resources of the literary and scientific world which are to-day so easily accessible.

Chautauqua took one farther step. If general education be a good thing for Sunday-school and other teachers ; if acquaintance with the every-day world, and ability to grapple its forces in the interests of our youth, — to ward off evil influences, and to use the good, — be so desirable on the part of those who teach in the schools one hour on Sunday, or five hours a day for five days in the week : how much more important is it that we reach with such helpful grace the homes in which children live for seven days a week, and the parents whose blood, opinions, personal authority, and unconscious influence mould character, fix creeds, and determine all the radical movements of early life ! It is an excellent thing to inspire and direct the godly teacher who puts his power into one hour a week, and the other teachers who bring their influence to bear upon youth for twenty or twenty-five hours a week ; but why is it not a much more excellent thing to take a firm hold, in wise way of grasping, upon the homes and parents who settle all the radical questions of life and character by a positive, a never-ceasing exercise of power, — power of every kind, — for one hundred and sixty-eight hours a week, and that from the moment of conception to the years of manhood and womanhood ? Why shall we not put salt of healing into the springs of Jericho? Why shall we not capture the citadel itself, and establish a reign of religion and culture and love and common-sense in the homes of the land? These questions came to Chautauqua. They must come. Such radical work as she attempted could not stop short of the most radical theories and agencies And Chautauqua made answer to the questions to which her initial work gave birth. The light she had started at the altar of the Sunday school, she took finally with bold hand, and lighted every one of the seven lamps on the golden candlestick in that "holy place,"—the HOME. The family circle was made a school Books were brought in, pictures were hung up, telescope and microscope were adjusted, the Bible was opened, the fires of devotion on the home altar kindled, and full-grown people were set at work reading, talking, teaching. New ideals were conceived, new tastes formed, new social regulations enacted, new ambitions for the middle-aged and the old awakened, and home was made an accessory and helper to school and church. From the five or six hundred elect students of 1874 who crowded the normal tent at Chautauqua for two weeks, we have come to the more than one hundred thousand readers, who for fifty-two weeks in the year turn the pages of useful books, sing songs of college fellowship, think in a larger world, and worship more intelligently the Creator and Father of the race. These are not at Chautauqua; but have made Chautauqua centres in their own homes, in all parts of the United States, in Canada, in England, in Russia, in India, in China, in Japan, in South Africa, and in the islands of the Pacific. From such small beginnings we trace such splendid expansions.

Children at Chautauqua have found a paradise, and amidst their pleasures they have learned useful lessons which are sure to help them everywhere else and always. Chautauqua is a veritable *kindergarten.*

When from this great army of readers and students gathered by Chautauqua, there come a few, who, unable to attend the established college, covet the highest scholastic and professional training, with rigid examinations, deserved promotions, and fairly-won diplomas and degrees, Chautauqua stands ready to receive and recognize them, to give guidance at every stage of the educational process, and to reward fidelity and ability with all legitimate college and university honors. Chartered by the State of New York, Chautauqua has full right to foster learning by the instructions and recognitions of the full-orbed university

Such is the simple story of the development of Chautauqua, by which it has become other than it was at the beginning. From the movement in 1874 have sprung the various organizations for the benefit of our large constituency, — organizations for the education of Sunday-school teachers, of secular teachers, of young people in school and young people out of school, of full-grown people who have heretofore cared too little for any school, of college men and women who are in danger of losing the impulse and benefit of the school once enjoyed, and for the help of homes, communities, secular schools, and churches We have the great banyan-tree with its bending boughs and forest of trunks, all from the original stock ; and these, like the banyan-tree, have taken root as individual and yet as united institutions, separate rather in name than in organization, — all under one administration, and yet meeting the demands of widely differing tastes and preferences. The list is formidable, but the depart- ments do not conflict. The work is one. With its wide reach of purpose, it was necessary that Chautau- qua should project the lines of its intention in plans and departments, that the world might see its magni- tude, and that the full territory it proposes to occupy might be pre-empted. Until this projection was made, the Chautauqua idea was irrepressible. And now Chau- tauqua with its variety of departments is not like a mere pile of buildings, with additions, lean-tos, unrelated edifices, and other after-thoughts, the results of un- manageable ingenuity. It is a growth and development, a provision according to the highest law, to meet the necessities which called it into existence. In this growth of twelve years, there have been no unnecessary additions. To have omitted any of them, would have made Chautauqua less than it is, and to have made Chautauqua less than it is, would have been a mistake — almost a disaster. Because of the broad and varied provisions now included in the Chautauqua movement, it will be greater and stronger for all time to come.

Let us glance at the long list : —

"The Chautauqua Sunday-school Normal Depart- ment" (now known as "The Assembly Normal Union"), for the training of officers and teachers, the increase of interest in Sunday-school teaching among the youth of the present who are to be the teachers of the future, and for the promotion of teacher-training by our pastors.

"The Chautauqua Teachers' Retreat," for the benefit of secular instructors, who, during a few weeks in the summer, may be quickened into new enthusiasm in their profession, and assisted in efforts for self-improvement.

"The Chautauqua Teachers' Reading Union," which provides a course of helpful reading and study for secular teachers, — a course extending through several years

"The Chautauqua (Summer) Schools of Language," (ancient and modern) for the illustration of method and the discussion of principles in connection with linguistic work.

"The Chautauqua Literary and Scientific Circle," for the promotion of reading-habits among all classes of people at their homes during the entire year.

"The Chautauqua Missionary Institute," for consultation by church people of all denominations, touching home and foreign missionary work, — its importance and demands.

"The Chautauqua College of Liberal Arts," for the assistance of earnest non-resident students who are ambitious to win college honors on merit, and to this end desire to prosecute most thorough courses of study, and to be subjected to most rigid examinations.

"The Chautauqua School of Theology," for the direction of ministers, who, in connection with pastoral work, wish to secure a training as complete as that given by any other theological seminary

"The Chautauqua Book-a-Month Reading Circle," for those who wish to read in general literature under wise direction.

"The Chautauqua Town and Country Club," for the

training of people, young and old, in the habits of observing and recording the phenomena of the physical
world, with a view to practical experience in agriculture,
and in the affairs of every-day life.

"The Chautauqua Society of Fine Arts," for teaching by correspondence and home practice the several
branches of art.

"The Chautauqua Young Folks' Reading Union,"
for promoting among young people the habit of reading
good books at home

"The Chautauqua Boys' and Girls' Class," held daily
at Chautauqua during the Assembly, for training the
children, who choose to attend, in Bible facts and
principles.

"The Chautauqua Temperance Classmates," for giving lessons during the Assembly, in the philosophy and
ethics of the temperance reform.

"The Chautauqua Society of Christian Ethics,"
holding a Sunday-afternoon session at Chautauqua during the season, for presenting to youth the ethical side
of Christian teaching.

"The Chautauqua Look-Up Legion," a · branch of
the Harry Wadsworth Ten Times One Club.

"The Chautauqua Cadets," a semi-military organization for boys, designed to promote physical training.

"The Chautauqua Calisthenics Corps," for the physical training of girls.

"The Chautauqua Musical Reading Circle," for the
reading of books bearing on the history and philosophy
of music.

"The Chautauqua Intermediate Class," for the study
of biblical themes by persons who do not care to take

up the normal branch of the "Assembly Normal Union "

"The Chautauqua American Church School of Church Work," for the training of ministers and lay-men in a broad and comprehensive system of practical theology

"The Chautauqua Press," which embraces all publications, periodical and permanent, issued under the auspices of the Chautauqua University in any of its departments

These associations, with more or less compactness of organization, enlist a variety of people   They are under one general management, are wisely classified, as will be seen later on, and are so adjusted as not at all to clash with each other   Persons interested in any one branch of study or effort find it more to their liking to have a department under the auspices of which that single branch may be taken up and pursued   Having completed one, they find it pleasant to begin another, and become in the transitions identified with successive departments of the one great Chautauqua work.

The movement at Chautauqua soon brought into existence similar assemblies   From Chautauqua came other Chautauquas   These were in some cases new meetings called from the beginning " Assemblies."   In other cases they were meetings of the Chautauqua type, held on old camp-grounds before or after the regular annual camp-meeting, or taking one or more days from the camp-meeting period for Chautauqua exercises

The alphabetical list of these " other Chautauquas " is given below, with the date of organization, or, at least, of the recognition of the Chautauqua idea and of the C.L.S.C. (Chautauqua Literary and Scientific Circle).

"Acton-Park Assembly," in Indiana, 1884.

"Arkansas Chautauqua Assembly," at Siloam Springs, Ark., 1885.

"Bay View," Petoskey, Mich.

"Canby Camp-ground," at Canby, Ore., 1885.

"Chautauqua Assembly of Southern California," Long Beach, near Los Angeles, Cal., 1884.

"Clear - Lake Assembly," Clear Lake, Ia., 1876 (C.L.S.C., 1879).

"Florida Chautauqua," De Funiak Springs, Fla., 1885.

"Genesee-County Assembly," Longlake, Mich., 1885.

"Inter-State Assembly," Ottawa, Kan , 1880.

"Island-Park Assembly," Rome City, Ind., 1879

"Kansas Methodist-Episcopal Assembly," Lawrence, Kan., 1885.

"Key-East Assembly," Key East, N.J., 1883.

"Lake-Bluff Assembly," Lake Bluff, Ill.

"Lakeside Encampment," Lakeside, O , 1877.

"Lakeview Assembly," Cazenovia, N Y.

"Loveland Encampment," Loveland, O , 1878.

"Mahtomedi Assembly," Mahtomedi, Minn., 1883.

"Maine Chautauqua Assembly," Fryeburg, Me., 1884.

"Maplewood-Park Assembly," Waseca, Minn., 1885.

"Monona-Lake Assembly," Madison, Wis , 1882

"Monteagle Assembly," Monteagle, Tenn., 1882.

"Mountain Grove," near Berwick, Penn., 1885.

"Mountain-Lake-Park Assembly," Mountain-Lake Park, Md., 1882.

"Nebraska Sunday-school Assembly," Crete, Neb., 1882

"New-England Sunday-school Assembly," South Framingham, Mass., 1880.

"North-western Chautauqua," Lake Minnetonka, Minn , 1879.

"Ocean Grove," N J , 1885

"Pacific Grove," Monterey, Cal., 1879.

"Piasa-Bluffs Assembly," Illinois, 1885.

"Pine-Tree C.L S C ," Maranocook, Me., 1885.

"Point-Chautauqua Baptist Union," Point Chau- tauqua, N.Y., 1878.

"Puget-Sound Assembly," Puget Sound, W.T., 1885.

"Round-Lake Assembly," Round Lake, N.Y , 1878

"South-Africa Chautauqua Assembly," Cape Colony, Africa, 1885.

"Sunday-school Parliament," Thousand Islands, N.Y.

"Tawawa Theological, Scientific, and Literary Asso- ciation," Wilberforce, O , 1883

"Texas Chautauqua," San Marcos, Tex , 1885

"Washington Court-House Assembly," camp-ground near Washington Court-House, O , 1885.

"Yosemite Assembly," in Yosemite Valley, Cal.: held only session in 1879

The expansion of the Chautauqua work is not to be fully estimated without taking into our thought the wide reach of the C. L. S C , the local circles and pri- vate members of which report to the central office at Plainfield, N J , from the Dominion of Canada ; from the island of Japan, where there are a thousand mem- bers ; from mission-stations in China, India, Bulgaria, Syria, Mexico, and Central America ; from Persia, Russia, France, England, Scotland, Ireland, and the Sandwich Islands.

Thus into all lands have the lines extended. The Chautauqua idea is emphatically "a touch of Nature that makes the whole world kin."

CHAPTER IV.

THE PLACE AND ITS INSTITUTIONS.

" *The greatest defect in common education is, that we are in the habit of putting pleasure all on one side, and weariness on the other, — all weariness in study, all pleasure in idleness.*" — FÉNELON.

IN the study of the " Chautauqua Idea," as developed in the institutions outlined in the last chapter, and to be more fully described in this and succeeding chapters, we may cast a glance at the locality itself, — CHAUTAUQUA , for Chautauqua is a place as well as an idea   The idea was before the place ; although it must be confessed that the embodiment of the thought in a physical frame-work of soil and forest had a most wholesome effect on the idea itself, giving it a chance to draw strength from its external conditions, to "ultimate" its conceptions in action, to experiment with raw material, to command the attention and elicit the commendation on which good things thrive, and to adapt its aim and energy to the variety of people and conditions with which it proposed to deal.

Chautauqua is beautiful, and grows more beautiful with the passing years   It is worthy of the service to the cause of religion and culture to which it has been consecrated.   The lake is lifted up fourteen hundred feet above the sea.   Green fields and beautiful forests surround it.   No river empties into it, nor any large

creek or brook. Its crystal waters are supplied by
natural springs. It has been compared to Lake Como
for beauty. The outlet is a winding channel, in a forest
of tall and thickly growing trees, — one of the most
remarkable little rivers in the country. What stories
might be told of the brave men, who, during the past
two hundred years, have roamed and made war, have
loved and wept and died, on these Chautauqua shores!
There are strange traditions lingering here, that wait
the summoning of some genius who shall do for them
what Irving has done for the Hudson, and Cooper for
the Mohawk.

It is interesting to trace the changes in the name
Chautauqua. Indian, Frenchman, and American have
had hard work to get it into its present shape. "Jat-te-
ca," "Chat-a-co-nit," "Tchad-a-ko-in," "Tjad-a-ko-in,"
"Chat-a-kou-in," "Shat-a-co-in," "Jad-ax-qua," "Ja-da-
qua," "Chaud-dawk-wa," "Chat-augh-que," "Chau-tau-
que," until a few years ago, by special legislative
enactment, the present name "Chautauqua" was given.

The real significance of the word is still, and will
always be, in doubt. It is a "foggy" problem, even
though the word Chautauqua may not signify, as some
assert, "the foggy place." It is the place "high up,"
according to the interpretation of some. The abundance of fish in its waters leads others to accept the
meaning, "fish taken out." The narrows at Bemis
Point, leaving two expansions of the lake, above and
below, favor the tradition that the Indians compared it
to "a bag tied in the middle," or "two moccasins tied
together." Interpret it as you will, Chautauqua is
CHAUTAUQUA, a place of clear light, of uplift, of abun-

dance, of even balances, of truth and righteousness, of faith and hope and charity.

Nature has not suspended her beneficent ministries since Art pitched her pavilion by the side of these waters   Trees still put forth branches and clothe them with foliage.   The old trees stand like venerable giants, with as much of hope as of memory in their hearts, and in their annual robe of verdure forget that for so many years they have watched the coming and the going of the seasons.   Young trees that have grown a dozen years older since the first Chautauqua song broke the silence are now stately and beautiful, ready to be witnesses for a hundred years of the strange things to be done here, and of which we, who are looking about for graves, only dream now.   The lake — who shall tell of its moods, its smiles and frowns, its loud murmurings of unrest when the fierce winds come down in power upon it ; its low sobbings after the storm, trying to for-give and forget ; its sweet answers to the toying breeze; its splendor when the moon flings a robe of silver over it, and when the sun, making it a mirror, rejoices in it (as Christ in the true saints) because it faithfully re-flects his own glorious image ?

OBED EDSON, Esq , of Chautauqua County, in an ex-ceedingly interesting historical sketch of Chautauqua published in "The Continent" for Aug. 22, 1883, re-cords the following legend of Lake Chautauqua : "Some Indians once encamped upon its shore   A young maiden of the party, having eaten of a root growing upon its banks which created great thirst, stooped to drink of its waters, when she disappeared forever.   Hence the name signifying 'the place of easy death,' or ' where

one vanishes away'" One might give to this legend
an interpretation, in the light of which the ministries of
the later Chautauqua would appear, — ministries under
the power of which, deep soul-thirst is excited and then
quenched, peace and rest secured, death made "easy"
indeed, under a view of life which makes death but a
"sleep," a "vanishing away," and an entrance into the
"rest that remaineth."

Art has not altogether been useless, although more
than once unwise Penuriousness has sometimes spoiled
lines and angles, and mixed bad colors; stupidity has
blundered into sad combinations and contrasts: but on
the whole, Art has clasped hands with Nature, and
made the place Chautauqua a lovely and fitting tabernacle for the Chautauqua Idea.

There is a Chautauqua within Chautauqua To see
this other Chautauqua, one must have eyes, — eyes that
look into the innermost things. He must see beyond
groves and crowds, beyond lake and sky, beyond buildings and programmes. He must be able to see necessities, intellectual and spiritual, in the individual and in
society, tendencies of thought, forces of conviction,
pressures of desire and ambition, the conflict of new
and old civilizations in the personal life, as circumstances bring a man face to face with the new, while yet
from habit and feeling he is held half-slave by the old.

He who sees Chautauqua must understand the relations (not generally understood, and to which I have
already called attention) between gracious culture and
the rough, unæsthetic services which people must render
each other and their own lives in this world; services
of feeding and clothing and cleaning and housing, —

low, gross, and humiliating, as judged from an artist's studio or a "poet's frenzied mood." He must find out that high and low, noble and ignoble, are relative terms; that a kitchen may for a time cage an angel whose hands dabble in dough, and whose tired feet in coarse shoes tread rough floors. She may serve her inferiors, and treasure the pittance they give her to buy books for her brain life; at least, that portion of the pittance she does not need to feed the fortunate people who depend upon her. When crowns are given out, a marvellous re-adjustment of relations will take place, and certain little neighborhoods will be shaken with surprise

Chautauquans with eyes see the distinctions in advance, and recognize the crowns that hover in mid-air over the saints, and they pay honors to "Alfreds in neat-herd's huts" before the throne is ready. A boot-black may be a king, — boot-black and king both at once Human eyes see only the black hands, patched knees, and crouching form, that bespeak servility. There are eyes that can see deeper and farther. Seeing so much, they extend a hand of greeting. Then kings and saints converse.

Chautauquans believe in wealth when honesty wins it, prudence protects it, and benevolence uses it. They believe in position when worth secures it, work honors it, and humility attends it. They believe in culture when teachableness goes before it, and all the faculties in true harmony receive it, and religion inspires and controls it. They believe in labor when true social relations distribute it, when no one family of faculties is abused by it, and when true, reverent, and philanthropic motives direct it.

Chautauquans are believers in a common brotherhood, but are not "communists." They are open to truth, and hold an inheritance in all truth, and are subject only to the truth. But they are not boastful free-thinkers in

"Realms remote, mysterious, divine,"

dogmatizing and denouncing. They believe in truth, God, and humanity. They seek the first, rejoice in the second, and serve the third.

These are some of the ideas which belong to the Chautauqua movement, the thoughts within the things, the theories of which phenomenal Chautauqua is a visible expression.

There is a Chautauqua farther on. First, there is a lake level; and just above it is the level of the "Point," with its pleasant grass, its winding walks, its old Auditorium, shaded and hallowed with memories that have grown through multiplying years. The old cottages, and many of the old cottagers, remain about this Auditorium, — reminders of the old times, and the oldest times, of Chautauqua, when the first vesper service announced that "The Day Goeth Away," and the "Nearer, my God, to Thee," rang out under these forest arches. Who that was there can ever forget that hour? The altars were aglow that night, and hearts on fire. It was an experiment, but from the first it was an assured success. The time will come when the remaining sharers in that first feast in the evening light will be very few, and the last of them will receive honor, and the children of Chautauqua will listen to their story as with quivering lips and kindling eye they speak about

that first evening under the trees, the words that broke
the sacred silence, the songs that bore praise and
wonder and joy to the heavens, and the friendships that
were formed there never to be broken

How many who joined in the first Chautauqua service
have already "fallen on sleep," and gone out into a
world sleepless and without nightfall, where for vesper
chant are substituted the hallelujahs of an eternal
morning!

But let us go up higher.   Beyond the Point and
Auditorium level, are the terraces that run along the
hillside, one above another, gardens and cottages, with
pathways and winding roads, leading up under welcome
shadows to a higher Chautauqua, — a long stretch of
table-land crowned now with Temple and Chapel, Pyramid, Normal Hall, Museum, and Hall of Philosophy;
while beyond, in the open fields toward the north, we
reach the highest point of our Assembly grounds, one
of the highest on the lake.

Thus from the landing and the beginning of our
journey we ascend from the lowest to the highest, and
find beauty, delight, pleasant welcomes and rewards, all
the way.

This study in the lay of the land which makes the
physical Chautauqua is an allegory.   There is an upper
Chautauqua; and not all who visit the place see it, and
not all who become Chautauquans reach it.

The Chautauqua movement is progressive, and its
friends and students are expected to make advancement
in the line of its conceptions and provisions.   It has
court beyond court, in which it unfolds its progressive
aims, and introduces its disciples to the higher privi-

leges of culture which it provides. No fences or lines mark these successive stages. They do not correspond with the topographical elevations, although we have found in the one a figure or symbol of the other. But such gradation exists, and I shall point it out.

THE CHAUTAUQUA UNIVERSITY embraces the following departments : —

    I — THE CHAUTAUQUA ASSEMBLY
      1. The Summer Meetings at Chautauqua
      2. The Sunday-school Normal Department.
      3 The Schools of Language.
      4 The Chautauqua Teachers' Retreat.
    II. — THE CHAUTAUQUA LITERARY AND SCIENTIFIC CIRCLE.
    III — THE CHAUTAUQUA COLLEGE OF LIBERAL ARTS, formerly known as "The Chautauqua University," and with powers as provided in its charter.
    IV. — THE CHAUTAUQUA SCHOOL OF THEOLOGY, with purposes and powers as in its charter.
    V. — THE CHAUTAUQUA PRESS.

THE CHAUTAUQUA ASSEMBLY was the original title of the Summer Meeting, and is the present title recognized in the Chautauqua Charter. The first "Assembly" began on the first Tuesday evening of August, 1874, and from that time the "Assembly" has opened at the same date When "Church Congress," "Scientific Congress," "Missionary Institute," etc , were introduced, they came "before the Assembly," — the " Saturday before," or the "Thursday before ," but the central date of the Chautauqua calendar has always been the "Assembly opening," which everybody at all enlightened in the ways of Chautauqua knows to be "the first Tuesday evening in August." When the "Teachers' Retreat" and the "Schools of Language" were opened two or three weeks before the "Assembly," the "Assembly opening" on the first Tuesday in August was recognized as the pivotal time-point of the whole summer's work. The Saturday before the first Tuesday is called the "Mid-season Celebration." The "Anniversary of the C M I " (Chautauqua Missionary Institute) comes on Monday before the first Tuesday in August, the great "Missionary Day," Thursday after the first Tuesday in August; "C L S C. Inauguration Day," first Saturday after the first Tuesday in August; "Denominational Congress and Look-up Legion Day," second Wednesday after the first Tuesday in August; "Alumni Re-union and Illuminated Fleet Day," second Thursday after the first Tuesday in August; and so on, and so on. And even now, where "Preliminary Week" gives us, with C T R and C S L, a whole month before "the first Tuesday in August," all eyes turn toward that date as the great and brilliant annual opening of the "Chautauqua Assembly." Formerly the "big bells" did not ring until that evening, the rigid laws of retiring and rising did not come in force until then, the most distinguished guests did not appear on the platform before that; and on the first Tuesday evening of August, the great crowds came from the regions round about, sure of a tempest of song and merriment, of wit and eloquence, on the auditorium platform under the trees, and later in the great Amphitheatre of Chautauqua.

Nor has the glory departed Whatever may have been the attractions of the platform during the month

of July, everybody in the vicinity of Chautauqua expects
a larger audience and a more intense enthusiasm on
"the first Tuesday evening in August" than at any
previous time. Old Chautauquans manage to "be at
the opening." Old residents along the lake run up
"for the opening;" and there are men and women who
always rise that evening when the call is made for "all
who have been present at every opening since 1874."
As the years go by, and richer programmes fill the July
season, this furor over the "opening" will somewhat
abate, but for all time there must gather about the
"first Tuesday evening in August" at Chautauqua a
peculiar charm, — the charm woven of precedent and
antiquity and association.

THE SUMMER MEETING with its "Preliminary Week,"
its "C. T. R," "C. S. L," "Assembly," and "After-
week," is the popular side of Chautauqua, — the first
point of approach to this remarkable educational centre.
It is the outer court, open to the whole world. It has
no restraints upon the incomers, save those which are
necessary to guarantee a financial support to the institution, and those rules of ordinary decorum which are
essential to the quiet enjoyment and profit of those
who pay their tribute and wait for the promised compensation. And ,this compensation comes in lectures
on the widest range of topics, from the "Philosophy of
Locke and Berkeley" to the light and cheery discussions about "Fools and their Folly;" music in all its
forms, — stringed instruments and organs; concerts by
gifted artists; characterizations by rare impersonators;
illustrations of life and manners in remote regions, by
the aid of costumers and *tableaux vivants*, stories of

travel, with photographic accompaniments colored, magnified, and illuminated; wanderings among fountains, models, and museums; uninterpreted chatter from classes in Latin, Greek, French, German, Hebrew, Anglo-Saxon; odd outcries from teacher and pupils in the School of Oratory; sermons by able ministers; lessons by competent teachers; attractions for light-hearted youth and wearied but rational age, in bonfires, banners, processions, fireworks, illuminated fleets, — these are the features of the outer court of Chautauqua, for the entertainment, awakening, and broadening of people who come with no far-reaching or serious purpose, but who come to "hear" and "see" and have "a good time." They are simply recipients. The will-power lies dormant, save as some stirring statement of lecture or sermon, or some unsyllabled passage in music, opens the soul to the worlds all about it replete with marvel, beauty, and power. So much for the outer Chautauqua. There are those who see this, — only this and nothing more. They come and go. They wonder why they and others come, and yet they think they may come again — but are not sure. They do not forget Chautauqua, and they do not "go wild" over it. They smile at other people, whom they call "fanatics" because they are full of it, and "bound to come again," and to "come every year," and always, and "would be willing to live there."

THE CHAUTAUQUA MISSIONARY INSTITUTE belongs to the "Summer-Meeting" department. It was organized in 1878, and begins regularly on the Saturday preceding "the first Tuesday in August," and lasts for four or five days. All aspects of the missionary question are discussed by men and women of the several denominations.

THE CHAUTAUQUA AMERICAN CHURCH SCHOOL OF CHURCH WORK, for the training of laymen and ministers in principles and methods of church life and work, suggested by Dr. GEORGE P. HAYS of Denver, Col., was conducted during the season of 1885 by Rev Dr J. A. WORDEN of Philadelphia, and will hereafter be a feature of the Summer Meetings.

THE CHAUTAUQUA YOUTHS' LEAGUE embraces the several classes and organizations designed for the benefit of children and youth: "The Boys' and Girls' Class;" "The Temperance Classmates;" "The Society of Christian Ethics;" "The Look-Up Legion;" "The Chautauqua Cadets;" and "The Chautauqua Calisthenic Corps."

THE CHAUTAUQUA BOYS' AND GIRLS' CLASS, meeting daily (except Sunday), opens on the second day of the Assembly (the Wednesday after the first Tuesday of August). The course of study is chiefly biblical, embracing lessons in the Bible as a book, and as a book of books; in Bible history, biography, geography, doctrines, etc.; in memorizing Scripture and hymns; in practical life, — laws of courtesy, deportment, etc. A certificate for each grade is given to any pupil who answers eighty per cent of the questions; and three competitive prizes are given for the three best examination-papers presented at Chautauqua in each class Lectures illustrated by costumes, by oxy-hydrogen light, by models, as of Jerusalem, Palestine, Herod's Temple, etc., are given frequently Pilgrimages by the children are made from time to time through the Park of Palestine, under the direction of experienced tourists who have visited and studied the actual Canaan

THE TEMPERANCE CLASSMATES meet for ten or twelve recitations during the Assembly, giving attention to educational topics which bear on the "Temperance cause."

THE SOCIETY OF CHRISTIAN ETHICS meets at four o'clock every Sunday afternoon during the season, in the "Temple," and with closed doors; only young people between twelve and twenty-one years of age admitted. Topics relating to every-day life and duty are discussed: "Duties of young people to mother," "to father," "to very old people," "to very young people, — the babies and very little children of the household;" "The place of conscience in day-school work;" "The care of the body;" "Self-respect," "Social amusements," "Conscience in the parlor;" "Habits of reading," etc

THE LOOK-UP LEGION is one of the many forms which the "Ten Times One" idea of Dr. Edward Everett Hale has assumed, and is devoted to the enforcement and illustration of his now famous motto: "Look up, and not down; Look out, and not in, Look forward, and not back, and, Lend a hand"

THE CADETS and CALISTHENIC CORPS are designed to promote physical training during the season at Chautauqua, and thus to render the place more attractive and profitable to the young people who spend the summers with us

THE SUNDAY-SCHOOL NORMAL DEPARTMENT, now known as the "Chautauqua Assembly Normal Union," was the basis of the original Chautauqua Assembly,

and its course of study the same that had been adopted
by the Sunday-school Union of the Methodist-Episcopal Church, and by representative leaders in other
Sunday-school organizations. Its farther development
is a matter of record.

At the "Chautauqua Sunday-school Assembly" in
August, 1876, a committee on a "Course of Normal
Class Lessons" was appointed.[1] That committee made
a report, which was unanimously adopted at a meeting
of persons of all denominations interested in the normal work. The report opens as follows : —

"With a view to greater interest, uniformity, and
efficiency in the work of normal class instruction for
Sabbath-school teachers among the various denominations of Christians, the undersigned committee, members of ten different denominations of Christians, appointed at the Chautauqua Sunday-school Assembly,
Aug 8, 1876, for the purpose of recommending a
course of normal class lessons, and suggesting a basis
of operations and plans of organization, respectfully
report : —

"That the course comprise forty lessons, to be called
the 'Chautauqua Course of Sabbath-school Normal
Lessons;' the time of each lesson to be divided between the consideration of the 'Bible and its contents,' and the 'theory and practice of teaching.'

"The Chautauqua Course of Sabbath-school Normal

---

[1] Names of the Committee J H. Vincent (M E), L M Kuhns
(Luth.), Richard Newton (P.E), J D Cooper (U.P), James M'Nab
(Pres), W Knox (Pres), O N Hartshorn (M E), A J Baird (Cumb
Pres), Charles Rhoads (Bap), O. F. Presbrey (Cong), W. G E. Cunnyng-
ham (M E. South).

Lessons may be adopted and used by any church, society, union, association, or institution of learning

"We recommend that normal classes organizing to study the Chautauqua Course of Sabbath-school Normal Lessons appoint a local committee of instruction, who shall have charge of the work of the class, conduct examinations, and who may issue diplomas to graduates

"Normal classes who desire to issue diplomas may obtain them from the Chautauqua Committee, with the heading ' Chautauqua Sabbath-school Normal Class Diploma,' and upon which may be placed the stamp or name of the church, society, union, association, or institution of learning, with which the class is connected ; these diplomas to be signed by the local committee of instruction.

"Normal classes organizing to study the Chautauqua Course of Sabbath-school Normal Lessons are requested to forward to the Rev. J H Vincent, 805 Broadway. New York, Superintendent of Instruction at Chautauqua, a statement of the name, location, church relation, numbers, and committee of instruction, thereof, to be filed and preserved "

"Normal Praxes" were required in this normal system, — a series of practice-exercises in writing, on the several processes of the teacher's work : thinking, memorizing, finding central and root thoughts, word-picturing, analogies, collecting illustrations, lines of approach, map-drawing, framing questions, and other exercises required in the work of teaching. No form of normal Sunday-school practice is more useful   I quote from some of the old praxis papers as illustrations of the valuable work done. On sheets, with ample space for the pupil's written answers, were printed the following, among many others. "Suppose the lesson were Deut. i. 19–33. *Imagine:* Class of six boys about twelve years of age. *Problem:* How fix in their minds the historical facts, relations, and geography of this lesson?" Again: "*Imagine:* Class of six young persons about sixteen years of age. *Problem:* What presumptive or direct argument in favor of the divine origin of the Bible may be found in each of the following facts: 1. Three towns in Syria, — El-Azariyeh, El-Khuds, El-Khalil; 2. Man at Athens, a Jew, delivering address on Mars Hill more than eighteen hundred years ago; 3 Three books written about Jesus within a few years, — Strauss, Renan, Farrar; 4 New York Hippodrome, ten thousand people, D L. Moody and Ira D. Sankey; 5 Queen Victoria giving a Bible to a pagan prince who asked her the secret of England's greatness, 6 Easter-day decorations in a Boston church; 7. A dying mother exclaiming, 'Precious Jesus!'" Again. "What religious comparisons or analogies are suggested by the following facts? and how could you turn them to account in religious teaching? Ripples and waves raised by the wind on the lake. At Chautauqua a fountain pours from a knothole in a tree. After a boat passes, there is a great rush of waves to the shore The electric lights cast dark shadows. It is more pleasant to hear the three Chautauqua bells than one." Another: "How illustrate and make clear to a class of children the following texts of Scripture? 'Except a man be born again,' etc.; 'Being justified by faith,' etc.; 'Where your treasure is, there will your heart be also.'"

A list of five hundred questions on biblical and Sunday-school themes was made out, and circulated widely. They were designed for self-testing by isolated pupils

The subjects comprised in the Chautauqua course of that day are here classified : —

I. PERTAINING TO THE BIBLE: 1. Its *names* 2 Its *books*. 3. The *classification* of books. 4. The *writers* 5 The *languages.* 6. The *gradual development.* 7. The *canon.* 8 The *identity* of its books. 9 Their *historic accuracy.* 10. Their *divine authority.* 11. Their *inspiration.* 12. The *principal versions.* 13 The *contents* of the Bible : History, chronology, geography, biography, manners and customs, divisions of time, natural history, institutions, prophecies, doctrines, weights, measures, etc 14. Its *interpretation.* 15. Its *mission, use,* and *power.*

2 PERTAINING TO THE SABBATH SCHOOL: 1. The *place* and *purpose* 2 The *relations* to home and church 3. The *organization* 4 The *management.* 5. The *classification.* 6. The *early lesson systems.* 7. The *international* lessons 8 The *supplemental* lessons 9 The *appliances.* 10 The Sabbath-school *superintendent.* 11. The other Sabbath-school *officers.* 12. The Sabbath-school *teacher* 13. The teacher's *helps* 14. The teacher's *difficulties* and *mistakes.* 15. The Sabbath-school *normal work,* — teachers' meeting, institute, normal class. 16 The *week-day power* of the school.

3. PERTAINING TO TEACHING: 1. The *soul* we teach. 2. The *acquisition* of knowledge. 3 The *retention* of knowledge 4. The *application* of knowledge 5 The *communication* of knowledge. 6. The preparation of

lesson matter. 7. The preparation to *teach* the lesson.
8. The pupils' *home-preparation.* 9 The *teaching process:* approach, attention, analysis, questioning, illustration, analogies, reviewing, memory training,
self-activity, self-application. 10. The *adaptation* to
classes : primary, intermediate, senior, adult, careless
pupils, insubordinate, etc. 11. *Normal Praxes :* acquisition of facts : specific lessons studied, — biblical
and normal, — analysis, analogies, root thoughts, central thought ; relation of Golden Text. Study of
theories : Educational and Sunday-school. Practice in
teaching : Approach, word-picturing, illustration, questioning. Memorizing Scripture.

4 BOOKS TO BE READ : Fitch on *Questioning.* Free-
man on *Illustration.* Trumbull on *Reviews.* Fitch on
Attention. Vincent's *Helpful Hints.* Chautauqua Text-
Books, No. 1. *How to Study the Bible.* No. 8. *What
Noted Men think of the Bible.* No. 10. *What is Educa-
tion?* No. 11. *Socrates.* No. 12. *Pestalozzi.* No. 15.
Froebel. No. 18. *Christian Evidences.* No. 19. *The
Book of Books.*

Adaptations of these lessons were made for pupils
of all grades, for students at Chautauqua, in "special
classes," as at other assemblies ; in "seminary classes,"
in the case of "individual teachers." There were also
"Teachers' Union" and "post-graduate" courses provided. Certificates and diplomas were given to successful candidates. The post-graduate course was
especially thorough. As announced in the Hand-book
for 1880, it was as follows : —

BOOKS to be studied : "Outlines of Church History," Dr. Hurst, price 50 cents ; "Short History of

English Bible," Dr. Freeman, price 50 cents ; "Companion to the Bible," Dr Barrow, price $1.75 ; "The Church School," Dr. Vincent, price 75 cents; "Christological Studies," Dr. D. D Buck.

Papers.— Each candidate is expected to present two papers containing not less than one thousand words each, one on a biblical, the other on a Sabbath-school theme.

A series of fifty questions based upon the above books must be answered in writing at Chautauqua.

At the Centenary Conference in London, in 1880, a still further development of the normal Sunday-school work took place by the appointment of an International Sunday-school Normal Committee, composed of workers in England, America, and France. A course of reading and study was outlined. This new course forms the basis of the "Assembly Normal Union" curriculum, recently adopted by most if not all of the Summer Assemblies. In competent hands this new departure is proving very successful.

THE CHAUTAUQUA INTERMEDIATE CLASS is an organization independent of the Normal Department, and for the benefit of youths and adults who elect training in the biblical rather than the normal studies. It meets daily in the Temple, beginning on Wednesday morning after the "opening."

CHAPTER V.

THE SUMMER SCHOOLS.

" The one exclusive sign of a thorough knowledge is the power of teach-ing." — ARISTOTLE.
" Cicero studied Plato and Demosthenes, but he resorted to no university."
— DR. TAPPAN.

THE CHAUTAUQUA TEACHERS' RETREAT aims to benefit secular teachers by combining with the recreative delights of the summer vacation the stimulating and quickening influence of the summer school. The professional part of the vacation thus utilized need not be exacting in its demands ; and under the law of the economy of teaching-force, one may, under the right conditions, receive from a teacher who is himself in good condition, a measure of help in an hour or a day, which will influence all the after-life of the teacher. Through lectures, lecture-lessons, biographical studies, illustrative exercises, scientific experiments, etc., under the direction of the foremost educators of the age, the " Retreat" presents to its students : 1. The *Philosophy* of teaching ; 2. The *Methods* which are the legitimate outgrowth of this philosophy ; 3. The *Application* of methods to the different branches of learning taught to the different grades of pupils in the schools ; 4. The *Biographical Centres,* or the study of those eminent educators who have from time to time embodied great

principles and illustrated distinctive methods; and, 5.
The "Retreat" also seeks to inspire its members to
develop their *individual powers and aptitudes* in the
study and practice of pedagogy.

The Chautauqua Teachers' Retreat was organized in
1879. The first meeting was held at 11 A.M., July 17,
in the "Temple;" the last, on the first day of August.
Dr William Phelps of Minnesota, Dr. J. W. Dickinson
of Boston, Dr. John Hancock of Ohio, Prof. R. S.
Holmes of Auburn, N.Y., Prof. George P. Beard of
California, Penn., Miss Morris of Brooklyn, Miss Leonard of Illinois, and Mrs. Ford of Cleveland, were the
instructors. *Conversazioni* were held on "The Teacher's Work," "Definitions of Education," "Defects in
Modern Education," "The Public Schools of Boston,"
"Asking Questions," "Normal Work," "Socrates,"
"Froebel," "Ascham," "Pestalozzi," "Object Teaching," "Teaching History," "Oral Teaching," "Teaching
in Pennsylvania," "Teaching in the West," "Building
Character," "The Higher Education," "A School
Week," "After-school Work," "Home Hinderances,"
etc, etc   A Sabbath Conference was held on "Jesus
as the Perfect Teacher."   Excursions on the lake,
social re-unions, lectures, music, and other attractive
features of the Chautauqua grounds and programme,
contributed to the pleasure and profit of the forty-five
teachers who constituted the first "Chautauqua Teachers' Retreat."

Since that first meeting in 1879, the Teachers' Retreat has steadily grown in favor among the educators.
Some of the most distinguished representatives of
theoretical and practical pedagogy have favored us with

their presence and counsel   The programme has been enriched by vigorous lectures, by expositions of principles and methods, by illustrative and experimental exercises, by conferences and question-drawers ; and from most of the States in the Union, pupils have come to enjoy for two weeks the benefits of contact with living leaders, and of actual observation in the "ways of doing things" by which the value of the teacher's service may be augmented

The development and expansion of the Retreat may be appreciated by a glance at the programme for 1885, in which we find provision for lessons in pedagogy and in the practical application of pedagogical science, studies in Shakspere; chemical practice in the laboratory ; peripatetic lessons in mineralogy, geology, forestry, and botany, training under the best teachers in elocution, vocal culture, calisthenics, stenography, microscopy, clay-modelling, and kindergarten. From this wide range of subjects, pupils will make a selection, and confine their attention to daily work in the direction of their choice for from two to six weeks

Fishing, sailing, rowing, bathing, roller-coasting, calisthenic practice, bicycling, croquet, archery, lawn-tennis ; spelling, pronouncing, and quotation matches ; camp-fires, debates, old style singing-schools, and the endless variety of entertainments provided by the management, — give sufficient recreation of an innocent and useful character, to the most laborious student.

Among the many exercises by which the Retreat has been rendered serviceable and attractive the past few years, is one deserving especial mention : The Ideal Summer Trip beyond the Sea. The first was conducted

in 1873. The idea of the "Summer Trip" is to impart
the instruction, and to some extent the pleasure, of foreign travel to those who are not able to make the actual
excursion; while for those who "expect one of these
days to go to Europe," the Ideal Trip becomes an
invaluable preparation.

By the power of imagination, a party of tourists pack
the delights and profit of one hundred and fifty days of
travel into fifteen; and all this by the aid of conversations, lecture-lessons, class-drills, blackboard outlines,
choice readings by gifted elocutionists, musical render-
ings by superior singers, personal reminiscences by
ladies and gentlemen who have travelled widely, a library of travel, a large number of card-photographs and
engravings, and by stereopticon illustrations.

The Amphitheatre, the Temple, the Hotel Athenæum
parlors, the Hall of Philosophy, and the lake steamers
are utilized in securing as fully as possible the realistic
features in this Ideal Trip.

The days of ocean travel are described in a Tourists'
Conference of one hour, and then illustrated in two
hours' display of stereopticon pictures explained by
old travellers who give the serious and ludicrous sides
of ocean-travel Storms, fogs, icebergs, moonlight on
placid waters, sailor's songs, the sports of voyagers, the
approach to the foreign shore, are graphically presented
By conferences, lectures, and whatever art can do to
assist, the Chautauqua Foreign Tourists are conducted
during successive days through the lands across the
ocean. In 1883 the tour was an extensive one, —
through Ireland, Scotland, England, and the Continent.
In 1884 the illustrated talks and the conferences were

limited to the British Isles, while instructive lectures were given on distinguished characters in English literature and in modern English history. In 1885, in anticipation of the dominating subjects of the Chautauqua Literary and Scientific Circle Course for the ensuing year, the field of the tourists' study and exploration was confined to Italy, ancient and modern, her great heroes, writers, and artists. The Tourists' Conference considered "Routes into Italy," "Italy — geographical and political," "Milan — Leonardo da Vinci's Last Supper; Cathedral; View of the Alps; King Humbert's Arcade; Walls;" "Rome." Lectures were delivered on "Venice, the Faded Queen of the Adriatic," "Florence, the Athens of Italy," "Naples, Pompeii, and Vesuvius," "Rome," "From Chautauqua to Casamicciola," "Around Vesuvius," "A Trip through Italy," "Memories of Life in Italy," "Leonardo da Vinci."

The Ideal Tour plan will be continued through the years, and must with increasing facilities provide an invaluable means of entertainment and of preparation for actual foreign travel.

THE CHAUTAUQUA TEACHERS' READING UNION is the most recent of the Chautauqua societies, and is an extension of the "Retreat" into a home-circle for professional reading and study during the entire year. It is the scheme of the C. L S C, adapted to the day-school teacher, and applied to his work. The plan of the "Reading Union" for secular teachers was discussed, and preliminary steps taken, in 1879, for organization, at Chautauqua. Owing to the pressure of other matters, and the success of the C. L. S. C. in engaging teachers in its course of reading, the Teachers' Reading Course was postponed. In December, 1884, the plan was revived, the "Chautauqua Teachers' Reading Union" established, and Dr. Thomas W. Bicknell of Boston appointed president. At this writing, the scheme is in process of development, and will in due time be officially announced. It will not conflict with or interrupt the work of State Teachers' Reading Unions already organized, but will co-operate with them. It will provide three regular and several advanced courses of reading and study, recognizing and honoring the work done by all other reading circles, supplementing such work by practical helps, and forwarding special counsels to its registered members. At the completion of the first prescribed course, a diploma will be given, and for every additional course a seal added. In case of special examinations on the several courses, special recognition will be made by the "gold seals" of the "Readers' Union." All persons joining the Chautauqua Teachers' Reading Union, and paying the annual fee of one dollar, will become members of the "Socratic League," and will receive seven valuable communications annually from the counsellors. The Union has already received the hearty indorsement of the leading educators of America.

THE CHAUTAUQUA SCHOOL OF LANGUAGES was opened in 1879, with classes in Greek, Latin, German, French, Anglo-Saxon, and the Oriental languages. A department of biblical exegesis was a feature of the first session. The announcement of the C. S. L. was accompanied by the statement that its object was "to make teachers familiar with 'the natural method' of teaching both the ancient and modern languages, and to increase popular interest in philological studies."

The "natural method" of teaching the languages had been successfully introduced and illustrated by Messrs. Henness and Sauveur. Other teachers of the system have been developed in this country, — born teachers, fertile in devices, enthusiastic and magnetic.

By this process, a person who has never known French or German may in six weeks conduct conversation on ordinary topics in the language ; while those who have known the grammar, but never dared to venture on pronunciation, may converse with very considerable fluency. The principles of the natural method have been applied to Italian and Spanish, and substantially to Latin and Greek, and with very remarkable success

My attention had been called to this system two years before, by a distinguished clergyman, who told of his daughter's marvellous success in the study of French under a skilful natural-method teacher. The enthusiasm of my friend, — a man of culture and of sober judgment, — and the facts which he presented in support of the new method, led to further inquiry. Case after case came to my knowledge, and to the theory on which the method is based I could make no serious objection.

The "natural method" does not claim to give its pupils the mastery of a language in six weeks or in six months. It is not a "labor-saving" device. It simply follows the ways of nature. Watching the process by which a child is enabled within a few years to speak his native tongue, the "natural method" recognizes the simple laws which he involuntarily observes, and applies them to mature persons, who with strong purpose and intense desire devote themselves to the acquisition of a new tongue. A child *associates* with certain words the objects and actions which they express He sees the fact, and hears the name. The frequent *repetition* of these words, in association with the objects, deepens his impression. He himself *pronounces* the words many times each day. His blunders are corrected. He corrects himself. Repetition gives facility. Language is a *reality*. The word answers for the thing. He succeeds in communicating his thought. Success inspires him with confidence. He ventures. His attempts are rewarded with new successes. Pronunciation, conversation, confidence, enthusiasm — and the pupil is prepared to study the *grammar*. He reads, talks, triumphs. He begins to be a Frenchman, a German. The language is not a series of pages in print, but a living verity, a practical, every-day help. He is now prepared to go forward for years, his efforts rewarded, his enthusiasm increasing with every week of study

The able teachers of language in our own Chautauqua schools have developed, modified, and improved this scheme, and show astonishing results

The school of languages at Chautauqua holds sessions for from four to six weeks every summer. Students of this school enjoy the privileges of the "Retreat" and the "Assembly" without additional expense. They may listen to literary lectures delivered in the language for the study of which they joined the school. In French *soirée*, or Latin *symposium*, they have a chance to test their knowledge of a foreign tongue, and their skill in the use of it. Gathered around a camp-fire, the school of German chats and sings in the language of *Vaterland.*

THE CHAUTAUQUA SUMMER SCHOOL FOR CHILDREN was an experiment for a single year, — 1883. Want of financial resources was the cause of a suspension which is, I trust, only temporary. It is the design of the C. S. S. C. to be a profitable vacation, full of rest of the right sort, for little people ; the perfection of recreation which shall be *re-creation;* a "garden" of wisdom, discipline, and delight ; a place for culture in language, science, manners, life and character.

The lessons of the C. S. S. C. are to be so given as to time, quantity, and manner, as not to be tasks ; so limited, that "ambitious" pupils cannot overwork ; so blended with play, that study will prove a pleasure ; so ably directed by superior teachers, that the exercises will be inspirations rather than recitations, and will prepare pupils to work on their own account at home and school, rather than to attempt larger results at the summer school itself.

Imagine a series of instructions, lessons, conversations, lectures, reviews, exercises, praxes, experiments, etc , under brilliant leaders (who know childhood), under the following departments : —

1 Lessons in Our Own Language, — or, how to speak, read, and write English.

2 Lessons in Our Own Neighborhood, — its botany, zoölogy, geology, and geography.

3 Lessons in Our Every-day Life, — or, how to conduct one's self ; how to make, save, and use money ;

how to keep accounts; how to act at home, in society, in travel, in business, at church, and at school.

Imagine the delights of Chautauqua days after two hours' work (and two hours only), with shady groves, lovely lake, fountains, lawn-tennis grounds, and roller-coaster. Think of microscopes, stereopticon, the evening "parlor hour," campfire, bonfire, fireworks, military drills for the boys, and calisthenics for the girls!

What has not yet been attained is only waiting for time and opportunity. The dream shall yet be realized.

CHAPTER VI.

THE C. L. S. C.

" Promote, as an object of primary importance, institutions for the general diffusion of knowledge " — GEORGE WASHINGTON.
" After I had read for memory, I read for hope." — MRS. BROWNING.

THE CHAUTAUQUA LITERARY AND SCIENTIFIC CIR-
CLE next claims our thought. In our pilgrimage
from the lake-level towards the loftiest altitudes, we
reach a most sacred and important part of Chautauqua.
It is another court, farther in and a little higher up,
with a white-pillared hall among the trees, — " The
Hall in the Grove," about which a book has been written, and in which songs are sung and weird services
held, and where strange inspirations fall on people.
For those who belong to the Circle — the " C. L. S. C."
as everybody calls it — are advanced Chautauquans.
They know why they come to the place. And they
know when to come. They keep a calendar, and they
mark the feasts, and they know what to do when
they are there. They seem at home. There are hosts
of them, all knowing each other, and apparently bound
together by some secret association which has a mystic
power. They wear badges on certain days, — badges
of different styles and colors and legends. In all this
there is something singular and beautiful.

This "Circle" is a company of pledged readers in

wide ranges of literature. The "Assembly" contains people who listen. The "Circle" is made up of people who read. The "Assembly" covers a few weeks. The "Circle" casts its canopy over the year and the years. The "Assembly" is at Chautauqua. The "Circle" carries Chautauqua to the world's end, — to the east and to the west, to Canada, to Florida, to Scotland, to the Sandwich Islands, to India and Japan, to Cape Colony, — everywhere. More than one hundred thousand names are now on its record-books, and more than half of them are pursuing with faithfulness one or more of its prescribed courses.

The members of the "Circle" stand on a higher plane than the visitors to the Assembly, because they put will into the work. They read what they ought, for months and years, everywhere, getting larger views of the world, and worthier views of life, and nobler views of the race, and of God the Father of all.

The "Circle" takes a wide sweep in the world of letters. Its themes are those of the college world. It puts the preparatory and college curricula into good readable English, and helps people out of college to know what is going on there; what the young people study in history, language, and literature; what authors they read, and what estimate is to be placed on them and their work. It gives glimpses of science, physical and metaphysical, pointing down to the rocks and up to the stars, and about to the fields and seas and the forms of life in plant and animal. Whatever college boys study, the "Circle" provides in some form and degree for parents to read, that home and college may be one in outlook and sympathy, in aim and delight.

The aim of the "Chautauqua Literary and Scientific Circle" is thus set forth in all of its circulars: This organization aims to promote habits of reading and study in nature, art, science, and in secular and sacred literature, in connection with the routine of daily life (especially among those whose educational advantages have been limited), so as to secure to them the college student's general outlook upon the world and life, and to develop the habit of close, connected, persistent thinking. It encourages individual study in lines and by text-books which shall be indicated; by local circles for mutual help and encouragement in such studies; by summer courses of lectures and "students' sessions" at Chautauqua; and by written reports and examinations.

The "C. L S. C." is a school at home, a school after school, a "college" for one's own house. It is for busy people who left school years ago, and who desire to pursue some systematic course of instruction It is for high-school and college graduates, for people who never entered either high school or college, for merchants, mechanics, apprentices, mothers, busy housekeepers, farmer-boys, shop-girls, and for people of leisure and wealth who do not know what to do with their time. Many college graduates, ministers, lawyers, physicians, and accomplished ladies are pursuing the course. They find the required books entertaining and useful, giving them a pleasant review of studies long ago laid aside. Several of the members are over eighty years of age; very few are under eighteen.

In the first chapter of this volume are presented the fundamental doctrines on which the C L. S. C. rests.

The right of every man and woman to all the education they have capacity, will, and opportunity to attain;
the educational possibilities of mind at its maturity;
the disciplinary value of every-day life, domestic and
commercial, promoting as these occupations do habits
of application and concentration, tending to the education of the various faculties, and needing only to be
supplemented by direction and inspiration in order to
open a wider range of thought than is usually enjoyed
by "busy" people; the importance of utilizing spare
minutes in literary endeavor; the comprehensiveness
of the preparatory and college curricula, affording as
these do a glance at the varied world of literatuie,
science, and art.

The writer of these pages, in the early years of his
ministry felt the importance and saw the practicability
of providing a course of popular reading which should
open the college world to the people deprived of college
training The student's "outlook" may be enjoyed by
those who have not been subjected to the student's
discipline. The discipline is far more valuable than
the outlook; but the latter is not to be lightly es-
teemed, since it is likely to lead to the other. It at
least brings the wide world of college thought so near
to the uneducated home, that that world is no longer
terra incognita, and is more likely later on to be explored
and possessed by youth who but for the "outlook"
enjoyed by their parents would never have been encouraged or prepared to enter it at all.

Business men and mechanics, hard-working women
in kitchen, nursery, or shop, may turn to good account
the training-power of every-day service, and rejoice in

a glorious possession of truth to which they have as
much right as professional students, or "favorites of
fortune."

College men and women who do the best work
during the four years in the study of languages and
mathematics, need to supplement that quadrennium of
digging, ploughing, and preparing the soil, by sowing
good seed wisely chosen and in abundance. The college course does not give much knowledge. It gives
power. Its mission is to prepare the student to appropriate knowledge. He who drops his books when he
gains his parchment might almost as well never have
started in his educational course The C. L. S. C. is
the after-school of the college It encourages men and
women who have passed through the full curriculum,
to review the field they have already surveyed ; to re-
read in good English the studies of the seven years,
and in doing this to sit by the side of less-favored
neighbors, giving them needed help in an unpretentious and unpatronizing way. It has been a source
of surprise and of pleasure to the managers of the
C. L S. C., to see how many college-graduates are enlisted in it, how faithful they are to the requirements
of the circle, and how helpful to their fellow-students
No man so highly prizes the college as he who has
acquired an education without its direct aid And
none sees the defects of the college so clearly, or so
heartily recognizes the possibilities of culture outside
of it, as he who has faithfully trodden the pathway
of the student from matriculation to mastership. He
well knows that a man's power is not to be measured
by the opportunities outside of himself. Circumstances

make *things :* personal resolve makes men The tiue
scholar remembers names, illustrious on the literary
lists, whose intellectual training did not come from
the schools, — Homer, Shakspere, Washington Irving,
Hugh Miller, Horace Greeley, Michael Faraday, Edward
Hitchcock, Herbert Spencer ; to say nothing of men of
our own day whose titles to fame are not won from any
college : Whipple, Trowbridge, Parton, Bayard Taylor,
Howells, Cable, Gilder, Stoddard, and a host besides.

One of the most important factors in college life is
to be found in the associations by which enthusiasm
is excited, friendships fostered, and the individual made
to feel that he is part and parcel of a great institution, —
an institution that was before him, and that will be
when he is no more Under its auspices are gathered
into a blessed and perpetual unity, individuals from all
parts of the land, who, with him, look up to and bless
Alma Mater. Songs are sung in her praise. Festive
days, observed from time immemorial, are still kept
sacred. He walks through the old groves, sings the
old songs, and follows precedents established by past
generations In all this there is an appeal to sentiment by which the educational power of the institution is enhanced, and the student's life enriched The
" class-spirit," " society " life, college songs, games,
ancient usages, are all important elements in college
power.

These elements of power are not lost when the
college goal is reached, and the student leaves the
classic halls With the passing years, enthusiasm increases. As he grows old, his heart grows more tender
at the memory of college customs and companionships

The sense of the non-collegian's loss in this respect is not appreciated by college men. In providing for the cultivation in the C. L. S. C. of the elements which make up the *esprit du corps* of the college, I had myself but little conception of their power and value.

The appeal to sentiment was an experiment. If it did not meet with a response from the mature men and women of our circle, — many of whom were well advanced in years, — it would prove both ridiculous and disastrous. With the college outlook in prescribed courses of reading and study, memoranda to be filled out, periodical reports to be made, explanatory and helpful notes to be provided, should we add features designed to create a bond of union between our widely separated members, and to excite in them mutual sympathy and affection, notwithstanding diversities in age, temporal circumstances, and social conditions? Shall the practical aims of the circle be brightened and warmed by devices appealing to the imagination and to the social nature? ·

The experiment was made, and was crowned with success. Heartily have our members indorsed the plans adopted. Memorial Days were appointed, commemorating distinguished characters in literature and history; significant mottoes selected; songs written and set to music; badges prepared; diplomas promised; class gatherings, alumni re-unions, round-tables held, and camp-fires lighted. All these provisions of the C. L. S. C. have contributed to its power. "Recognition Day" at Chautauqua, and at the other Assemblies, is the great day of the annual gathering.

The C. L. S. C. was formally organized at Chautau-

qua, on the 10th of August, 1878. The importance of
the movement was recognized at the time. "The Daily
Assembly Herald" for Monday, Aug. 12, made editorial
allusion to the new departure in the following terms ·—

"'The Chautauqua Literary and Scientific Circle'
(a beautiful name for a society which represents a
beautiful idea) will add strength to the great organization already effected in this grove. The design, as
explained in Dr. Vincent's lecture, which appears in
this paper, will commend it to the favor of parents
and young people, scholars and professional men,
everywhere. Already over seven hundred persons
have sent in their names as candidates for membership in the C. L. S. C., which is not yet three days
old ; and already we hear individuals declaring with
emphasis, 'We shall have a *local* C. L. S. C. organized
in our town very soon after the Assembly is over.'
Eminent men from the colleges and professions and
marts of trade have identified themselves with this
new movement. Now, let every Chautauquan present and absent read Dr Vincent's lecture. In it he
states the nature and design of the Circle. . . . Every
educator and parent in the land should second his
efforts as mapped out here, because he seeks to re-
deem the young people of the country from the corrupting influence of pernicious literature, which has
no tendency to lift them up intellectually or morally.
This address will be an historical document in time
to come, and we trust the bold and daring prophecies
the doctor has made will be more than realized.
Send in your names from near and from far, if you
are ready to become members of the Circle. From

present indications, before we come to Chautauqua in 1879, we shall have two thousand names enrolled. With this new and useful, practical and popular departure, Chautauqua will put on new life "

The opening meeting of the C. L. S. C. was reported in "The Assembly Herald" for Aug. 12, as follows : —

"On Saturday morning, Aug. 10, at ten o'clock, in the Pavilion, was held the first public meeting in the interest of the Chautauqua Literary and Scientific Circle. This is a new organization, for the purpose of spreading more fully the Chautauqua idea, and providing for the Chautauquans a course of study to be pursued during the interim of the Assemblies, as well as while the Assembly is in session. The interest taken in the movement was manifested by an attendance of people which crowded the Pavilion in every part, and large numbers stood on the outside, the wall-curtains being lifted so that the speakers could be seen from every direction On the platform were seated Dr. Vincent and Bishop R. S. Foster, with many other distinguished educators ; and over two hundred ministers of different denominations were in the audience The opening exercise was the following address by the Rev. Dr. Vincent."

(The address given on the occasion by the author of the present volume is here very much condensed from the " Herald " report.)

Knowledge promotes power. It gives to a man wide vision, enlarging the world into which he was born, and multiplying worlds to which from time to time he is introduced. It is microscope and telescope to the man who possesses it. In the scheme of redemption, God has connected all grace and spiritual power with knowledge. "Grow in grace, and in the knowledge of our Lord and Saviour Jesus Christ."

Provisions are made in human society for growth in knowledge. A high estimate is placed upon it. Even the ignorant look up with awe to the men who know, and always the knowing men have advantage. In every community there are four classes of people.

First, those who are born into large intellectual opportunities, to whom the vast realm of knowledge is pointed out at the very beginning of life. Home authority directs them towards it, home example inspires them to enter it. I felt, a few weeks ago, as I stood in Westminster school, under the shadow of Westminster Abbey, in London, the power of this hereditary influence, as I might call it. A boy looks upon the walls of that Westminster school, and reads the name of his great-great-great-great-grandfather, who in 1526 was a graduate from this Westminster school. In succession, every generation, all the way down to two or three years ago, is recorded in that list. The family which has the literary taste, the hereditary influence, the parental example, gives large opportunity to the new candidates for immortality who come into it. Blessed is the home that has intellectual antecedents! The atmosphere of these homes tends largely to the awakening of literary tastes and purposes in the children. Education is systematically sought. Time is specified, places are provided, teachers are employed, books and every needed appliance are procured for the use of the pupils. Rivalry in the class-room, from the primary

class all the way to the senior class, secures intensity
and strength of purpose The very limitation which
characterizes the grammar school, with its completed
course ; the high school, with its specified curriculum ;
the college, with its four years, — tends to increase the
zeal and energy of the student I am surprised that
so few of the sons and daughters of our most cultivated
families, and of those families who, lacking the culture
and the intelligence, have the financial resources, are
found entering the college and prosecuting the college
course The man makes a great mistake who allows
his son to think, at any period of his boy life, of any
thing less than a complete college education.

Second, There are those born under the necessity
of daily toil For them educational opportunity is provided. Even where home has no literary tone, where
parents have no special delight in culture, the public
school provides tasks and teachers. But this education
is limited, and but rarely appreciated. Children go to
school to get knowledge enough for trade and bread-
winning : no more.

Third, There are those who, born under necessity,
struggle into opportunity. There are valiant souls who
without family prestige, without incitement on the part
of father or mother, seem early in life to take a wide
view, feel the necessity, and say, "By God's help, with
our own right hand, and what brain-power we have, we
will attain what culture we can" And those hard-
working fellows manage to go through college. They
fight their way up into power ; and while children of
wealth pass through the college life, very often, simply
because of the authority which puts them there, these

brave souls that feed on plain fare, and make no great
show in society, work their way up into places of power,
and are the intellectual heroes of our time. And there
are those who, not having enjoyed the opportunities of
college, and not having had the inspiration early enough,
in the later years acquire culture by some means or
other, determined to have intellectual power as their
privilege and as the heritage of their children.

Fourth, There are those born under the necessity to
which I have referred, who lack the vision at the beginning ; who need help and stimulus in the acquisition of
personal culture. They go into a trade early in life.
They early go into family life, and find it too late to go
back from business into the school. But these need
culture as parents, as citizens, as members of the
church, as workers in the various departments of
church activity, — culture as immortal souls, who by
dint of perseverance here would carry a certain measure
of intellectual force into the life eternal. Many of these
men acquire property, and pass, through the power of
property, into larger social spheres, for, as a general
rule, with property goes culture. And as these men
come up through dint of hard work into a larger sphere,
and among intellectual people, they feel a certain embarrassment, as they mingle with the better class of
society, — an embarrassment which arises from their
early lack, and their want of familiarity with the world
of art, of science, and of letters. These people are the
very ones who deplore their lack of early opportunities,
and become discouraged. The field is so vast to them,
that they do not know what to do, what to read, where
to begin. They have no teachers ; they have no facili-

ties; they have no intellectual fellowships; they have
no stimulus. And meanwhile, with this other section
of society for which no provisions are made in the line
of intellectual culture, influences are at work misdirect-
ing their intellectual forces Our young people are
reading weak, dissipating, cheap, sensational, corrupting
literature You see mothers going home on a Saturday
evening with cheap ten-cent papers and novels, with
which they propose to while away the hours of the
coming Sabbath. They have a thirst for something;
nobody directs or corrects it They follow their own
tastes and desires; and the children are brought up in
the atmosphere of that home, reading the same books,
and suffering the same mental deterioration. That is
not the worst of it Into this large, uncultivated, and
non-studious part of society, there comes an element
which threatens the very foundations of home life and
of religious life, — the popular forms of modern scepticism, in books, tracts, and papers written in the interest
of a negative theory of this life and the life to come.

Now, here are the four classes. The organization
which I have now to present for your consideration
aims to reach, uplift, inspire, and stimulate that large
class of the community which needs culture, but for
which no provision is made anywhere or by any educational institution. The name of our proposed institution
is the "Chautauqua Literary and Scientific Circle,"
which aims to give the college student's outlook upon
the world of thought, by the studies of primers of literature and science, by the reading of books, by the preparation of syllabi of books read, by written reports of
progress, and by correspondence with professors of the

several departments, who shall consent to occupy the chairs to which we shall invite them. I hold in my hand the outlines of the plan of the Chautauqua Literary and Scientific Circle. I have been assisted in its preparation by two eminent and cultivated men, whose judgment, scholarship, and practical wisdom will commend the scheme to your favorable consideration.

[Having presented the outlines, the speaker continued.]

Chautauqua is to be the centre of this course of study. Lectures are here to be delivered. Students' sessions, as at this series of meetings, will be held from year to year. I foresee a laboratory. I foresee a telescope, belonging to Chautauqua. I foresee a department of microscopy. I foresee a valuable library of scientific and religious works. I foresee a museum of art. I have already staked out a charming grove into which we shall come in a few evenings, — those of us who are willing to accept the proposed course of study, — and in what we shall call "St. Paul's Grove" we shall find a centre for our students of nature, art, science, and the most holy Word. We shall constitute the blessed brotherhood of the "Chautauqua Literary and Scientific Circle." We look forward to the organization all over the country, of local circles, with libraries, where a few persons may come together, and if they are not able each to purchase all the books which shall be read in the four-years' course, a fund may be raised, and the books be loaned, and one after another read. Circles may be organized for reading together aloud many of these books. The detailed plans of this organization will be hereafter presented.

By individual study the influence of the Circle may be promoted. A system of correspondence with professors of departments will be arranged. Monthly reports will be made by those who engage in the study. Local institutions, high schools, seminaries, colleges with their courses of lectures, will in many cases contribute towards the assistance of those who, living in the vicinity, propose to pursue this course; and by the time the student reaches the beginning of the third year he will be able to say, "I find that my tastes run in the line of natural science," say of geology, "and by your consent, members of the faculty, I will make geology my specialty for the remaining two years." In that case, where the specialty is developed, and the man wishes to prosecute a most thorough course of reading, such provision will be made for his accommodation

Here are some of the advantages of this organization: It will develop higher and nobler tastes; increase mental power; exalt home-life, giving authority and home-help in public-school studies, and organizing home into reading circles. It will counteract the influence of our modern popular pernicious literature, and sweeten and enrich the daily lives of poor and hard-working people It will bring the more cultivated people into contact with the less scholarly, promote a true appreciation of science, and tend to increase the spiritual life and power of the Church. All knowledge becomes glorified in the man whose heart is consecrated to God.

[The speaker answered the objection to the plan of study based upon its superficiality.] Superficial it is, and so is any college course of study. The boy who stands at the close of his senior year, on Commence-

ment Day, to receive his parchment and whatever
honors belong to him, who does not feel that his whole
course has been superficial, will not be likely to succeed in the after-struggle of life. But superficiality is
better than absolute ignorance. It is better for a man
to take a general survey, to catch somewhere a point
that arrests him ; for the man who never takes a survey
never catches the point in which dwell the possibilities of power for him. By this superficial view he
develops taste and power. When you sow seed, it is
not the weight of the seed put into the soil that tells,
but it is the weight of the harvest that comes after.

Let me give you a fact concerning Prof. Joseph
Henry, of the Smithsonian Institute : "As a boy he
was an inveterate novel-reader, until at sixteen an English book of scientific lectures happened to fall into his
hands. He was so interested in it, that the owner presented it to him, and he kept it ever afterwards among
his treasures. On the fly-leaf is written this paragraph,.
written by him in 1837: 'This book, although by no
means a profound work, has, under Providence, exerted
a remarkable influence upon my life. It accidentally
fell into my hands when I was about sixteen years old,
and was the first book, with the exception of books of
fiction, that I ever read with attention. It opened to
me a new world of thought and enjoyment, invested
things almost unnoticed with the highest interest, fixed
my mind on the study of nature, and caused me to
resolve, at the time of reading it, that I would devote
my life to the acquisition of knowledge.'"

Suppose our Chautauqua Literary and Scientific Circle had dropped that book into the hands of the boy

Joseph Henry, where is your learned professor who is to say, "Ah, that is doing nothing. That is superficial work"? When I place, within four years, fifty books into the hands of a thousand young and old people over this land, with a prescribed course for reading and study, first to discover their special power, and then to inspire them to prosecute a course of study in that direction, who will dare to say that I am doing superficial work?

But some one objects that "this does not promote spiritual life. It is not legitimate work for an encampment originally established for devotional meetings, and now existing under the auspices of a Sunday-school association." Away with this dividing-up of things! All things that are legitimate are of God. The human intellect belongs to God, and is to be cultivated for him. And when I see John Wesley, on fire with zeal to save souls, sitting down to write Hebrew grammars, and Greek grammars, and French grammars; when I see John Wesley taking Shakspere's plays, and so selecting, abridging, and modifying that he could put them into the hands of young people for their culture; when I see what John Wesley did in the promotion of secular culture among his people, that they might be broad as well as intense, — I say again, Away with the heresy that a man is stepping aside from his legitimate work as a Christian minister when he is trying to turn all secular nature into an altar for the glory of God!

I met a friend in Europe a few weeks ago, who said to me as I described this Chautauqua Literary and Scientific Circle, "I will present to your Circle as elegant a banner as I can procure in Europe. I will have the silk woven for it in France, I will have the design painted upon it in Italy." And we selected, after consultation, the motto for our banner, — the motto, the watchword of our Chautauqua Literary and Scientific Society. It is as follows: " WE STUDY THE WORD AND THE WORKS OF GOD." And last year, when my venerable friend Dr. Vail came into this tent, and sitting down here, in the competitive examination, picked up the fifty questions, and wrote his answers to them, as he passed in his examination-papers to me, I shall never forget how he looked, and how his voice trembled, as he bade me good-by, not knowing that he should ever return ; he said to me (and I have taken this as the second motto for the Chautauqua Literary and Scientific Circle), " LET US KEEP OUR HEAVENLY FATHER IN THE MIDST."

In our studies in the school that is to be, let us keep the thought of our Father in the midst of nature, the thought of our Father in the midst of literature, and the thought of our Father in every-day life.

So this "every-day college," this Chautauqua Literary and Scientific Circle, will grow. It must grow. I have had a few candidates present their names. I do not know how many. If we have ten to begin with, I shall think it quite a success. We shall invite people all over the United States to unite with us. We shall not make it expensive ; we shall not actually require a pilgrimage to Chautauqua, although we shall greatly aid and inspire those who do come. But student-lamps will be trimmed on many a little table over this land the coming winter. Fellowships will be formed. The thought that we are one, engaged in a common purpose of culture for God's glory, will help us; and we shall return to Chautauqua year after year, members and alumni in the Chautauqua Literary and Scientific Circle, proud of our *Alma Mater*, and determined to exalt and honor her wherever we are.

And now, a few words to those who may sign their names to the blanks which will be distributed before the close of this service To you who are old, and want to undertake the course: Finish in heaven if you cannot finish on earth. You are never too old to begin. I do not believe in the idea of people getting old.

See a man sixty, seventy, or eighty years old. Who will call a man eighty years old an old man, when he is destined to live forever in the presence of God? I admire the record of the venerable man who began studying Latin at sixty years of age. I admire the spirit of the man who says, "Too old? Never too old while my heart beats, and I have the heavens overhead, and God's great Book open before me."

How glad I should be if I should find in the future years, that more boys and girls are going to our high schools and universities because of the impulse in this line received here at Chautauqua! And I say to you: With all your getting, get understanding Look through microscopes, but find God. Look through telescopes, but find God. Look for him revealed in the throbbing life about you, in the palpitating stars above, in the marvellous records of the earth beneath you, and in your own souls. Study the possibilities which God unfolds, and make of yourselves all that you can.

To those of you who, with circumstances against you, are about to enter this course of reading, let me say:

The harder the struggle, the brighter the crown. Go on! Have faith and holy purpose. Go on to *know* and *will*, to *do* and *be;* and when outward circumstances discourage, trample the circumstances under foot. Be master of circumstances, like the king that God has called you to be.

> "I see a youth whom God has crowned with power,
> And cursed with poverty. With bravest heart
> He struggles with his lot through toilsome years,
> Kept to his task by daily want of bread,
> And kept to virtue by his daily task;
> Till, gaining manhood in the manly strife,
> The fire that fills him smitten from a flint,
> The strength that arms him wrested from a fiend,
> He stands at last a master of himself,
> And in that grace a master of his kind."

God give you such hearts, such toil, such triumphs, and give you such masterhood, as shall one of these days place you among the kings and priests of a redeemed and purified universe! [Great applause.]

At the close of Dr. Vincent's address, Rev. M. L. Williston of Jamestown, N.Y., read the following poem, written for the occasion by Miss Mary A. Lathbury, of New York, entitled

LIGHT.

> Jerusalem the olden,
>   Asleep among her hills,
> Hath many a dream prophetic
>   The waking world fulfils, —
> Her pride and desolation;
>   Her bondage and her tears;

Her dream of battles, flashing
  Across the lurid years
A light on cross and crescent,
  And on the knightly throngs
Who wage our bloodless battles
  To the old Crusader's songs.
For all that is — ay, even
  The texture of a dream —
Is wrought in wondrous pattern
  Beneath the things that seem;
Until His hand, who cometh
  And maketh "all things new,"
Shall lift the veil that gave us
  But "figures of the true."

Within the Holy City,
  Beneath a pagan dome,
Once every year "the Faithful"
  In thronging thousands come;
With faces raised, exalted,
  In each uplifted hand
A taper yet unlighted,
  A silent host they stand,
With eyes of expectation
  Upon the vaulted wall,
Whence, from the blue above it,
  The holy fire shall fall.
And when at last, descending,
  They mark the floating flame,
A thousand hands are lifted
  In holy Allah's name;
And blessed he whose taper,
  First kindling in the glow
Of that descending marvel,
  Shall lend its light, and so
From hand to hand, from torch
  To taper in its flight,
The sacred fire of heaven
  Has spread, and all is light.

Jerusalem the olden
  Sleeps like a stagnant stream:
To her the falling of the fire
  Is but a fitful dream.
And if across her vision
  Unholy hands have tossed
Unholy fire, to kindle
  A pagan Pentecost,
No less is ours the glory
  And gladness of that sight;
Not less to us the promise
  Of the coming of the Light.

O friends whose hope and longing
  Outrun the years, to meet
That age whose coming footsteps
  Are heard in every street!
You in whose eyes the shining
  Of love and faith is set,
To light dark souls who wander
  Along the lowlands yet;
Think not because the hill-tops
  Are glowing in the dawn,
That glory cometh only
  With the coming of the morn.
God shineth in the darkness:
  And through the rayless skies,
Because his voice hath called them,
  A thousand stars shall rise.
And if from the mid-heavens
  A light above the sun
Shall fall with sudden glory,
  The light is still but one;
For that which over Bethlehem
  And o'er Damascus shone,
Shines in the world's fair dawning,
  And the rainbow round the throne.

O friends and brothers, gathered
  Around the open Word,
The heavens are rent above us
  With the glory of the Lord!
No eye of sense may see it,
  No human hand aspire
To lay on earthly altars
  That pure immortal fire;
But to the heart that waiteth,
  To eyes athirst for light,
Descends the blessed vision,
  And there is "no more night!"
Then each to each transmitting
  The light, the life, the truth,
What wonder if the beauty
  And the glory of a youth
Born of spirit, and eternal,
  Shine o'er all the earth again,
And the Bride, the holy city
  Of the heavens, is with men!

Humanity is lifting
  Her waiting face to God,
And in her hand she beareth
  The old divining-rod
Which sprang in early Eden, —
  A scion of that tree
Whose fruit might only ripen
  With earth's maturity.
With it the old magicians
  Once sought to touch the stars,
When Science groped for knowledge
  Behind her prison-bars;
Across it creeds and systems
  Have stumbled to their fall;
To win it, men and nations
  Have staked and lost their all.

Religion, weak and weary,
    Cast as a broken reed
The rod of knowledge from her,
    And leaned upon her creed.
But, dawning o'er the ages,
    The Light and Life of God
Have stirred with spring-time pulses
    The world's divining-rod;
And she — the human — standing
    Upon her latest height,
Bears it with eyes of patience
    Uplifted to the light.
And lo! the rod has budded,
    To blossom, as of old
The rod of Aaron blossomed
    Beside the ark of gold!
No longer through the shadows
    She seeketh for a sign;
She needeth not her wise men,
    Her oracles divine.
The Life of God is shining
    Upon her where she stands;
And, leaf by leaf unfolding
    Within her reverent hands,
The earth and seas and heavens
    Disclose her secrets old,
And every force of Nature
    Reveals its heart of gold!
Now knoweth she the answer
    That ends the schoolmen's strife, —
That knowledge bears no blossom
    Till quickened by the Life.

O holy, holy city!
    The Life of God with men!
Descending out of heaven
    To ne'er ascend again.
O Light — O Life immortal!
    One sea above, below!

If unto us be given
That blessed thing, — TO KNOW, —
Hope's beatific vision
And Faith's prophetic sight
Shall die before the fulness
Of that unclouded Light.

After the reading of the poem, Dr. Vincent said: "In the preparation for this important occasion, I have consulted some of the most experienced and practical educators of the country; and from a number of distinguished gentlemen I have received letters relating to this movement."

The letters were then read by Rev. H. W. Warren, D.D., of Philadelphia, who prefaced the reading by saying, "These letters being written to Dr. Vincent, some of them are naturally complimentary to him. He thought best to leave out those portions. I insisted that he could stand having them read, and that he ought to be crucified if need be; that the men who had written the letters had a right to have them read as they are, and so they shall be read. [Applause] Of course it is expected that the press would indorse an enterprise like this; so I bring you the letter of an editor, first of all, — an editor you have often seen here, with a very large head and a little body, but an enormously large heart, — the Rev. Lyman Abbott, D.D., of "The Christian Union," New York.

"THE KNOLL," CORNWALL-ON-THE-HUDSON,
July 25, 1878.

MY DEAR DR. VINCENT, — Your letter of July 10 did not in the least surprise me, because all your friends have learned to expect surprises from you : nothing is unexpected except the expected.

Chautauqua proves its right to be called immortal, by continually growing larger and better.

Your plan for making it a university for the year, instead of a mere summer university, is worthy of the spirit of Methodism, which is certainly ubiquitous if not omnipresent.

It seems to me if you can lay out such plans of study, particularly in the departments of practical science, as will fit our boys and young men in the mining, manufacturing, and agricultural districts, to become, in a true though not ambitious sense of the term, scientific and intelligent miners, mechanics, and farmers, you will have done more to put down strikes and labor-riots than an army could ; and more to solve the labor problem than will be done by the Babel-builders of a hundred labor-reform conventions.

You have my heartiest sympathies, and my most earnest good wishes, in this new endeavor to preach the gospel, which includes, as Christ defines it, "opening the eyes of the blind," as well as setting free the captive.

Yours very sincerely,   LYMAN ABBOTT.

Dr. Warren said, "There is another class of men from whom we shall expect indorsement ; that is, the theological professors. I bring you one from a man, black hair, dark-complexioned, but full of fire as if he were covered with a crown of gold. I refer to Dr. Townsend, of Boston University, whom you have often heard."

BOSTON, July 30, 1878.

MY DEAR VINCENT, — Your plan for the promotion of Christian culture in art, science, and literature, among the masses of the American people, strikes me as one of the grandest conceptions of the nineteenth century. The so-called common people of our country are showing themselves ripe and qualified for such culture, as never before, in their desire for and comprehension of the latest results of scientific research. I predict for the movement great success and grand results.

Would not the Atlantic coast be an excellent place for such a school?

Very truly yours, L. T. TOWNSEND.

DR. WARREN — "Another theological professor, whom you have heard here with great pleasure, — Dr. A. A. Hodge, of Princeton."

PRINCETON, N.J., July 23, 1878.

MY DEAR DR VINCENT, — I am delighted to hear of your movement for increasing the influence for good of your Chautauqua Assembly. The scheme is a grand one, and only needs, to assure its success, that efficient administration which has so eminently characterized all your enterprises. History and nature are the spheres in which God exercises his perfections, through which they are manifested to us. All human knowledge should be comprehended in the one system of which Christ is the centre, and illuminated with the light of revelation. And revelation itself will appear more certainly divine, and its sphere more complete, when it is viewed in all its natural relations to the works of God in creation and providence. Truth is the great instrument by which the God of light works, and the whole truth is the only pure truth. We need all the broad lights and all the side lights to sweep away the shadows in which alone scepticism and superstition lurk. The workers in the Christian Church, above all others, need this comprehensive illumination. As dispensers of the light of God as it shines in the face of Jesus Christ, they should cultivate the faculty of casting that light abroad over all his works, and thus, making the entire universe his temple, irradiate it with his glory. May God guide you, and crown all the endeavors with which he inspires you with complete success.

Yours sincerely,   A. A. HODGE.

DR. WARREN. — "Now I bring you a letter fragrant with the breezes of the Berkshire hills, full of the ozone of those forests, as the atmosphere is full of the ozone of this forest. I refer to the letter of Arthur Gilman."

LANESBOROUGH, BERKSHIRE CO, MASS.,
July 25, 1878.

MY DEAR SIR, — Your letter in which you bring to my attention your plan for a Literary and Scientific Circle at Chautauqua has found me here, having been forwarded from Cambridge.

I have learned the details of your plan with interest. There are many who have not the advantage of the home circle, nor the stimulus of a literary atmosphere, to whom you can in the way you propose give a start in the way upward.

Your fears of "superficiality" do not trouble me. For your course will probably aim rather to direct the mind toward the way in which you wish it to develop, than store it with the details of knowledge. You wish to awaken, rather than to cultivate ; to show what can be done to create curiosity to know and an ambition to do.

When once you have given the mind a start, and have pointed out the way to knowledge, you will have laid a foundation upon which you may confidently believe that something worthy will be erected.

I thank you for letting me know your plans, and shall be interested to learn of their success, for which I look.

Sincerely yours,   ARTHUR GILMAN.

DR. WARREN. — "But do these college men think that such a plan is feasible ? They with their cloister walks, their quiet places, and four years exclusive study, — what do they say can be done in the midst of such as these, in the region of ordinary and every-day life ? I will read you a manly letter from Dr. Howard Crosby, a man who believes in his own opinions, and, if he does not believe in other people's opinions, attacks the gigantic sins of civilization single-handed and alone, that he may do, his part in accordance with his own opinions."

MY DEAR DR. VINCENT, — Your scheme to induce business men and others to pursue useful courses of reading in science and history is worthy of all commen- dation. While we cannot expect to make such persons scientists or scholars, we may expect them to become appreciative of things scientific and scholarly, and to be able to discriminate between the false and the true.

The books for such a curriculum should be very carefully chosen. In science they should be such as only
give the aspects of nature and a few fundamental principles. Any thing technically scientific would either
disgust or mislead. In history they should be clear
outlines, rather than exhaustive philosophic treatises.
No one can make up for the want of a college education. The four-years attrition with other minds is a
sharpening process that nothing else will furnish. If
you can make parents comprehend this so that they
will not let their sons slip by the college, you will do a
great thing. Your plan will warn people against the
waste of time and the injury to mind and soul in the
reading of low sensational stories, when useful and
elevating knowledge is within their reach.

Trusting that you may carry out your scheme to
perfection, I am

Yours very truly,   HOWARD CROSBY.

116 East Nineteenth Street, New York,
    July 15, 1878.

Dr. Warren. — "Another college president. Dr.
Foss, President of the Wesleyan University, at Middletown, Conn., — what does he say can be done?"

Middletown, Conn., July 25, 1878.

My dear Dr. Vincent, — Yours received. I hasten
to say that your plan of "The Chautauqua Literary and
Scientific Circle" has my hearty approval. If executed
according to your idea, and with the enthusiasm generally manifested by those who marshal themselves under
your leadership, I think it will be good and only good,
and that continually, so far as it goes; and I trust it

will go far enough to be a great help to Sunday-school teachers, and to inspire a multitude of the choice youth of the Church to seek a liberal education.

Yours very truly,   C D FOSS.

DR WARREN — "Let us now hear from William C Wilkinson, professor of sacred rhetoric in the Rochester Theological Seminary"

TARRYTOWN, Aug. 3, 1878.

REV J. H. VINCENT, D D.

My dear Sir, — The movement which you propose, under the title of "Chautauqua Literary and Scientific Circle," is one that must command the earnest sympathy and respect of every intelligent well-wisher to his kind. There is even an air of boldness and breadth about it which excites my admiration I cordially wish it the largest measure of success

It will doubtless be disparaged by many as visionary and impracticable. But so, before its present brilliant realization, would have been the whole idea of the Chautauqua Sunday-school Assembly Too many derivative enterprises like it are now springing into existence all over the country, for that to be any longer dismissed from thought as chimerical. If your new and nobler conception should prove correspondingly successful, the multiplication of kindred popular "circles" may be looked for as a legitimate, fruitful, diffusive result of your public-spirited and generous initiative at Chautauqua Certainly you have created auspices for the proposed movement, under which success, if success be possible at all, is well assured beforehand.

I believe you will succeed; and if you do, the true measure of your success, it will remain for many future generations to witness and to appreciate.

In addition to the many important utilities of your plan which the terms of your prospectus suggest, I anticipate others of scarcely inferior value. The practical working of the movement will tend to create for it a peculiar literature of its own. This in itself will be a great gain to the cause of popular enlightenment. The model of style appropriate to primers of science, of letters, of history, of political economy, and of other such branches of human knowledge as will be likely to engage the attention of your " Circle," must necessarily exert a most salutary influence for clearness, directness, and simplicity, on all the current literary production of the times. Besides, the success of your enterprise will multiply readers of books, and so stimulate writers to produce. It will be very sure also to awaken and develop literary and scientific ability in minds where it would otherwise lie dormant and useless, and thus increase the intellectual wealth of mankind. It will enlighten and invigorate public sentiment to favor institutions of higher education.

In short, your proposal, in degree as it is carried into successful execution, will prove a useful agency in helping forward the always exigent cause of mental, moral, social, political, and religious progress among men. I send you my heartiest God-speed in the good work to which you have now given the pledge of your reputation worthily won in kindred undertakings for the public advantage.

Most cordially,   **WILLIAM C. WILKINSON.**

DR. WARREN — "And now, as indicating how the thing may be done, how every church may be a centre from which all these influences may go out ; as indicating the acceptance of the idea by one of the most practical minds in the great city of New York, — I read you a letter from the pastor of the Church of the Strangers. This pastor is no stranger to you, however. I refer to the Rev. Dr. Charles F. Deems of New York."

NEW YORK, July 15, 1878.

MY DEAR DOCTOR, — Your plan for the organization of a Chautauqua Literary and Scientific Circle meets my heartiest approbation. For some weeks I have been pondering a similar idea. The difficulties which suggested themselves to me would have disappeared if I had connected the idea with the resources of Chautauqua. I now wonder that I was not bright enough to do so. In the "Church of the Strangers" are all the classes enumerated in your letter to me. We have business men who have not enjoyed collegiate advantages, to whom one hour devoted to literary and scientific culture, with a purpose, would be an intellectual tonic of great advantage to their hours of trade. We have also the class of mothers you describe, and of the young men engaged at trades and in business. We have a few "young ladies of leisure ;" but we have many more young ladies who have little leisure, and have as bright minds as their more favored sisters, and perhaps a greater desire for culture, because, it may be, they have a greater sense of its need. It was this class especially for which I desired to provide. Your plan meets this want. A four-years' course might be arranged, with thorough annual examinations, and a diploma at the close. You may rely upon my hearty co-operation.

Wishing the scheme the most complete success, I remain

Cordially your friend,   CHARLES F. DEEMS.

DR. WARREN. — "Years ago our ears were dinned to weariness with the glories of the Prussian system of common-school education. A few years afterwards it was discovered, excellent as that system of education was, that in consequence of the lack of books, of papers, of stimulus to read, many of those perfectly trained children forgot their instruction, and ceased to remember how to read To start a soul upward in the ways of knowledge, and then leave it with no incitement to go forward, is certainly a great blunder. I am not sure but the last state of that man would be worse than the first. Let us remember, God has spread the great pages of his work above us, and says to every one of us, as he said unto Abraham, 'Lift up now thine eyes on high, and behold and number the stars, if thou be able.' Let us remember he has put the Word in the pages that are at our feet, and has said, 'Consider the lilies of the field.' Referring to life and zoölogy, he wants us to take note of the very sparrows. The people are ready; all that is needed is the presentation of a plan. The plan is before you: take it to your heads, take it to your hearts. [Applause.]"

Dr. Vincent then read the following letter from the President of Boston University : —

BOSTON, July 20, 1878.

REV. DR. VINCENT, Plainfield, N.J.

My dear Brother, — The proposal set forth in yours of the 10th inst. strikes me as a legitimate and promising supplement to that vast system of home education which you have done so much to stimulate and direct. When some of the would-be Thomas Carlyles hear of it, they will no doubt essay to project some unutterable volcanic protest against it, stigmatizing it as a new device of the evil spirit of scientific and literary democracy for the purpose of multiplying pygmies and propagating sciolism, but when the genuine old Thomas himself shall come to inquire into it, who that has read his only Lord Rector's address to young folk, and seen the importance he attaches to books and self-instruction, can for a moment doubt that he will give the plan one of his toughest, heartiest, and most ursine benedictions? Would you could have him with you Aug. 10, to give the undertaking the right kind of a launch!

You are aiming to secure that without which every system of education is weak, and with which any is strong; namely, interested personal home work the year round. And you seem to carry these young home students forward to the point where they can go alone, if they cannot have the help of the schools. In many cases there will, of course, be failures, but in many more there will be success. In proportion to the success, I shall be more than ever proud of my country, and confident as to its future. With best wishes, ever

Yours fraternally,   W. F. WARREN.

Dr. Vincent then said, "I hold a very delicate bit of paper in my hand. Last summer I enjoyed the pleasure of an interview with William Cullen Bryant. I explained to him fully the system which we contemplated. I wrote him afterward a long letter, defining it more clearly, if possible; and through friends that were conversant with the scheme, that distinguished man became thoroughly acquainted with our aims and methods. While in London a few weeks ago, I received from him the following letter, written in his own hand, — written but a few weeks before his death. This letter has never been read in public, and has never appeared in print."

NEW YORK, May 18, 1878.

MY DEAR SIR, — I cannot be present at the meeting called to organize the Chautauqua Literary and Scientific Circle; but I am glad that such a movement is on foot, and wish it the fullest success. There is an attempt to make science, or a knowledge of the laws of the material universe, an ally of the school which denies a separate spiritual existence and a future life; in short, to borrow of science weapons to be used against Christianity. The friends of religion, therefore, confident that one truth never contradicts another, are doing wisely when they seek to accustom the people at large to think and to weigh evidence as well as believe. By giving a portion of their time to a vigorous training of the intellect, and a study of the best books, men gain the power to deal satisfactorily with questions with which the mind might otherwise become bewildered. It is true that there is no branch of human knowledge so important as that which teaches the duties that we owe to God and to each other, and that there is no law of the universe, sublime and wonderful as it may be, so worthy of being fully known as the law of love, which makes him who obeys it a blessing to his species, and the universal observance of which would put an end to a large proportion of the evils which affect mankind. Yet is a knowledge of the results of science, and such of its processes as lie most open to the popular mind, important for the purpose of showing the different spheres occupied by science and religion, and preventing the inquirer from mistaking their divergence from each other for opposition.

I perceive this important advantage in the proposed organization ; namely, that those who engage in it will mutually encourage each other. It will give the members a common pursuit, which always begets a feeling of brotherhood ; they will have a common topic of conversation and discussion : and the consequence will be, that many who, if they stood alone, might soon grow weary of the studies which are recommended to them, will be incited to perseverance by the interest which they see others taking in them. It may happen, in rare instances, that a person of eminent mental endowments, which otherwise might have remained uncultivated and unknown, will be stimulated in this manner to diligence, and put forth unexpected powers, and, passing rapidly beyond the rest, become greatly distinguished, and take a place among the luminaries of the age.

I shall be interested to watch, during the little space of life that may yet remain to me, the progress and results of the plan which has drawn from me this letter.

I am, sir,   Very truly yours,   W. C. BRYANT.

REV. DR. JOHN H VINCENT

After the reading of the letter of Mr. Bryant, Bishop Foster of Boston said, " We live to learn.   Were it not for the history of Chautauqua, I should look upon the scheme which has been opened to you to-day as one of the most gigantic chimeras I ever heard of ; but with that history lying back of me, . . . I begin to look upon it as a grand and glorious something that has a future to it.   One of the saddest spectacles to my mind, despite the beauty of our civilization, — a civilization unsurpassed by any recorded in the history of time, — is the vast outlying acres and continents of fallow mind ; mind unapprised of its power and of its heritage ; and, if possible, still more sad, the vast fields of hungry and unhappy mind, not knowing where to look for help.   I have long believed that in the uneducated, — I do not mean now the term in a strict sense, but the uneducated in the higher walks of learning, — there is a state of hunger, of desire, that is unappreciated by educated men.   I have recognized it in my ministry, bringing before the people from time to time the great fundamental and grand truths of religion which are so generally ignored and neglected by the pulpit.   I have heard time and again, that the people cannot appreciate discussion, — that they will weary of discussions of that kind.   I am here to say, after an experience of forty years, that the profoundest discussions my mind has ever been able to elaborate have been the most entrancing to the common people.   They have listened to them with the greatest possible eagerness, and I believe they have produced the most profound and blessed truths.   I am thoroughly convinced that there is a hunger of mind abroad in the land, — in the rural districts, in the villages, among the working-people, and the trades-people, the people that are not acquainted with school thought and school learning in the higher forms, — that we do not understand or appreciate; and I believe that this movement which is now launched will succeed in accomplishing two things that will be very beneficial. It will minister to a vast number of minds that have gone beyond an age to initiate collegiate study and prosecute it to the end. It will bring to them an outlook into the fields of truth. Mere school education in the ordinary form serves simply to put into the hands of men instruments to prosecute the pursuit of knowledge. It does not minister knowledge, but furnishes the means of further attaining it. It opens the door to lead out the thought, to lay before the mind the map of what is to be conquered, — what is to be possessed. When men pass out of the school without this information, I do not wonder that they subside into utter inanity and inaction, and lapse back again into an ignorance perhaps worse than if they had never been educated at all. The mind should have the doors opened to it, that it should be able to look out into the great world of truth in every direction, and see its vastness and infinitude; and it should allow the information to go out and possess it. I believe this school will furnish this information to a large number of those who have passed beyond the age of school study. I therefore congratulate you and our country, and our great civilization, on the inception of this new movement, and pray it may advance to a glorious culmination."

The first year's course of reading was announced. It embraced the following books. Green's Short History of the English People; Chautauqua Text-Book No. 4, Outlines of English History; Chautauqua Text-Book No. 5, Outlines of Greek History, Mahaffey's Old Greek Life; Stopford Brooke's Primer of English Literature; Chautauqua Text-Book No 6, Greek Literature; Chautauqua Text-Book No 2, on Studies of the Stars; Warren's Recreations in Astronomy; J. Dorman Steele's Human Physiology; Hurst's Outlines of Bible History; and Pierce's Word of God Opened.   Over eight thousand four hundred names were enrolled the first year, in the class of 1882.   At the suggestion of wise and practical friends of the C. L S. C., a modification was made in the plan of study, by which the readings of the several classes for any one year should be substantially the same, thus securing the benefit of unity in the classes of the several years

Many who undertook the course of study became discouraged, and dropped out entirely   Many continued to read portions of the course, keeping up their relation to the Circle, but not attempting to graduate at the end of four years.   In 1882, 1,718 members of the first class received their diploma   "Recognition Day" (Commencement Day, as it was then called) was a great day at Chautauqua.   A report of the proceedings as published in "The Chautauquan" will give some idea of the enthusiasm which prevailed.

Graduation in the C L S C simply means that the college outlook has been completed, and that the reader, having received his diploma, begins a more thorough course of reading in lines of his own choice. A large number of reading courses are provided.   On the diploma are thirty-one blank spaces on which seals are to be placed as the holder completes the successive courses outlined for him.

The following is the report in "The Chautauquan" for October, 1882 : —

All through the past year, members of the C L S.C. class of 1882 looked forward to the 12th of August as their day of graduation   When the day came round, about eight hundred members of the class, each with the C.L.S.C. badge pinned over the heart, were in the procession, marching through the arches ·to the inspiring music of the North-western Band.   The day was beautiful ; Nature was in accord with the Chautauqua idea.   The sun shone from a cloudless sky, the air was cool, the lake was calm, the grove appeared in its best dress, and cottages and public buildings were handsomely decorated with flags and banners and evergreens   A great multitude of people had gathered, representing every State in the Union, and most of the Territories.   Many were present from Canada, some from England and India, and other distant lands.   And yet the interested parties were not all present   More than one thousand members of the class of 1882, who were counted among the graduates, were detained at their homes, scattered far and wide over the country ; but they were not forgotten by their classmates, by the orators of the day, by the singers in their songs, nor by the officers of the C L S C , for ere this time they have sent out to the thousand absent ones their diplomas   No verse of song or passage of an oration was more appropriate to the day than this first verse of the C.L.S.C. Song of 1880 : —

"A song is thrilling through the trees,
 And vibrant through the air;
Ten thousand hearts turn hitherward,
 And greet us from afar;
And through the happy tide of song,
 That blends our hearts in one,
The voices of the absent flow
 In tender undertone.
Then bear along, O wings of song,
 Our happy greeting glee,
From centre to the golden verge,
 Chautauqua to the sea."

St. Paul's Grove, in the centre of which is located the Hall of Philosophy, seemed to breathe the spirit of the day. Four years ago, in this place, the C. L. S. C. was organized, before the Hall of Philosophy was erected, or the grove was cleared, improved, or beautified. The Hall was adorned for the day, and all the surroundings wore a classic air. On its supporting pillars, looking inward, were the busts of "vast Plato," the great philosopher of Greece, Socrates his master, Homer the poet of the world, Virgil of noble song, Goethe the greatest genius of Germany, and Shakspere the greater genius of England. Between the pillars were suspended sixteen hanging baskets filled with choicest plants, beautiful in flower and foliage. Large urns filled with rare plants were placed on either side of the arch-guarded walk. The line of march for the class from Merrill Avenue to the Hall passed beneath four high and broad arches, — the first golden, passed by the class of 1882, and to be passed by every graduating class in the future; the second evergreen; the third floral; and the fourth rustic, — all magnificently

trimmed with evergreens, flowers, and moss, and rich
in symbolic meaning. Eight great pillars, iron-clad,
surround the Hall on either side. On these were the
lamp-stands and lamps on which at night burned the
Athenian watch-fires. The plan was most original and
full of meaning, and the arrangements were complete.
Too much praise cannot be ascribed to Lewis Miller,
Esq., Dr. Vincent, and others who brought to a successful issue this important work.

At precisely 9.45, on Saturday, the 12th of August,
the Third Division of the great anniversary procession
was organized in front of the cottage of Dr. J. H. Vincent, and marched in the following order : The Chief
of Police of Chautauqua ; the North-western Band, of
Meadville, Penn., with seventeen pieces, Prof. Luc
Houze leader ; the Banner of the Chautauqua Literary
and Scientific Circle, veiled in white, and borne by
Messrs. W. E. H. Massey and Will Butler. Then came
Dr. J. H. Vincent, Superintendent of Instruction, the
Counsellors of the C.L.S.C., Bishop Henry W. Warren,
Dr. Lyman Abbott, followed by Rev. A. H. Gillett
(messenger), and others. The line of march was out
Lake Avenue to Cookman, up Cookman to Fletcher,
through Fletcher to Haven, up Haven to the Hall of
Philosophy. Many of the cottages and tents on the
line of march were gayly decorated with flags and
streamers, while mottoes and hanging plants served to
lend an unusual charm to the route.

When the head of the procession approached Fletcher
Avenue, the solid mass of eight hundred members of
the class of 1882, gathered in the neighborhood of the
gate of St. Paul's Grove, parted to permit the passage

of the honored Superintendent and Counsellors, giving them the warmest expressions of regard and honor as they passed. On reaching the junction of Clark and Haven Avenues, the band took its position on the outer field, while the Superintendent and Counsellors passed into the great Hall, being soon joined by Dr. W. C. Wilkinson, the third of the Counsellors able to be present. The Hall of Philosophy was well guarded by the faithful keepers of the grove, under the direction of Marshal J. D. Pepper, and none were permitted to cross the sacred lines save the officials of the day.

Promptly at 9 58, Division No. IV — composed of the "C. L. S. C. Glee Club," eight members, Prof. C. C. Case conductor; and the "Choir of the Hall in the Grove," thirty-seven members, Prof. W. F. Sherwin conductor — entered the sacred enclosure, and took appointed positions, the "Choir of the Hall in the Grove" in the rear of the Floral Procession, and facing the walk from St. Paul's Gate; the "Glee Club" at the right of the platform in the Hall of Philosophy, Miss Fannie A. Compton presiding at the organ.

At the stroke of the great Chautauqua bell announcing the hour of ten o'clock, the members of the graduating class, standing together outside of St. Paul's Grove, read responsively, Dr. S. J. M Eaton leading in the first section, and Rev J. L. Hurlbut leading in the second section, as follows : —

FIRST SECTION. — Surely there is a vein for the silver, and a place for gold where they fine it.

SECOND SECTION. — Iron is taken out of the earth, and brass is molten out of the stone.

FIRST SECTION — He setteth an end to darkness, and searcheth out all perfection: the stones of darkness, and the shadow of death.

SECOND SECTION. — The flood breaketh out from the inhabitant; even the waters forgotten of the foot; they are dried up, they are gone away from men.

FIRST SECTION. — As for the earth, out of it cometh bread: and under is turned up as it were fire

SECOND SECTION. — The stones of it are the place of sapphires, and it hath dust of gold.

FIRST SECTION. — There is a path which no fowl knoweth, and which the vulture's eye hath not seen.

SECOND SECTION. — The lion's whelps have not trodden it, nor the fierce lion passed by it.

FIRST SECTION. — He putteth forth his hand upon the rock; he overturneth the mountains by the roots.

SECOND SECTION. — He cutteth out rivers among the rocks; and his eye seeth every precious thing.

FIRST SECTION. — He bindeth the floods from overflowing; and the thing that is hid bringeth he forth to light.

SECOND SECTION. — But where shall wisdom be found? and where is the place of understanding?

FIRST SECTION. — Man knoweth not the price thereof; neither is it found in the land of the living.

SECOND SECTION. — The depth saith, It is not in me; and the sea saith, It is not with me.

FIRST SECTION. — It cannot be gotten for gold, neither shall silver be weighed for the price thereof.

SECOND SECTION. — It cannot be valued with the gold of Ophir, with the precious onyx, or the sapphire.

FIRST SECTION. — The gold and the crystal cannot equal it; and the exchange of it shall not be for jewels of fine gold.

SECOND SECTION. — No mention shall be made of corals or of pearls; for the price of wisdom is above rubies.

FIRST SECTION. — The topaz of Ethiopia shall not equal it, neither shall it be valued with pure gold.

Rev A. H. Gillet, Messenger, standing outside the great gate, said, —

"I come to inform all candidates for enrolment in the 'Society of the Hall in the Grove,' that the hour appointed for your reception has arrived; the Hall has been set in order; the Path through the Grove has been opened; the Arches under which you must pass have been erected; the Key which will open this Gate has been placed in my hands. And to you who, as members of the Chautauqua Literary and Scientific Circle, have completed the four years' course of reading, and now hold in your hands a pledge of the same, I extend, in the name of the authorities, a welcome into St. Paul's Grove, under the First Arch. And let the watchmen guard carefully the Gate."

The immense throng gathered on all sides of the grove gazed with astonishment upon the scene, as the parted gates admitted to the sacred enclosure the throng of candidates for the high honors of the Chautauqua Literary and Scientific Circle. Suspended over the great archway of the gates, was the memorial silk flag borne by Dr. A. D. Vail through all the great educational and religious centres of Europe and Asia, unfurled by him on the Pyramids and the heights of Jerusalem, and swung aloft from the spires of Rome and London. On the keystone of the gateway arch, stood out in bold relief the sculptured green leaf, the badge of the C. L. S. C. fraternity. Beneath these memorials and emblems, slowly, four abreast, led by the Marshal, W. A. Duncan, the grand body of the class passed up the walk under the "Second" and "Third" arches, halting for a moment just before reaching the "Fourth" arch. Over this arch and inwrought with it, were the talismanic figures "1882," surmounted by the Cross.

Just outside of the Hall, the procession was met by thirty-six little girls, dressed in white, and crowned with wreaths, bearing each, for baskets, a chip hat filled with flowers and hung on the arm by a pink ribbon. From their baskets the "wee bit lassies" cast their flowers in the pathway of the class of '82. You could see the men "kind o' choke up" and turn away in embarrassment, and women begin to act as if there was to be a Chautauqua salute when these "angels and ministers of grace" approached. And at the strewing, the grave, earnest faces of the graduates lit up with smiles. But never a smile on a child's face; it was earnest business to them. No one that day more intent to act well his part. In the Amphitheatre the graduates returned the homage by enthusiastic rounds of applause for them, whom Professor Hurlbut happily named "the C. L. S. C. of the future." Mrs. Beard's department was the poetry of the procession. She was efficiently assisted by Miss Helen Savage and Mr. William Burroughs of Brooklyn, and Mr G. E. Ryckman of Brocton, who furnished the flowers.

Out upon the sweet air of the morning poured forth the "Song of To-Day" from the Choir of the Hall in the Grove, while the column passed on into the Hall, filling it to repletion.

A SONG OF TO-DAY

"All things are yours." — 1 Cor. iii. 22.

Sing pæans over the Past !
We bury the dead years tenderly,
To find them again in eternity,
Safe in its circle vast.
Sing pæans over the Past !

Farewell, farewell to the Old!
Beneath the arches, and one by one,
From sun to shade, and from shade to sun,
   We pass, and the years are told.
  Farewell, farewell to the Old!

Arise and possess the land!
Not one shall fail in the march of life,
Not one shall fail in the hour of strife,
   Who trusts in the Lord's right hand.
  Arise and possess the land!

And hail, all hail to the New!
The future lies like a world new-born,
All steeped in sunshine and dews of morn,
   And arched with a cloudless blue.
  All hail, all hail to the New!

All things, all things are yours!
The spoil of nations, the arts sublime
That arch the ages from eldest time,
   The Word that for aye endures, —
  All things, all things are yours!

The Lord shall divide the sea,
And open a way in the wilderness
To faith that follows, to feet that press
   Into the great To Be.
  The Lord shall divide the sea!

               M A. LATHBURY, 1882.

  While the graduates were taking their places in the
Hall, the C. L. S. C. Glee Club sang No 17, the "Song
of the C. L. S. C. for 1880;" all the officials upon the
platform, joined by all the members of the class, heartily
uniting in the outburst of melody.

" A song is thrilling through the trees,
   And vibiant through the air ;
Ten thousand hearts turn hitherward,
   And gieet us fiom afar;
And through the happy tide of song,
   That blends our hearts in one,
The voices of the absent flow
   In tendei undertone
       Then bear along, O wings of song,
         Our happy greeting glee,
       From centie to the golden verge,
         Chautauqua to the sea.

" Fair Wisdom builds her temple here,
   Her seven-pillared dome ;
Towaid all lands she spreads her hands,
   And greets her children home;
Not all may gather at her shrine
   To sing of victories won,
Their names are graven on her walls —
   God bless them, every one ! — *Chorus.*

" O happy circle, ever wide
   And wider be thy sweep,
Till peace and knowledge fill the earth
   As waters fill the deep;
Till hearts and homes are touched to life,
   And happier heights are won ;
Till that fair day, clasp hands and say —
   God bless us, every one ! — *Chorus.*"

Standing on the platform were the Superintendent
of Instruction, Dr. Vincent ; Lewis Miller, President
of the Chautauqua Board ; and Counsellors Warren,
Abbott, and Wilkinson.

The following selections were read responsively by
Dr. Vincent and the class : —

SUPT. — Whence then cometh wisdom? and where is the place of understanding?

CLASS. — Seeing it is hid from the eyes of all living, and kept close from the fowls of the air.

SUPT. — Destruction and death say, We have heard the fame thereof with our ears.

CLASS — God understandeth the way thereof, and he knoweth the place thereof.

SUPT. — For he looketh to the ends of the earth, and seeth under the whole heaven:

CLASS. — To make the weight for the winds;

SUPT. — And he weigheth the waters by measure.

CLASS. — When he made a decree for the rain, and a way for the lightning of the thunder:

SUPT. — Then did he see it, and declare it: he prepared it, yea, and searched it out.

CLASS. — And unto man he said, Behold, the fear of the Lord, that is wisdom; and to depart from evil is understanding.

SUP1. — Add to your faith virtue, and to virtue knowledge.

CLASS. — Happy is the man that findeth wisdom;

SUPT. — And the man that getteth understanding (Prov. iii. 13).

CLASS. — For the merchandise of it is better than the merchandise of silver, and the gain thereof than fine gold (Prov. iii. 14).

SUPT. — She is more precious than rubies:

CLASS. — And all things thou canst desire are not to be compared unto her (Prov. iii. 15).

SUPT. — Length of days is in her right hand;

CLASS — And in her left hand riches and honor (Prov. iii. 16).

SUPT — Her ways are ways of pleasantness, and all her paths are peace (Prov. iii. 17).

CLASS — She is a tree of life to them that lay hold upon her; and happy is every one that retaineth her (Prov. iii. 18).

At this point the beautiful banner of the C. L S C., never before disclosed to the public eye, was unveiled, and placed in front of the platform, and its uncovering was received with rapturous applause.

Dr. Vincent said, "This banner is a gift to the Circle by Miss Jennie Miller, daughter of Lewis Miller President of Chautauqua" [Applause]

The Superintendent of Instruction addressed the graduating class as follows : —

Fellow-students of the Chautauqua Literary and Scientific Circle.

DEARLY BELOVED, — You have finished the appointed and accepted course of reading; you have been admitted to this sacred grove; you have passed the arches dedicated to Faith, Science, Literature, and Art; you have entered in due form this hall, — the centre of the "Chautauqua Literary and Scientific Circle."

And now, as Superintendent of Instruction, with these my associates, the Counsellors of our Fraternity, I greet you; and hereby announce that you, and your brethren and sisters absent from us this day, who have completed with you the prescribed course of reading, are accepted and approved graduates of the Chautauqua Literary and Scientific Circle; and that you are entitled to membership in the "Society of the Hall in the Grove."

"The Lord bless thee, and keep thee; The Lord make his face shine upon thee, and be gracious unto thee; the Lord lift up his countenance upon thee, and give thee peace."

"THE ANNIVERSARY ODE OF 1879" was sung with heartiest fervor by the class of graduates, as follows : —

> " Bright beams again Chautauqua's wave,
>   And green her forest arches,
> As with glad heart and purpose brave,
>   The student homeward marches.

Before him rose the pleasant goal,
  Through all the years' endeavor,
Blest inspiration of the soul!
  For light aspiring ever.

Refrain

    Once more we stand, a joyous band,
      Our songs to heaven up-sending;
    They freely rise, a sacrifice
      Of prayer and praises blending.

"Our college halls are grand and free,
  Her charter heaven-granted;
Her roof the summer crownèd tree,
  Where nature's hymns are chanted;
And round her shall her children cling
  With loyal love and duty,
And yearly all their offerings bring,
  Of gathered wealth and beauty.— *Refrain*.

"From the vast ocean shore of thought,
  We bring our earliest treasure,
With many a golden memory fraught,
  And many a lofty pleasure.
We offer now our work to Him
  Whose loving light hath guided,
Through pathways to our knowledge dim,
  From His great thought divided — *Refrain*."

DR. VINCENT — "We are now prepared to move, according to the order of the Marshal, to the Amphitheatre. I hope to greet you all at this place, according to programme, this evening — Mr. Marshal, we are now ready."

The procession then took up the line of march in the following order (1) the Band; (2) Floral Division, with their emptied baskets (whose contents had strewn the way from the Fourth Arch to the Hall during the entrance of the graduates) ; (3) the C. L S C Class of 1882 ; (4) Dr Vincent, Superintendent of Instruction, and Lewis Miller, President of Chautauqua, arm-in-arm ; (5) the Counsellors, H. W Warren, Lyman Abbott, and W. C. Wilkinson, in line , (6) the Messenger, Rev. A H. Gillett, the General Secretary of the C. L. S. C., A. M. Martin, the Recorder, Rev. W. D. Bridge.

The procession left the Hall *via* gate on Haven Avenue, four abreast, marching up Haven to Clark Avenue, out Clark to Cookman Avenue, where it met the "Chautauqua Procession," standing with open ranks, through which the C. L. S C procession passed with uncovered heads, receiving through all its passage the Chautauqua salute, and heartiest expressions of good-will. The Chautauqua Trustees, waiting at the head of the Chautauqua procession, fell in at the rear of the C L S C. procession, and passed with the latter through the opened ranks After the passage of the graduates, etc , the Chautauqua procession, A. K. Warren, Marshal, closed ranks, countermarched, and followed behind the Chautauqua Trustees.

Many were the groups gathered on cottage balconies, and by the line of march, all joining in warmest congratulations as the procession passed.

When the head of the procession reached the gate of the Amphitheatre, the band took up its position on the left of the walk, the graduates opened ranks, through which, amid a constant Chautauqua salute, the President, the Superintendent of Instruction, Counsellors, etc., passed to the Amphitheatre, and to their place on the platform.

The banner of the C. L. S C was placed inside the Amphitheatre, facing the entrance, the streamers pendent from its cross-bar being held by four little girls, — Kittie Schofield, Rebie Flood, Winnie Massey, and Mabel Rice

After the entrance of the floral company, the officers of the C. L. S C., the Chautauqua Trustees, etc, the classes followed and took their seats in the following order: 1882, 1883, 1884, 1885, 1886

On the platform were grouped the above-named officers, the faculty of the C S. L, Prof B. P. Bowne, Miss J E. Bulkley (Secretary of the C. T. R), Bishop R. S. Foster (who was received with rounds of applause), and others

When the outer entrances of the Amphitheatre were opened, and the crowds of expectant lookers-on had filled every available inch of space, the Marshal of the Day, W. A Duncan, said, "The further services are placed in the hands of the President of the Chautauqua Association, Lewis Miller."

No further description of the first Recognition Day is here necessary. Songs were sung, the "Commencement Oration" was delivered by Bishop H W Warren, and in the afternoon the Diplomas were presented. It was a day of the greatest enthusiasm that had ever been witnessed at Chautauqua.

The correspondence of the Central Office at Plainfield, N J, and the columns of THE CHAUTAUQUAN (the official organ of the C. L. S C.), afford many testimonies to the value of Chautauqua work. It is impossible to publish a hundredth part of the hearty words which come from members in all parts of the world. I shall

give a few pages of them as specimens of the acknowl-
edgments coming to cheer and inspire the leaders in this
good work These are introduced with the design of
showing how the C L S C has been a blessing to
people of the most widely varied educational and social
standing ; how it has gone into homes of plenty and of
poverty, into parlors and into kitchens ; how the local
circles have helped communities ; and how beyond the
seas, in foreign lands, the beneficent ministries of the
Circle have been felt. I am largely indebted to our
Secretary, Miss K. F. Kimball, for the selection, compilation, and transcription of this body of testimony.

A member in Connecticut — a college graduate —
writes : "I have had to do the most of the C. L. S. C
work during vacations, which accounts for my being
behind I thoroughly believe in the plan, because it
tends as much to quicken and keep alive college graduates as any thing else. It is just what they need.
I found that for me it bridged over many a break,
and filled up many an awkward opening, left by a
college course. And I must further avail myself of
odd minutes for systematic reading in the line of special courses. An uneducated dry-goods clerk, whom
I told of the plan, said he could not express his
pleasure in knowing of the scheme. In my dry and
technical studies, I found a great need of just such
reading as our course provides. I know from personal observation, that a lawyer who knows nothing
but law is a mean and narrow-minded person ; and so
I resolved to be not only a good lawyer, but a well-
read man. The influence of the Circle has opened
up to me a future of glorious possibilities, and has

aroused my ambition.   I am endeavoring to rise above
my present circumstances, and to gain a place of
influence and usefulness in the world, that it may
be better for my having lived.   If I succeed, I shall
have to thank the C. L S. C for a great part of the
success.   Many of the young men associated with me
in the church have experienced the same benefit."

A member writes from Ohio : " I desire to tell you
how completely I am captivated by the C L S C.
course of study.   I have been all my life for forty
years a great reader, and for the last twenty years
have made a specialty of history and the sciences.
But my reading has hitherto been too careless, and
without sufficient thought.   I realize an immense
benefit from my present systematic course."

A graduate of Michigan University writes : "I wish
to thank you for the note of congratulation which
I received from you, just before leaving Michigan
University, and to tell you that I owe my degree in
large measure to you The inspiration to continue
my studies in some Eastern college came to me at
Monterey, when you invited me to Chautauqua, and
expressed the hope that I would be there in '82 to
receive my diploma I said I would work for that
end, and I also resolved to go, if possible, prepared to
enter some college At Michigan University I have
taken a four-years' course in three years, owing largely
to the knowledge and strength I gained from the
C. L S C. For this I am deeply grateful to you, and
above all to our Heavenly Father who has crowned
each effort with success, and has showered blessings
manifold I feel the responsibility which has come

with these added benefits, and I desire in return to give a life of happy, faithful service.   I remain a most loyal Chautauquan."

A woman writes: "I am one of the 'lone' C. L. S. C.'s.   I have long wanted to take up this course of reading, but could not see where the time was to come from.   Last August, worn out both in body and mind, I went to Chautauqua.   Just how I felt while there, would be difficult for me to tell; my heart was stirred within me as never before.   I came home invigorated in mind and body, ready to step at once into my place, and take up my work again with a *full* determination to make room and time for the C. L. S. C."

Another from another sphere of life: "Last January a lady spoke to me about reading.   I told her that I read all that I had time for.   I work in a factory ten hours a day, and it did not seem as though my reading amounted to much.   She told me about the C. L. S. C., and sent 'The Chautauquan' to me   As soon as I read it, I concluded that it would be well worth the while to join.   For myself, I can now say, that with a dictionary by my side, and a 'Chautauquan' in my hand, I am more than contented."

From a Methodist Episcopal minister: "My duties as a pastor and my conference studies are enough to take all my time, but I cannot afford to give up the course of the C. L. S. C.   It gives me a leverage upon the younger members of my congregation, and the more intelligent part of the community, which as a pastor I desire to hold."

From a seaman: "The first I learned of the won-

ders of Chautauqua was in the city of New Orleans,
where I met an old shipmate who was thoroughly
imbued with the 'idea.' As I had always been of a
reading and studious disposition, he told me all about
it. God bless him for it! I have found hundreds of
persons, young and old, all over the United States,
who think almost as much of the 'idea' as they do of
their business. Let the good work go on."

A professional man writes : "I mean to read the
books, whether my work for this present year passes
or not; for this is the only way that I can do any
systematic reading, being very busy with professional
work. It is just the thing for me."

A woman writes : "I have always felt that there
were people in the world somewhere, if I could only
find them, who would understand that poverty-strick-
en people may have aspirations, and yet be honest
and true, and that we may wish for wealth in order to
make progress, and not to enable us to live idle and
vicious lives. I presume you will say, 'of course;'
but I have so often been exhorted to 'be content in
the station in life in which it has pleased God to call
you' But I do hunger and thirst after knowledge,
whether right or wrong; and I cannot subdue that
hunger unless I crush out all that is purest and best
in me." To such as these, the C. L. S. C. comes as
an angel of mercy and of strength.

From a manufacturing city : "In this city, conditions are peculiarly favorable to the success of the
C. L. S.C., — a manufacturing place where a large proportion of the inhabitants depend on their wages for
their living; there are many who, having partially

completed their education, have found it necessary to begin work in the mills. As a member of the School Board, I have noticed this fact particularly. Our high school contains about one hundred and ninety pupils, while there are more than one thousand in the grammar grades. Many who are thus obliged to give up study for the business of life have acquired a keen desire for knowledge. The C. L. S. C. has many recruits from their number, and is satisfying, I believe, their demand for a broader culture. Many of our public-school teachers have also taken the course, to supplement their work in the schoolroom. I am convinced that it is not a thing of a day, but is destined to occupy a permanent place among our educational institutions."

A student of the C. L. S. C. in Idaho writes : "The pupils of the public school will one day be Chautauquans. There is enthusiasm over every thing in the course that we enjoy together, and that is a considerable portion of it. We talked over the air, when the loveliest blue mist hung for days between us and our most beautiful mountain's snowy peak. My pupils have treated our very near Chinese neighbors with more consideration since the reading of 'China, Corea, and Japan.' This is only the second year of school-life in our place, and we are largely indebted to the C. L. S. C. for help in overcoming some difficulties incident to a first struggle."

From one of the leading Chautauqua workers : "I was in Missouri, March last, and was compelled to take a freight-train to make connection. As I entered the caboose, I noticed a little candle on a cracker-box on the side of the car.   There was a door on hinges made out of bits of leather ; and a rough button, held in its place by a screw, closed the door.   After the train started, the conductor came in, and after attending to his duties, stepped to the box, turned the button, opened the door, and took out a package of C. L. S. C. books (recognizable as such anywhere), sat down on a bench, and began working with one of the Chautauqua text-books.   Of course it was an absolute necessity that I should make his acquaintance.   I approached him, and asked what he was doing.   He said, 'A friend of mine in St. Louis called my attention to this Chautauqua course of reading.   I did not know what it meant, but I knew I ought to read. So finally I joined the circle, bought the books, and put them in the box.   My brakemen read with me. One of us keeps watch, and the others read.   Sometimes it is pretty hard work when we have an unusually long run and much freight ; but for the sake of the help it is, I am going to hold on to it.'   I felt like giving the fellow a round of applause, all alone as I was in the car."

A member from a large city writes : " Please excuse my sending the memoranda at this late hour: if you knew how fully my time was employed each day, you would not wonder   I am engaged from 8.15 A. M. until 6 P. M. in a store, besides keeping house.   My time for reading the C. L. S. C course is when I ride to and from the store, twenty minutes each way, and during noon-hour.   I do not tell you this to complain, or gain credit : it is simply to let you know, if I am sometimes a little tardy, it is not because I have lost

interest, or given up. I think I never enjoyed reading so much in my life. It gives me a broader outlook, and I am more interested in every thing. The
pleasure I derive more than pays for all the time it
takes."

From the Far West, a woman writes: "I live on
a farm, and my husband has no help except what
I give him. All of the time I am not doing housework, I am obliged to drive the horse at the horse-
power while my husband irrigates the land. I have
done my reading while driving the horse for the past
two months, but I cannot write while driving."

From a mother: "I return to you my memoranda,
filled to the best of my ability without consulting
helps. These four years of C L. S. C studies have
been a pleasure as well as an incalculable profit to
myself and my family. I was born and educated in
Germany. Through these studies I am now able to
assist my boys in their studies in the English language. The Grecian schools of philosophy were as
nothing compared to this system of educating the
people. It is the grandest educational movement in
the world!"

Another: "Enclosed you will find the memoranda
for the past year I did intend to have sent them
sooner *this* year, but have the same old excuse to
plead, — ill health and many cares. The Chautauqua
reading has been a 'godsend' to me; for confined
almost entirely to the house, and often to my room,
it has passed away many otherwise lonely hours. I
shall hope to graduate another year, but am sure
I shall continue the reading."

A member from Idaho writes: "I am studying alone, do my own housework, practise my music every day. I have about a hundred chickens of choice breed. We are almost never without company, and I drive from one to two hours a day when at home. We have travelled from ten thousand to twenty-five thousand miles every year for the past eight years. You will see that I have to be rather systematic, but I assure you I have had to almost turn my head inside out to get at the results of my reading of last year; for I did not refer to any helps, except on Question 28 when I referred to the cyclopædia."

A mother, after alluding to the sudden death of her boy, says: "My object in taking up the C. L. S. C. course was to keep pace with that gifted boy, for I had always felt that I could not be left behind; and, while he at school was reading Latin and Greek, I at home was reading the same works in English, so that I might have an outlook from as nearly the same standpoint as possible. I hardly had a thought but for him, and around him centred and clustered every hope. With this great incentive gone, you can readily see that it has been very hard to read or study, and for a long time I had given up all hope of ever finishing; but friends urged me on, and I find it is just what I need, and I often thank God that you ever thought of the plan of the C. L. S. C."

From a member in Alabama: "I want to thank you for the C. L. S. C., which has opened to me such a new and wonderful source of pleasure and improvement; and to tell you how lonely I feel away down here in the backwoods among the mountains of North

Alabama, prosecuting the studies all alone. I have tried to organize a local circle, but failed, owing to the fact that there is so little accessible material of which to form one. We could not even form a triangle, as they did in Michigan, but only a straight line extending from me to my neighbor over the hills ; and, so far as I know, she and I are the only members in Alabama · but perhaps in thinking so, I am as greatly mistaken as the prophet Elijah when he said, 'And I, even I only, am left.' "

A lady applying for membership says: "The C. L. S. C. promises to meet a want I have realized for some years. Graduating at the —— Institute in 1864, I have spent eight of the intervening years in travelling. Your schedule suggests a wider scope than any course of reading I could plan for myself."

A member from New-York City writes : "I joined this circle with a view of interesting my young people in it ; and, as a result, in our mission school we have a circle of thirty, all very much interested in the work, and, as one of the outcomes of it, a Young Ladies' Christian Association and Flower Mission, the members making weekly visits to Randall's Island, the Old Ladies' Home, and other charities, receiving not only the smiles and prayers of the inmates, but the blessedness of doing good."

A student at Williams College writes : "One year ago I began the Chautauqua course in connection with my regular college duties. While for me a great part of the work was a review, I found that it served to clinch and make fast my previous knowledge of the subjects taken up, and also gave me much infor-

mation that was new, and not to be obtained in my
college course. I have just entered on my senior
year; and, although I am very busy, I shall keep up
my C. L. S. C. work, believing that any time I can
take to devote to that will be spent to the best possible advantage. To one who has the advantages of
a college education, the C. L. S. C. course furnishes
a valuable auxiliary and material aid."

From an enthusiastic reader: "Since I began to
study in the C. L. S. C., I have spent a summer in
England and Scotland. Thanks to you and Green,
I was thoroughly steeped in English history and literature, which made every place alive with interest.
At Oxford, did we not wander along the lovely Isis
where Addison loved to walk, to ponder and study?
and did we not revel, in a mild way, under the solemn
shade of the venerable trees, and gaze with intense
interest at the manuscripts and books of the Bod-
leian Library? and did we not hear Gray's Elegy in
that very country churchyard? Then, too, we made
a pilgrimage to Canterbury, 'The holy blisful martir
for to seeke.' · There were six of us, and we were all
of one mind. We crossed the border, and made a
short tour through Scotland, which included a visit
to unfrequented Ayr, and to Kirk Alloway where poor
Tam saw such a bewitching sight. The last weeks
of the summer were spent in the English Lake District, and long shall I remember the wonderful pictures seen from our windows at Keswick. To the
C. L. S. C. is due much of the pleasure of the summer. Through the C. L. S. C., I received the first
impulse to study systematically at home."

A mother writes : "As I glanced over the plan of study for the year, and saw 'Biology,' my heart was thrilled with joy ; for but a short time previous, my oldest daughter had said, 'We have biology this year in high school : what is it ?' And I had been forced to answer, 'I don't know.' . . . The year began . . . My daughter studied biology in May and June. Our books did not arrive until late in June. So we studied in July and August, the vacation months ; and, as she was fresh from the study, and had her blank-book of notes, we studied aloud ; and you cannot tell how the hearts of mother and daughter were knit together in those days. Forty years and sixteen years ! . . . My daughter is a Christian ; and, as she read aloud in my book, she would exclaim, 'How beautiful ! I thought biology couldn't have any thing to do with the Bible.' . . . And I blessed the wisdom and sagacity which included this book in the course."

A lady of sixty-four years says : "Enclosed please find 'Memoranda Outline,' and a paper, 'Mary Queen of Scots.' Will you make some allowance for sixty-four years ? and the past year is the first attempt for study since I was twelve and one-half years, and not in very good health It is a new departure, and one I enjoy, as I live very retired."

Another lady : "I enjoy the C. L. S C. very much. It gives me courage to feel, that, although I am forty-five years old, I am a scholar, and am in a school, and really learning something. My chance for school-education was but little. After I was twelve years old, I staid at home, and worked summers, and then had only three or four months of schooling in winter, and for that had to walk a mile and a half through unbroken snow roads. Do you wonder that the C. L. S. C. comes to me like a God-given gift? Those that have been 'scrimped' as I, can appreciate what it is to have a course of reading laid out for them. I do get discouraged at times when the work is hard, and I am so tired I cannot understand what I am reading. I hope to go to Chautauqua for a week next summer. That seems to me to be the nearest heaven I shall ever get on this earth."

From California: "When I read the C. L. S. C. testimony in 'The Chautauquan,' I always think Chautauqua has been all that and more to me; for it has led me from cold, dark scepticism to my Bible, and my Father in heaven, and it is gradually leading some of my friends into the light. I prize my C. L. S. C. books more highly, that they are worn and soiled by many readers; and I believe I can do no better missionary work than by enlarging the Circle."

Persons who imagine that the tendency of the C. L. S. C. is to diminish interest in college should read the following: "I will say that the reading which I have done in the C. L. S. C. has been a great help to me, and has been an incentive to further study. The 'Preparatory Greek Course in English' aroused in me a desire to learn Greek. The other books which I read made me desire to know more. The result was that I determined to take a classical course in —— University. Therefore I shall not be able to keep up the C. L. S. C. studies for the next few years."

From a lady member of the class of '82 : "Several years ago, I was very anxious to pursue a regular course of study, but was unable to do so Last year I joined the C. L. S C. It brought back the old desire for knowledge, and I determined if possible to attend some good school. My brother graduated that year at the —— high school, and as he wished to go to —— College, we talked it over, and concluded that if I could keep house we could both attend for about the same amount it would cost one to board We made the experiment To-morrow is Commencement, and as I look over the year's work there is thanksgiving in my heart I passed a good examination in all the studies I had in the C L. S C. When I entered college, Dr —— gave me two hundred questions. I think he wanted to try the C L S. C workers in English history"

A young man writes from California : "After two years with the class of 1887, I feel that I must, for the present at least, give it up You will be glad to know, however, that it is only that I may give more attention to other studies, for which the C. L S C has in some measure prepared me. I am most grateful for the help and stimulus received from the C L. S. C God bless it !"

A young business-man, considering the question of entering college, says : "I have been a member of the C. L S C for one year This is a wonderful encouragement, and has really awakened me. I am happy in reading, and send my papers this week. Aside from business hours, and my almost daily study of Latin, my time is very short ; but I use every second in perfect enjoyment, looking into the Chautauqua studies."

And now we turn to the lands beyond the seas, and read the entertaining and inspiring story of the good work in Japan, South Africa, and Russia —

Early in the summer of 1884, a letter from Mrs. A. M. DRENNAN, a member of the C. L. S. C., and an active missionary worker in Japan, brought the following most welcome announcement. "From this far-off land I send you some names for enrolment upon the C. L. S. C. books, at least as knockers at the door for admission into your — *our* — Circle." The eight applications for membership enclosed with this letter marked the beginning of a movement, the rapidity of whose development has been most remarkable. The aim of the Japan Literary and Scientific Circle is primarily to reach the young men of Japan. Concerning the special needs of this class, Mrs. Drennan writes: "The young men whose names I send are students, but have not the money to buy books if they could even get the books here. Many of them can read English, but many will have to read in Japanese; and it is a lamentable fact, that few books of a religious class have been translated. Infidelity has been busy, and such books are spread broadcast. The young men here *will* read. If we do not give them good reading, they will take that which is pernicious. I am trying to direct the reading of ambitious young men, who read and study and think. They *will* read. If they do not have the right kind of books thrown in their way, they will read the works of such men as Ingersoll. Those in our society desired to study for the sake of learning, and not simply to pass time.

Any one of them would pursue the full Chautauqua course if he could get the books. When you think of Japanese young men, do not think of a set of rough heathen, but of a class of aspiring youth, who, having cast off their old ideas and religion, are seeking earnestly for a new, — something satisfying to the intellect as well as to the conscience"

The success which has thus far attended the efforts of Mrs. Drennan and her associates in firmly establishing the C. L. S. C. in Japan has been attained amid many discouragements and obstacles which would have disheartened less earnest workers. The utter lack of suitable literature, and the fact that English books would be available for but a small proportion of the young men to whom this opportunity would be priceless, convinced the officers of the Circle that no immediate foot-hold could be gained unless suitable works could be translated. In an early letter, Mrs Drennan wrote : " I wish I could impress upon the minds of the thousands of Chautauquans in the dear home-land the great importance of this work among the young men of Japan now ; and I wish I could tell them how earnestly we have, for some months, been seeking for books that will at all meet the demands of the C. L. S. C., and yet how almost entirely we have failed. There are fifty names upon the roll for the organization of a Circle here ; but our long delay and fruitless search for books, I fear, will discourage many "

With some aid from the Central Office of the C. L. S. C., and the active co-operation of Japanese members, the work of translation was commenced early in 1885. As a delay of three months must elapse after application to the government, before a magazine could be published, the first number of the Japanese "Chautauquan" was issued in book form soon after the 1st of April, 1885. Concerning this first number of "The Chautauquan," Mrs. Drennan writes: "The first article in the book is an editorial by the editor of the largest paper in this part of Japan He is a very fine writer, and highly educated. He is perfectly enthusiastic over the work, and all say his article is very fine. It is an argument favoring this plan, and giving his views as to the good it will accomplish in Japan."

March 30, 1885, Mrs. Drennan writes : "I wish I could convey to your mind something of an idea of the enthusiasm in reference to our Chautauqua society here. In much less than a week after the first advertisement in the papers, our secretary had received nearly three hundred letters of inquiry, and on application had given out every copy of the first five hundred copies of the Hand-book [a small pamphlet explaining the work of the C L. S. C.]. A second edition of five hundred was made ; and now, in less than a week after, only about two hundred copies remain." Two weeks later, another letter reports as follows : "I wish I had time to-night to write you a long letter, for it would take a very long one to tell you all the good things about our 'J. L S C.' I know your heart would be full of joy if you could know the deep interest that has been awakened in our work here. We have just to-day from the press our third edition of the Hand-book, a copy of which I sent you last mail. This makes two thousand five hundred copies of the Hand-book. There have been over three hundred applicants for membership About one hundred and fifty have paid up all dues. Our secretary has answered over seven hundred letters of inquiry. Applications have come from several cities, for the privilege of organizing branch societies. With your kind aid for a little while, we will have an influence that will spread over this entire land, doing great things for this people. My heart was thrilled with delight the other day, on receiving some letters as applications for membership from some soldiers in a distant city."

The membership at this time (April, 1885) had reached one hundred and seventy-five, and was rapidly increasing. The students were enthusiastic, and anxious to be recognized by the Central Office in America; and, although they were supplied with membership-cards printed in Japanese, they were very eager for the regular membership-card of the class of '88, sent to them from this country. In the next two months the circle took a long step forward. Mrs Drennan wrote, June 29, 1885 : "We now, after carefully looking over all names, and writing down only such as we feel are really paid up, find on our books seven hundred and fifty carefully written and beautifully arranged names, enrolled as Chautauquans, whose aim• and ambition is to read this course, and thus link themselves with the intelligent of other nations, and also to secure for themselves the coveted prize of a diploma from America. The 'J. L. S. C.' is flourishing beyond our most sanguine expectations. Think of a class in Japan, numbering seven hundred and fifty members ! It is simply wonderful. Our president told me that many letters come from different sections, where the books have gone, asking, 'Who is this Jesus of whom you spoke in the book'? What do you mean by 'Christian era'? What is the 'Christian Church'? etc., thus giving him opportunity to preach Christ to many whom he may never see. These questions he answers by letter, and also in the magazine under the head of " Questions and Answers." As I wrote before, many soldiers are now reading the books; and even *jinrikisha* men are seen sitting on their *jinrikishas*, waiting for custom, with their dictionary and 'Chautauquan' in hand, studying the course Praise God for this gift to Japan !

"You would be interested if you could see us at study in Chautauqua meetings. To save expense, we are now using my schoolroom. All desks, etc., are removed. I have the floor covered with soft mats such as they have in their houses (these I rent for the night), then I decorate with flowers, pictures, books, etc, and light up brilliantly. At the gate have two large oiled-paper lanterns three feet or more long, on which in large Chinese and Japanese characters is written the name of our society. These lighted give a very pretty effect. I have tables for the secretary, president, and reporter, at these tables are chairs All the members come in with shoes off, and take their seats in order upon the floor. At the appointed hour we open with singing and prayer. Then each member takes out his book, and, beginning with the first article, they ask any questions they have marked in their reading during the week These the president is expected to answer. Thus they go over each article. Many questions are asked by different persons, on the same article; thus, by the time they are through, each article is well discussed. After this, some one appointed gives a lecture,

or a short talk; then singing, and a prayer to close. It
is very interesting to me to see so many intelligent-
looking young men earnestly studying, and asking questions, that show that a new field of thought is being
opened up to them. Last meeting they discussed
Egypt, the Pyramids, Assyria, America," etc.

A summer assembly was planned by the officers of
the J. L. S. C.; but owing to a disastrous flood which
swept over the city of Osaka and vicinity, destroying
much property and thousands of lives, the circle were
for a time compelled to abandon the idea. The latest
reports from this vigorous branch of the C. L. S. C.,
received within a few weeks, show that the interest in
Chautauqua work is still growing rapidly. Difficulties
and discouragements have not in the least diminished
their enthusiasm.

Mrs Drennan writes in November, 1885: "In the
beginning of the society meetings, we always opened
and closed with singing and prayer. Many young men
came in, who were very much opposed to Christianity,
and had heard none of its teachings. At first, many
would not kneel; others laughed aloud, not boisterously
but audibly. It was the first prayer they had ever
heard. Now many of those young men are in the
churches. Our president told me that a short time ago
he baptized in his church one of those young men, who
said his first religious instruction was in our little Chautauqua meetings in my room. There are now over one
thousand members. They are scattered in all parts of
Japan. There are six local circles formed, and others
will be formed soon. A majority of the members of
our society are not Christians. There are all grades of

society, from the *jinrikisha* men up to lawyers, judges, and government officials.   There are a number of soldiers, also young students, pastors, editors, and men of forty-five or more ; our secretary is forty-five.   Many ladies also are members, and many in the schools."

From Japan, let us pass to the far South on the Eastern hemisphere.   The work begun in South Africa was, like that in Japan, the result of active effort on the part of a member of the C. L. S. C.

Miss Theresa M. Campbell, a member of the class of 1884 in Tennessee, sailed for Africa in June, 1881, to take charge of a public school for girls at Riversdale, Cape Colony.   In spite of the delay consequent upon the long journey, distance from America, and the difficulties attending work in a new school in a strange land, this enthusiastic member of the Circle worked steadily on, and in due time reported to the American office her completion of the four-years' course.   In April, 1884, Miss Campbell left her position at Riversdale, to take charge of a school at Wellington.   From this place the following letter was received, dated Dec. 17, 1884 : —

"Eureka !   At last my day-dream for the last three and a half years has been fulfilled, and there is a South African Branch of the C. L. S. C.   From the day I left New York on my way here, I have talked about the C. L. S. C., until I imagine some of my friends thought I had C. L. S. C. on the brain.   I must confess I had begun to think it was all wasted breath : so you may fancy my delight when I was invited to meet a committee from the Huguenot seminary, to confer with them in regard to the C. L. S. C.   The members of the senior class had been to some of the teachers, and asked them if some plan could not be devised so that they could go on studying after they left. A faculty meeting was held; and, as they all knew my feelings in regard to the C. L. S. C., the committee was at once appointed with instructions to interview me. . . . The result of the interview was that a meeting of all those who were leaving school, and wished to have their home reading and study directed, was called, and I was invited to meet them, and explain the Chautauqua plan. Before the meeting closed, the South African Branch was born. On last Thursday I was invited to meet the alumnæ of the seminary who were back to the anniversary exercises, and explain our plan to them. We are hoping great things from our branch, as, with the exception of the teachers at the seminary, every member will be the point from which new circles will be formed. The young ladies are very enthusiastic over it, and I hope I shall be able to report the forming of new circles in every one of the places now represented. Some of the members I know you will be very much interested in knowing something about. Miss —— is a daughter of a French missionary. She was sent home when ten years old, to receive a part of her education, and three years ago came back to South Africa, and entered the seminary. She graduated last Thursday. She is a very talented young lady; and, best of all, her talents are all dedicated to the service of the Master . . . Remember this new Branch of the C. L. S. C. very tenderly in your prayers, that it may be a light to illumine this end of the Dark Continent." This letter enclosed twenty-five names for enrolment in the class of '88. Two months later fifteen more names were received, and Miss Campbell wrote, "We do not despair of getting our hundred in another three months."

In July, Miss Campbell received the government appointment of principal of the Rockland Seminary at Cradock, Cape Colony, leaving the care of the Wellington Local Circle in the hands of Miss Landfear, the secretary. The C. L. S. C. has steadily increased in numbers, and a letter written in November reports the total membership in South Africa as eighty-seven.

Miss Landfear writes in October: "Our Wellington Circle holds meetings once in two weeks, and very pleasant gatherings they are, with selections of readings, original papers, and music. This is the only local circle that has yet been started. We feel that we are at a disadvantage in being so far away from Chautauqua, but we are glad that its help can reach out to this distant end of the earth. The other members are mostly solitary ones."

The following sketch of the First Chautauqua Assembly in South Africa will give an idea of the interest awakened, and the character of the work which is being accomplished.

The greetings of the South Africa Assembly were received in time to be read at the opening of our Chautauqua Assembly in August, 1885.

HUGUENOT SEMINARY, WELLINGTON,
June 30, 1885

The Chautauqua Assembly of South Africa, to the Chautauqua Assembly of Chautauqua, U.S.A., sendeth greeting.

BELOVED, our prayer before God is that you may prosper and be in health, even as your souls prosper. Our beloved leader, Chancellor Vincent, will tell you how the slip — a little one — which was taken from your vine has taken root and grown, and spread forth its branches abroad. To-morrow morning closes the first Assembly in South Africa. How we wish that we could give you an adequate idea of the delight and pleasures of the few days which "according to the good hand of our God upon us" have passed away! We ask you for your prayers that the Chautauqua idea may grow, and become as great a blessing to our beloved South Africa as it has to America.

In behalf of the South African Branch of the Chautauqua Circle,

THERESA M. CAMPBELL, *Vice-President.*

HUGUENOT SEMINARY, WELLINGTON,
June 30, 1885.

DEAR CHANCELLOR VINCENT, — We are just bringing to a close our first Sunday-school Assembly. We consider it a great success. We commenced on Saturday at 2 P.M., and close to-morrow at 10.30 A M. Our friends have helped us most beautifully. On Saturday afternoon we had the welcome address from the president of the local circle; a lecture by Mr. Heale, the South African historian; a paper explaining the Circle, which I had the pleasure of reading; and a Round Table In the evening we had a vesper-service, the same you use on the first evening of the Assembly. Sunday, delightful conference and prayer meetings, normal Sunday-school teaching illustrated, Bible-readings, and, to crown it all, a most delightful communion-service Monday morning, two papers on "Impressions of America," by some friends who have recently returned from a trip there;

and a model of the "Tabernacle" was exhibited and explained. In the afternoon, a lecture on "Number," by one of the professors in the Theological Seminary, and a paper. In the evening, a most charming lecture on "Poetry and Wordsworth," by the principal of the Normal College in Cape Town. This morning we had a lecture on "Frances Ridley Havergal," illustrated by her music and hymns; and a paper on the missionary work in Africa. This afternoon, a fine lecture, given by one of the professors from the Stellerbosch College, on "Memory." This evening, a lecture on "The Higher Education of Women, its Duties and Responsibilities," by our one lady physician. To-morrow morning we have an address on "The Needs of Africa," and the president's farewell words. Sunday, at six o'clock, we had the vesper-service. It was a great success. Besides what I have mentioned, we have had classes in kindergarten, drawing, etc. The weather has been simply perfect, and our audiences remarkably good; between two and three hundred have crowded in to every thing that has been going on. I resigned my position as president, but found myself at once elected as vice-president. Rev. G. R. Ferguson has been elected as our president. The secretary remains the same. Our sessions at the Round Table have been very interesting. You must please excuse this hastily written account, but I wanted you to get it in time for the Assembly, so it must go by this mail, and I am writing after midnight so as to catch the mail to-morrow morning. With kindest regards, I remain

Yours truly,   THERESA M. CAMPBELL.

Turning from these two flourishing Chautauqua col-
onies in Japan and in South Africa, our attention is
arrested by news of a remarkable movement which is
taking place in Europe. The leader in this latest enterprise is Russia; a strange fact, when we consider that
England, at this time, could boast not one Chautauqua
Circle, and but few individual members. The first impulse given to Chautauqua work in Russia was the effect
of an illustrated article explaining the various Chautauqua organizations, which appeared in the March number
of a Russian magazine, "Nov." This magazine is published by an old and reliable firm in St. Petersburg.
The best writers contribute to its columns, and it has
a wide circulation throughout the country. The article
was written by a Russian lady, long a resident of America, and at present political correspondent from New
York for St. Petersburg and Moscow papers. While
in Ohio she became greatly interested in the work of
the Chautauqua Circles, and as a result of that interest
sent a carefully prepared article on Chautauqua to the
"Nov," that Russian readers might know what was
being accomplished by this great American institution.

The effects of this article were at once apparent.
Many inquiries reached the author of the article The
publishers in St. Petersburg were almost overwhelmed
with requests for programmes of the Chautauqua studies; while a few letters addressed rather indefinitely to
"Chautauqua, America," etc., found their way in time
to the Central Office These communications were
written in French, German, or Russian , and here at
once a serious difficulty presented itself. But few of
the applicants could write or even *read* the English

language. The interest manifested is shown by the fact that several applicants enclosed membership-fees in Russian stamps, while another directed his banker in New York to remit the necessary fee without waiting for further information

Meanwhile the "Nov," to meet the great demands made upon it for a course of study, published a list of text-books on various subjects, and announced that students might send their names for enrolment to that office. Peculiar difficulties present themselves when we consider the possibilities of extending Chautauqua work in Russia; such as, the language, the peculiar characteristics of the people, and certain government restrictions. And although the present movement is in no way under Chautauqua control, it is the outgrowth of the Chautauqua idea; and in the not far distant future we are confident that a Russian Chautauqua Circle will be a reality. Already several names from Russia (English-speaking students) have been enrolled in America. The following extract from a letter written by the author of the article in "Nov" shows emphatically that the desire for knowledge is as keen among the multitudes of young men and women in Russia, as in our own country or in other foreign lands : —

"The editor of that magazine (Nov) has recently published a list of ninety-four names of persons (among whom four women) who have joined the Russian Chautauqua Circle, and have begun to read the regular course of study. These people range in age from seventeen to fifty-two, belong to all conditions of life, and are the only ones who allowed their names to be published. Two hundred and eight more persons have joined the circle, follow the course of studies, but don't allow their names to be published; and, again, forty-two other persons have bought the books, determined to follow the course of the studies, but choose to preserve the strictest *incognito*, even in their correspondence with the editors of the 'Nov,' who are also the organizers and conductors of the Russian circle. If all these people that follow systematically the course of self-instruction are to be counted, their number amounts to three hundred and forty-four, — a most respectable showing, considering that the movement has been started only a few months. The majority of these open students are of ages ranging from twenty-five to thirty-five. A few are in their twenty-first and twenty-second years, and but two or three of nineteen and seventeen, before which age members are not enlisted."

Homeward bound by way of the Pacific, let us look for Chautauqua work in the Sandwich Islands. A New Yorker writes: "I found 'The Chautauquan' on a planter's table in the Sandwich Islands, and learned of a circle in Honolulu." And the president of the Honolulu circle writes: "Having observed the degree of interest manifested by 'The Chautauquan' in collecting and disseminating items of news concerning the different 'sub-circles' which own fealty to and gather inspiration from our now mighty parent circle, I take pleasure in reporting the continued prosperity of the 'Maile' (Mī'-le), located here in the metropolis of the occidental tropics. Our circle's name is taken from the fragrant and beautiful *maile*-vine, with *leis* (or wreaths) of which the Hawaiians are fond of decorating themselves on

festal occasions   We number seven enthusiastic members, who have reaped great benefit from the prescribed
course during the past year, and we expect a largely
increased membership at the opening of the coming
term.   The interest in the C. L. S. C. course of study
is extending rapidly in the Islands, and promises the
formation of several new circles in the near future.
The coming vacation will be utilized by a party of the
ladies of our circle, to visit the world-renowned volcano
and burning lake of 'Kilauea (Kee-lau-ā-a)' on the
island of Hawaii; to which the late establishment of a
new and easy route is attracting crowds of visitors, both
local and foreign.   Please accept the cordial '*aloha*' of
the Maile Club."

Although I have allowed these interesting quotations
to multiply much beyond my purpose when I began, it
will not do to omit the following testimonials concerning the value of the work done by local circles, which
have now become centres of great social and literary
influence all over the land.   From an Illinois circle we
have this report : "This circle was formed over a year
ago, and closed its first year's work in June last, with
a positively brilliant entertainment.   The affair was a
great success; as, indeed, the whole year had been
The ninety members went into it with a will.   The
church in which the exercises came off was beautifully
decorated, programmes were printed, the best of music
and literary performances provided ; and to crown all, in
spite of the fact that our town is a literary centre where
people are lectured and essayed and entertained year out
and year in, a magnificent audience greeted them.   Not
strange that the members are proud of their success."

From a local circle in Maine: "We have a constitution, and keep a record of each meeting. Our motto (one of Garfield's) is, 'Be fit for more than the thing you are now doing.' At each meeting, each member pays one cent or more, and if the money is not used in the circle it goes toward paying our annual fee. The president is a dressmaker; and 'we girls,' or at least four of us, work for her. We have reading in the shop nearly every day, forty minutes or more, and then talk of what we read. Almost a Socratic school in a dressmaker's shop! Friday evening of each week, the shop takes on another look. The work is put away, the table drawn out, the bright cloth laid, the lamps 'trimmed and burning.' Soon the members take their seats and place at the 'table square,' and for two or more hours we spend a refreshing and enjoyable evening."

From a local circle in Missouri: "I have delayed writing you, in order that I might tell how Chautauqua wears with us. We organized Sept 12, with six members; and although our number is still the same, our enthusiasm has steadily increased, and you may count on signing six diplomas for our little circle in '89. Nor will we stop then. A broad field is opening before us, and we are going on and on. We will 'never be discouraged.'"

A circle in Iowa, organized in 1878, reported four years later as follows: "Our class started with fifteen, and we graduate fifteen strong. None faltered or fell out by the wayside." A year later, the secretary of this circle writes: "The graduates of 1882 still remain banded together, and are this year pursuing the special course of modern history. 'Fifteen' is still a favorite number, — the number with which the class was organized in 1878, the number that graduated, and the number that are at present pursuing the special course."

"A circle in Kansas started off on its opening night with twenty-six members, who at the next meeting increased to forty-one. The Kansas State Agricultural College is in their town, and professors and students are taking hold of the club with interest."

From Michigan comes the following : "Our circle of eight members has been nameless until our last meeting, when it was decided to call it the 'Thorn-apple Circle.' Our meetings have been held semi-monthly, at the home of an invalid member who is very zealous in the work. Two of our members live at a distance of five miles from the village, but have regularly attended the circle gatherings, though much of the time the weather has been such as would have discouraged any one not blessed with the Chautauqua spirit. Our meetings have been exceedingly profitable, and the prospect is flattering for a much larger class the coming year; as much interest has been manifested by those who have visited our semi-monthly meetings."

The student of statistics will be pleased to examine the following reports from the Plainfield office (compiled by Miss K. F. KIMBALL, the Secretary), concerning several classes of the C. L. S. C. I present the figures without comment.

Of the original enrolment of the class of 1882, there were under twenty years of age 881 persons ; between twenty and thirty years, 3,805 ; between thirty and forty years, 2,346; over forty years of age, 1,214; of the graduates of this class of '82, there were 27 under twenty,

628 between twenty and thirty, 567 between thirty and forty, 472 over forty years of age. In the class of '82, there were three men to five women who joined, and one man to three women who graduated. One-fifth of the entire class of '82 graduated. One-seventh of the men, and one-fourth of the women, enrolled at the beginning of the class of '82, received diplomas.

Of the three classes '82, '83, and '84, there were enrolled, under twenty years of age, 2,943; between twenty and thirty years, 11,713; between thirty and forty years, 5,874; over forty years, 3,166.

The C. L. S C. is a school for people out of school, and its success in the future is to be secured by a wise adaptation of its methods to this special class.

From the C. L. S. C. we turn to another plan:—

THE CHAUTAUQUA BOOK-A-MONTH READING CIRCLE, under the supervision of Dr. J. L. Hurlbut, aims to supply the needs of a large class of people, who desire a course of reading less extensive than that of the C. L. S. C. Its works are a little more recreative and popular in their style, and chosen rather for reading than for close study; and with the design of supplementing the C. L. S. C. for some, and of substituting an easier line of literature for others. It embraces a course of thirty-six volumes, one for each month during three years, in the various departments of literature; so arranged that it may be accomplished by reading from twelve to twenty pages each day. There are few people who cannot spare the time requisite for such a course of reading, especially if the books chosen are interesting in their subjects, and attractive in their style. The works selected for the course include the history of the most important nations, and a few of the greatest epochs ; biographies of the men most famous for their achievements in statesmanship, conquest, and literature ; a few choice books of travel in the unfrequented portions of the earth , some works of popular science; the great essays of the greatest essayists ; and a small number of works of fiction, the masterpieces of romance, several of them historical pictures of past ages.   A course of reading embracing so wide a range in so small a compass must necessarily be limited in the number of its selections from any one author, however distinguished ; but it is hoped that the works selected may lead many of the readers to seek a closer acquaintance with their writers.

THE CHAUTAUQUA MUSICAL READING CLUB is an experiment which has not received sufficient attention from the management to justify a decision as to its practicability. A prospectus, prepared by Prof. W. F. Sherwin of Boston, states its objects and methods as follows : —

"There are thousands of earnest students of music among us, who sincerely desire to know something of the literature of their art. There are thousands of others in whose hearts such desires would burn if they only knew how much of fascination there is in the pursuit of this literature

"The true lover of music, who would gain an entrance into the secret realms of the 'divine art,' must know the history of its evolution, and as well also the history of the lives and struggles of those whom we by common consent call 'masters'

"He must also study the history of great compositions, by watching carefully their gradual development, the pains-taking labor bestowed upon them, and by reading the analyses and criticisms of celebrated musical scholars and profound thinkers. By such study he is sure to gain access to a world of beauty that is yet only known and fully appreciated by a favored few. But while there are so many who really desire just such knowledge, they do not know how to begin.

"Even learned musicians, when suddenly surprised by the question, 'What musical literature shall I read?' stop to think, and lament the fact that the few that have read were compelled to grope their way in the dark without the advantage of any systematic arrangement.

"Then, even when a small catalogue of books is furnished, the beginner in musical literature finds himself greatly in need of directions, explanations, suggestions, and almost endless assistance.

"The C. M. R. C. proposes, 1st, To furnish such a course of study as we think will yield the greatest amount of genuine instruction and entertainment to the music-loving reader; the great desire being to quicken the musical understanding, and arouse the enthusiasm. 2d, To conduct the classes, examinations, etc., on the same plan as that so successfully pursued by the C. L. S. C.

"A course of study is provided for two classes of readers : 1st, For those who are practical students of music, who have already made some progress in the elements of music, and who desire not only to be intelligent concerning music, but also to acquire a knowledge of science for practical purposes. For such the

'Scientific Course' is prescribed. To successfully prosecute this course, at least one hour per day of earnest study will be necessary. The reading in this course is precisely the same as that found in the 'Literary Course,' omitting the 'Musical Romance,' and substituting therefor the 'Science List' All who desire to make their knowledge of music thorough should attempt this course.

" 2d, The 'Literary Course' is prepared especially for those who are simply lovers of the art, having no desire to prosecute its study into the science of harmony, etc. This is emphatically a course intended for the musical culture of the minds of knowledge-loving people. It is intended for those who would be intelligent concerning music and musical matters, without being scientific musicians themselves In this course, simply the 'Romance List' is read with the regular literature (history, etc), omitting the 'Science List.' Forty minutes per day will suffice for this course."

CHAPTER VII.

THE "UNION," THE "CLUB," AND THE C. S. F. A.

" The real object of education is to give children resources that will endure as long as life endures; habits that time will ameliorate, not destroy; occupation that will render sickness tolerable, solitude pleasant, age venerable, life more dignified and useful, and death less terrible." — SYDNEY SMITH.

THE CHAUTAUQUA YOUNG FOLKS' READING UNION is in brief a Chautauqua reading-circle for the young people. It is a miniature C. L. S. C.

Whole families come to Chautauqua annually to spend the "season;" and, of course, in the families are children, — little children and big, boys that might as well be girls, and girls that might as well be boys, for all the difference that it makes in the freedom and joyousness of their young lives. And there are the after-boys and the after-girls, who are not yet men and women, but who manage to unite the proprieties of age with the buoyancy and gladsomeness of youth.

Recreation is one of the principal features of this delightful summer retreat. Wandering through the woods, the little people gather ferns, mosses, and wild flowers; in the lake they may bathe or fish, and over its crystal surface row or sail. Games already described in this volume are provided for them.

Many of the children, who come by the hundred to

Chautauqua every summer, have asked why there might not be a *circle* organized for them also, to suggest attractive and useful reading, to help them in the sometimes wearisome studies of the day-school, and to cultivate a taste for the right kind of reading.

On Thursday morning, Aug. 18, 1881, the "Chautauqua Young Folks' Reading Union" was formally organized. By taking the initials of this long name we have C. Y. F. R. U., which is the way the Union is usually designated. It is the purpose of the C. Y. F. R. U. to aid children and young people in forming correct tastes, and in making judicious selection of reading with which to occupy their spare time. The selections are made with special reference to wholesome and delightful recreation ; to instruction in the many ways of doing things with the hands, so as to make them quick and ready in helpful ministries ; to the illustration of the practical relations of religion to every-day duties and pleasures , to the awakening and direction of a normal desire for knowledge, so often repressed and misdirected to the permanent injury of a child. The very best writers for children and young people are engaged to prepare articles and books on topics related to this general plan.

The organ of the C. Y. F. R. U. is "The Chautauqua Young Folks' Journal," published by D. Lothrop & Co., Boston. The "Journal" and books required cost less than three dollars a year, including the office-fee. The subjects are substantially the same embraced in the current course of the C. L. S. C., so that parents and children may follow the same line of reading, and by conversation at home help each other, and thus make home much happier than where old and young have nothing in common. To all new members, a certificate of membership is forwarded. It is a beautiful albertype, embodying the light-bearing Spirit of the Union.

THE CHAUTAUQUA TOWN AND COUNTRY CLUB, under the direction of Charles Barnard, Esq., of New York, who thus states its aims and work, "is a town and country association of young people who wish to know something, and be something, and do something. It is a garden-school, with plants and animals for companions, and friends and books for guides. For teachers it has a farmer, a gardener, a florist, a herdsman, a shepherd, a dairy-maid, a poultry-keeper, and other people who know all about dogs, birds, ducks, rabbits, fish, and every plant and useful creature on the farm or in the water The C. T. C. C. is for boys and girls, young men and young women, at home, in town, at school, in the shop or on the farm, in the house or out of doors. One can join as soon as he knows how to read, and he can join at any time, and be a member until death. He can join alone, or form a local circle and join with others There are no entrance examinations, no requirements whatever, except that one wishes to know something, and be something, and do something, and is willing to take up the Chautauqua Town and Country Club's course of reading, and perform one of the C. T. C. C. works, and pay the small fees for two years.

"The objects of the C. T. C. C. are fivefold, — first, to help its members to learn something about the earth on which we live, its plants, flowers, and fruits, and to make the acquaintance of the plants and animals on

the farm and in the house; secondly, to help its members to become trained, skilful, and accomplished;
thirdly, to show them how to use their skill and knowledge in gaining health and happiness; fourthly, to show
its members how money is earned, to point out the way
to many useful trades and arts, and to show them the
value of good and honest work; lastly, to show by the
study of nature something of the Creator's wonderful
ways in managing this beautiful world.

"The members of the C. T. C. C. will be expected to
take up during the winter evenings a prescribed course
of instructive and interesting readings, and to give at
least one month, and as much more as they wish, to the
C. T. C. C. work. This course of reading and work
will extend over two summers and two winters, when
all who have faithfully carried out the rules of the Club
will receive a diploma, and become graduates of the
Club. After that they can still remain members of the
C. T. C. C. as long as they wish. The C. T. C. C.
course of readings is specially for winter evenings.

"The home of the C. T. C. C., or headquarters for
work and information concerning all matters excepting
the entrance of new members, will be at Houghton
Farm, Mountainville, Orange County, N.Y. Houghton
Farm is a large, first-class farm, devoted to all kinds of
farm crops and garden work. Every thing is carried
on at the farm that can be found in any farm in the
Northern States, including cattle-raising, horses, pigs,
and sheep, orchards, greenhouses, poultry-yards, ken-
nels, and dairy, and fruit, flower, and vegetable gardens.
There is, besides all these branches, a first-rate meteor-
ological and experimental station. Each department

is carried on to obtain the very best results possible
There is also a good library, from which the C. T. C. C.
course of reading will be prepared, and all the work laid
out in the C. T. C. C. programme of work will be actually
performed on the farm   All enrolled members of the
Club will be welcome to visit Houghton Farm at any
time, and can there see more or less of the C. T. C. C.
work actually going on.   There will also be at the Club
Headquarters a question-box or bureau of information.
Every member of the Club will be free to ask any question about farm, garden, greenhouse, or in fact any agricultural or horticultural work ; and each question will
be answered by some one in charge of the many departments of the farm.   For instance, all questions about
sheep will be answered by the shepherd, all concerning
the dairy by the dairy-maid, and so on   All members
of the C. T. C. C. will give their full name in asking
questions, and, if belonging to a social C. T. C. C. circle,
the name of the circle   There will be no charge for
use of the question-box.

"It is expected that every one that joins the Chautauqua Town and Country Club, whether young or old,
young man or young woman, will become an observer
and a worker ; that is, will select from the programme
of work something to do for every day for one whole
month in each year.   This will be to observe the
weather, observe the height of the thermometer at the
same hour every day from the first to the last day of
any month in the year, or observe and report the height
of the barometer, direction of the wind, amount of
clouds, or any other fact concerning the weather   At
the same time they will also, if they wish, select from

the programme one or as many more pieces of work as they like.   This work and observation should be done at the same time, so that you may learn to see the relation between the weather and all processes in plant and animal life.   The C. T. C. C. programme of work and observation is arranged in a series of easy labors that can be done in town or country at different times in the year.   Every member may select any observatory work, any farm, garden, house, kennel, or other work that he or she thinks can be done.   All members are also at liberty to do as many more of the works on the programme as they like, provided they do them well.   None of this work extends over more than four months in the year, and none will take less than thirty consecutive days. The work can be done at home, out of doors, in the garden, on the farm, in the front yard before the village house, in the brook, in the fish-pond, in the window, in the barn, in town or country, and all of it is easy, interesting, and well worth the doing.   The work may be the care of a horse, a dog, a bird, some chickens, pigeons, or even carp in a pond.   It may be the planting of some corn, some lettuce in a frame, flowers in the garden or in a flower-pot, or testing some seeds, or the care of a geranium in a raisin-box in a tenement-house window. One may take any thing he likes from the programme, provided he does it well, and reports it correctly."

THE CHAUTAUQUA SOCIETY OF FINE ARTS is under the direction of Mr. Frank Fowler of New York; Miss Jeannette L. Gilder, editor of "The Critic," conductor.   The interest in the study of art in its various branches being one that is growing, and extending to every town and hamlet in the country, the University proposes to add an Art Annex to its other departments, which will provide for the study of art under the best instructors, so that persons living at the farthest distance from the metropolis may have the same advantages in this particular as are to be had in the most expensive schools.

A plan of work will be laid out for each month, and the students in each branch of art-study will report progress in their work at stated periods.

It is not only the purpose of the C. S. F. A. to teach the decorative and ornamental arts, but to teach art to artisans so that they can pursue their trades with the intelligent interest that comes of cultivation.

The course of study will extend over two years. Special courses may be made for special studies for a longer period. The classes will be as follows: in elementary drawing; free-hand drawing and perspective; figure drawing from life; painting in water-colors; painting in oil; crayon portraits; crayon drawing.

CHAPTER VIII.

THE COLLEGE OF LIBERAL ARTS.

"Do not ask if a man has been through college. Ask if a college has been through him." — CHAPIN

"The best and most important part of every man's education is that which he gives himself" — GIBBON.

BEYOND the "Assembly" and the "Circle," and beyond the "Inner Circle," which leads to the "Upper Chautauqua," we come to the uppermost Chautauqua, — the "University" proper, with its "School of Liberal Arts," and its "School of Theology."

We have wandered with members of "The Society of the Hall in the Grove;" have saluted "The Order of the White Seal;" and here we find members of "The League of the Round Table," whose seven seals on the C. L. S. C. diploma entitle them to this higher honor. Here, too, are advanced students in the "Chautauqua School of Languages;" these walk in the outer courts and among the sacred corridors adjoining the University itself. Chautauqua now means more than ever to them. The towers of the University proper rise above them. They ask why its doors may not open to them, and why they may not rejoice in work, real work, with after-tests in genuine examinations, and after-honors in diploma and degrees.

Some remain in this goodly place, hearing the songs

that float down from the higher halls, enjoying converse
with their fellows of the grander degree, and encouraging other and younger and more vigorous companions
to go up and possess the land. Others knock at the
door by the upper step, and as it opens, they enter
the highest form of the Chautauqua movement, — THE
CHAUTAUQUA COLLEGE OF LIBERAL ARTS.

Here we find provision made for college training of
a thorough sort. Students all over the world may turn
their homes into dormitories, refectories, and rooms for
study, in connection with the great University which
has its local habitation at Chautauqua. Thus "hear-
ers" and "recipients" in the Assembly, "readers" in
the C L S C, "student readers" in the "inner circle," the "League of the Round Table," may go beyond,
even to the College of Liberal Arts, the *bona fide* College of Chautauqua.

Chautauqua exalts the college. She believes that
the benefits of a college training are manifold.

1. The action by which a youth becomes a college-
student — the simple going-forth, leaving one set of
circumstances, and voluntarily entering another, with
a specific purpose — is an action which has educating
influence in it. It is a distinct recognition of an object,
and a deliberate effort to secure it. The judgment is
convinced, the will makes a decision, and corresponding
action follows. We have the thought, the aim, the
standards, the resolve, the surrender, and the embodiment of all in an actual physical movement. There
must follow these activities a reflex influence on the
youth himself. It becomes a "new birth" in his life.
He has gone to another plane. His every-day conduct

is modified by it. He looks up and on. According to
the standard he has set, the idea he entertains of education, and the motives which impel him, will be the
subjective effects of his action, — the real power of his
new life.

2. There is educating power in the complete plan of
study provided in the college curriculum, covering as it
does the wide world of thought, distributed over the
years, with subdivisions into terms, with specific assign-
ments of subjects, with a beginning and an ending of
each division, and many beginnings and endings, with
promotions according to merit, and final reviews, recognitions, and honors. There is great value in the
enforced system of the college. It tends to sustain
and confirm new life, begun when the student made his
first movement toward an institution

3 The association of students in college life is another
educating factor   Mind meets mind in a fellowship of
aim, purpose, and experience   They have left the same
world ; they now together enter another world. They
look up to the heights and to the shining of crowns
which await the gifted and faithful. They are brothers now : one *Alma Mater* to nourish them   They
sing their songs, — songs which, although without much
sense, have power to awake and foster sympathy. Even
a man of sense loves to listen to them   He laughs at
the folly, and, though himself a sage, wishes he were
one of the company of singers   The laws of affinity
work out. Soul inspires soul. Memories grow apace.
Attachments that endure, adventures seasoned with fun
or touched with sadness, absurdities, failures, heroisms,
triumphs, are crowded into the four years, and like

fruitage of bloom and fragrance from a conservatory may go forth to bless many an hour of wandering, of sorrow, of re-union, of remembrance, in the later years. There was something pathetic in the return of the famous Yale College class of 1853 to their *Alma Mater* two summers ago. As they wandered about the scenes of their youth, under the old elms, through recitation-rooms and chapel, singing the old songs, reviving the old friendships, recalling faces to be seen no more, no wonder that tears fell down furrowed cheeks, from eyes unused to weep. Is there any stronger or sweeter friendship than that born under the ivied towers and spreading elms of college hall and campus?

In college, mind meets mind in the severe competition of recitation and annual examination. The bright boy — one of a small class at home, who had it all his own way there — now finds a score or more of leaders whose unvoiced challenge he is compelled to accept; and how he does knit his brow, close his eyes, summon his strength, school his will, force his flagging energies, and grapple problems, that he may hold his own, out-strip his rivals, and win prize and place for the sake of his family's fame and for his personal satisfaction !

There is nothing that so discovers to a youth the weak points of his character as the association of college life. There are no wasted courtesies among students. Folly is soon detected, and by blunt speech, bold caricature, and merciless satire exposed. Sensitiveness is cured by ridicule, cowardice never condoned, and meanness branded beyond the possibility of concealment or pardon. College associations stimulate the best elements in a man, expose weak and wicked ones, and tend to the pruning and strengthening of character.

4 Then there is in college life association with professors and tutors ; and this is, I confess, sometimes of little value, as when teachers are mere machines, but in it, at its best, are distinguishing benefits.   When teachers are full men, apt men, and enthusiastic men, — as college professors, and for that matter all teachers, ought to be, — the place of recitation soon becomes a centre of power   Tact tests attainment, exposes ignorance, foils deceit, develops strength, indicates lines of discovery, and inspires courage   A living teacher supplies at once model and motive.   He has gone on among the labyrinths, and up the steeps of knowledge ; has tried and toiled and triumphed   He sought, and he *is.* And now by wise questioning, by judicious revelation, by skilful concealment, by ingenious supposition, by generous raillery, by banter, by jest, by argument and by magnetic energies, the teacher stirs the student into supreme conditions of receptivity and activity. Such teachers make the college   As President Garfield said, "Give me an old schoolhouse, and a log for a bench ; put Mark Hopkins on one end, and let me as student sit on the other, and I have all the college I need."   When an institution is able to employ men of superior knowledge, power, and tact, students must be trained, and all their after-lives are affected by the influence   For memory magnifies the worth of a true teacher, and the hero of the college quadrennium becomes a demigod through the post-graduate years.   A dozen men of this mould, if once they could be gotten together, would make a college the like of which has

not yet been seen on the planet. Shall Chautauqua one of these days find them?

5. The college life promotes mental discipline. It drills, and drills, and draws out. It compels effort, and effort strengthens. It provides a system of mental gymnastics. What was difficult at first soon becomes easy, until severer tests are sought from the very delight the student finds in concentration and persistency. Thus development takes place in the varied faculties of the soul. The student acquires power to observe with scientific exactness, to generalize wisely from accumulated data, to project hypotheses, to watch psychical processes, to reason with accuracy, to distinguish between the false and the true, both in the inner and the outer world; to grasp protracted and complicated processes of mathematical thought; to trace linguistic evolutions, — remembering, analyzing, philosophizing; to study the students of the ages, and the products of their genius in art, poetry, jurisprudence, and discovery, in the facts of history and the great principles of sociology. All the powers employed in this manifold work during the college term are trained and thus prepared for work after the college term is ended. It is not so much the amount of knowledge acquired during the four years, as it is the power at will ever after to acquire knowledge, that marks the benefits of the college course.

6. With discipline comes the comprehensive survey of the universe. The college outlook takes the student backward along the line of historical development. It shows him the heights and the depths, the manifold varieties and inter-relations of knowledge. It gives him

tools and the training to use them, and a glance at the material on which he is to use them. The student through college is a traveller, sometimes examining in detail, sometimes superficially. He gives a glance, and remembers ; he takes notes, and thinks closely. He sees the all-surrounding regions of knowledge ; and although he may make but slight researches in particular lines, he knows where to return in the after-years for deeper research and ampler knowledge.

7. College life leads to self-discovery. It tests a man's powers, and reveals to him his weakness. It shows him what he is best fitted to do, and the showing may not be in harmony either with his ambitions or his preconceived notions. A boy born for mercantile pursuits, who comes out of college a lawyer or preacher, proves that the college failed to do its legitimate and most important work for him. Professors who merely glorify intellectual attainment, and who neglect to show students their true place in the world, are little better than cranks or hobbyists. College life is the whole of life packed into a brief period, with the elements that make life, magnified and intensified, so that tests of character may easily be made. It is a laboratory of experiment, where natural laws and conditions are pressed into rapid though normal operation, and processes otherwise extending over long periods of time are crowded to speedy consummation. Twenty years of ordinary life, so far as they constitute a testing period of character, are, by college life, crowded into four years. A boy who is a failure then would, for the same reasons, be a failure through the longer probation, unless the early discovery of peculiar weakness may be a protection

against the perils which this weakness involves Therefore it is a good thing for a youth to subject himself
thus early to a testing; for from it may come self-
discovery, when latent powers may be developed, and
impending evils avoided.

8 The true power of the college is in the will that
makes way to it, and makes way in it, and makes way
through it The tasks are mastered, the knowledge
acquired, the recitations made, the examinations passed,
the honors won, by personal, persevering will. The discipline by which the will brings all other powers into
practised submission and service is the best end of a
college education. The actual knowledge is valuable,
and there is a great deal of it; but that is not the chief
or the best result of the educational institution.

The college is not a *museum,* — literary, æsthetic, historic, scientific, — but a *gymnasium,* intellectual, moral,
personal. Its value is to be determined by the measure
of the man who comes out of it, — the measure of his
mental, executive, and moral force.

It will be evident from all this, that all college men
do not thus estimate the institution ; at least, they give
no proof of such estimate They do not show it when
they enter, while they stay, or after they leave College
life being a "fashion" in their choice circle of society,
they follow it ; a precedent in their family, they sustain
it ; a gilt-edge to the snobbery they fancy, they put it
on. They go to get through Dissipation, not discipline, is the rule of their college life. A diploma that
testifies to a falsehood, in a tongue they cannot trans-
late, is the trophy they bear away, — the only sign that
they were ever enrolled as college students. There are

such as these. Let us believe, as we declare, to the honor of the institutions they misrepresent, that the number of them is not great.

It must not be forgotten that there are "masters of themselves and of their kind," who have never been at college They awoke too late to the conviction of its need, or they found a line of life with opportunities of study and of work outside of a university, or they made the compromise with circumstance by which it became "a helper and a slave." They did not go to college ; but by transcendent genius, by heroic purpose, by protracted and unflinching effort, they won place and name that few of the favored sons of the universities might not envy.

On the other hand, the success of self-made men, as they are styled, must not weigh too much in favor of the path they trod, nor must it lead for a moment to the depreciation of the advantages they lacked. Great as they were without the higher school and the living teacher, they and the world would probably have been the gainers by a complete opportunity on their part for personal training. At least, so they thought ; for, if there be men more enthusiastic in favor of the college than college men themselves, they are to be found in the ranks of the successful self-made scholars, who know what they have lost by what they have won, and by the manner of the winning

Of other advantages of educational institutions, I shall not now speak. They are manifold. Our youth of both sexes, whatever their callings in life, would do well to seek these advantages. Therefore parents, primary teachers, and older persons who influence youth, should constantly place before them the benefits of college education, and inspire them to reach after and attain it. Arguments should be used, appeals made, assistance proffered, that a larger percentage of American youth may aspire after college privileges, or at least remain for a longer term in the best schools of a higher grade. Haste to be rich, restiveness under restraint during the age of unwisdom, inability to regulate by authority at home the eager and ambitious life of our youth, together with false, mercenary notions of parents, who "cannot afford to have so much time spent by the young folks in studying, because they must be doing something for themselves," — these are some of the causes of the depreciation and neglect of the American college; a neglect lamentable enough, and fraught with harm to the nation.

Chautauqua lifts up her voice in favor of liberal education for a larger number of people. She would pack existing institutions until wings must be added to old buildings, and new buildings be put up, to accommodate young men and maidens who are determined to be educated.

Chautauqua would exalt the profession of the teacher until the highest genius, the richest scholarship, and the broadest manhood and womanhood of the nation would be consecrated to this service.

Chautauqua would give munificent salaries, and put a premium on merit, sense, tact, and culture in the teacher's office. She would turn the eyes of all the people — poor and rich, mechanics, and men of other if not higher degree — toward the high school and the college, urging house-builders, house-owners, housekeep-

ers, farmers, blacksmiths, bankers, millionnaires, to
prepare themselves by a true culture, whatever niche
they fill in life, to be men and women, citizens, parents,
members of society, members of the church, candidates
for immortal progress

To promote these ends, the Chautauqua Literary and
Scientific Circle was organized.   By its courses of popular reading it gives a college outlook to the uncult-
vated, and exalts the higher learning   It is a John the
Baptist, preparing the way for seminary and university.

The managers of the Chautauqua movement, however, recognize the fact that there are thousands of
full-grown men and women who are at their best intellectually, and who, with some leisure and much longing,
believe they could do more than read.   They want to
study, to study in downright earnest; to develop
mental power; to cultivate taste, to increase knowledge,
to make use of it by tongue and pen and life.   There
are tens of thousands of young people out of school by
necessities commercial and filial, who are awakened to
the power within and the possibilities beyond   They
believe they could learn a language, and enjoy the literature of it   They believe they could think and grow,
speak and write   They are willing and eager to try.
Out of minutes they could construct college terms.
They have will enough, heart enough, brain enough, to
begin, to go on, to go through; and all this, while the
every-day life continues with its duty for this hour and
for that.   They believe that into the closely woven
texture of every-day home and business life, there may
be drawn threads of scarlet, crimson, blue and gold,
until their homespun walls become radiant with form

and color worthy to decorate the royal chamber, — the chamber of their King, God the Father of earnest souls.

Chautauqua recognizes the fact that there are many such persons, who covet educational opportunities of the best kind, who cannot leave home to enjoy them. Parents are old or feeble, and son or daughter is needed to keep the place, carry on the business, and care for father and mother. Now, they could leave the old people to fate, or to the neighbors, or to the tender mercies of hired servants; they could go to college, and stay, and get gain of culture — but it would be at a sacrifice too sad to think upon. What good in a gain made at such a price? To these self-denying, loyal souls, the "Chautauqua College of Liberal Arts" comes, — not with courses of reading, but with prescribed studies, just such as are pursued in the best colleges of the country, — and encourages and assists them at their own homes to study, and to take all the time they need in order to do the required work well. Letters and lessons frequently pass between professors and pupils. Difficulties are removed, suggestions offered, will-power developed, knowledge and intellectual power secured. In course of time they read Greek and Latin as well, as intelligently, as do other college students. They read as wide a range of collecteral ancient classic literature. They study mathematics, putting time and thought into the process, and getting power out of it. They perform more experiments in chemistry than the average resident college student. In physics they read, observe, think, and make report. On every part of the college curriculum they pass written examinations in the presence of eye-witnesses, and they prepare theses;

all of which go on file, and remain in the University office as proofs of patience, fidelity, and ability. They find scholars among their nearest neighbors, — lovers of knowledge, college-graduates, specialists in various lines of science and literature. By frequent conversations they elicit cordial criticisms, get encouragement and information, and that quickening influence which comes from contact with the living teacher, and which a youth of twenty, working for examination, under compulsion, in a "division" or class of forty or fifty students, does not always to any greater degree secure. These students of the C. C. L. A. pass examination alone, and MUST answer or try to answer, not one or two out of forty, but every one of the list of forty questions. They study with high ambition. The very limitation put upon them tends to discipline. They cannot do as they would. They *must* do what they can. The "cannot" and the "must" beget purpose and invention, and out of these come strength and the joy of achievement. To this class of ambitious people comes the Chautauqua College of Liberal Arts. It gives them help, direction, incentive, instruction, encouragement. The teacher, though absent, is, by a mystic law of soul, present with his pupils, following, inspiring, quickening them. By the swift and steady shuttle of the post, threads are crossed and intertwined, till distance dwindles into neighborhood, and under a woven pavilion master and learner sit together, questioning, answering, thinking, reasoning, developing, finding delight in the world of truth and in the processes by which it becomes their own. The end comes after a while, and upon the faithful student honor and reward are put — in diploma and degree. Why should it not be so? Are these not scholars? Have they not gained discipline? Are they not lovers of learning, with an insight into the way of gaining knowledge? Are they not all that "Bachelors of Art" are? Have they not honorably worked their way through? Why should a dissipated stripling in the fourth division of a college class, who has gone "through" by special helps of "chums" and "ponies," receive a degree, and these filial, faithful students at home be denied it? They know more than he does. They have honestly explored the field over which he has hurried. They have more power and grip in every intellectual process. Why shall they not have parchment and degree? To such as these, Chautauqua guarantees both. In the Chautauqua way the stripling just described could not win them at all. The diplomas which the C. C. L. A. will give, few members of the lowest third of an average college class in America could either merit or secure.

Besides the class I have described, there are men and women in business and domestic life, some of them in positions of influence which wealth secures, some of them on the highway to such state of prosperity, who deplore their deficiencies, and desire to enjoy college privileges. Among these one will find lawyers, ministers, merchants, and women of leisure. To all of them the C. C. L. A. is a benediction. College residence is impracticable. One hour's study a day for a few years will give them long-coveted honor.

The C. C. L. A. recognizes and fosters the college spirit. In a very important sense, Chautauqua students cannot be isolated. They are "Chautauquans," and as

such are united. They are one in the fellowship of that
unique and remarkable movement now known all over
the world ; one in consecration to a splendid work, —
the promotion of symmetrical culture among the people
everywhere ; one in a guild that has chosen its "local
habitation " among the primeval forests on the shores
of one of the loveliest lakes on the continent, where
Art has clasped hands with Nature, and bidden Literature, Science, and Faith abide.   Here the "Academia,"
a beautiful grove, has been laid out ; and here every
matriculated student of the CHAUTAUQUA COLLEGE has
a home where altar-fires burn, and the songs of his
mystic brotherhood ring out   The C. C. L A. gives to
its members a peculiar pre-eminence. They occupy
the height which crowns the Chautauqua movement.
Looking down, they see the great army of C. L. S. C.
readers and students who compose "The Assembly,"
"The Circle," and "The Inner Circle," — successive
steps in the University towards the heights now occupied by the "College" itself. It is something to be
surrounded by such a constituency, and to be its foremost representatives !

The "Chautauqua College of Liberal Arts" has
power to confer degrees, — all university degrees.
The Board of Trustees has decided by a unanimous
vote, not to bestow an honorary degree. They are
willing to defer that official act for twenty years if need
be. They are resolved to honor no man whose attainments under Chautauqua auspices would not be an
honor to Chautauqua   The circumstances under which
the work is done render it imperative that the work
be well done. Chautauqua is determined, in these

higher departments of educational effort, to command the respect of the scholars who care to examine her theory and methods of work.

The system of "Correspondence," on which the "Chautauqua College of Liberal Arts" must depend for success and reputation, is, at my request, stated and defended by one of its ablest representatives, Dr W. R Harper, who as a teacher of Hebrew has for years been pre-eminent, and to whom has been intrusted the department of Greek and Latin in the C. C. L A.

"Four questions may be considered: (1) What *is* the correspondence-system of teaching? (2) What disadvantages attend this system, as compared with oral teaching? (3) What advantages, if any, does the correspondence-system have over oral teaching? (4) What results have thus far been accomplished in the line of teaching by correspondence? In the statements made, special reference is had to the teaching of languages.

I. WHAT IS THE CORRESPONDENCE-SYSTEM?

"A brief explanation of the plan of study by correspondence is first in order.

"1. An *instruction-sheet* is mailed to the student each week. This instruction-sheet (*a*) assigns the tasks which are to be performed, — e g., the chapters of the text to be translated, the sections in the grammar to be learned; (*b*) indicates an order of work which the student is required to follow; (*c*) offers suggestions on points in the lesson which are liable to be misunderstood; (*d*) furnishes special

assistance wherever such assistance is deemed necessary, (*e*) marks out a specified amount of review-
work ; (*f*) contains an examination-paper which the
student, after having prepared the lesson, is required
to write out. The instruction-sheet is intended, therefore, to guide and help the student just as an oral
teacher would guide and help him

"2. The *examination-paper* is so constructed, that, in
order to its preparation for criticism, one must have
prepared beforehand most thoroughly the lesson on
which it is based. An examination-paper on Cæsar,
for example, requires of the student (*a*) the translation of certain chapters into English ; (*b*) the translation into Latin of a list of English sentences based
on the Latin which has just been translated ; (*c*) the
explanation of the more important constructions,
with the grammatical reference for each construc-
tion ; (*d*) the placing of forms ; (*e*) the change to
'direct discourse' of a corresponding passage in 'in-
direct discourse ;' (*f*) the explanation of geographical and historical allusions ; (*g*) the statement of
grammatical principles, etc., etc.

"3 In the *recitation-paper* submitted to the instruct-
or, besides writing out the matter called for in the
examination-paper, the student asks such questions,
and notes such difficulties, as may have presented
themselves to him in his study of the lesson. This
recitation-paper is promptly returned with all errors
corrected, and questions answered, and with special
suggestions, suited to each individual case.

"In this manner each lesson of the course is
assigned and studied ; and the results of the study

submitted to the instructor for correction, criticism, and suggestion.

"From this it will be seen that the correspondence-teacher must be pains-taking, patient, sympathetic, and *alive;* and that the correspondence-pupil must be earnest, ambitious, appreciative, and likewise *alive.* Whatever a *dead* teacher may accomplish in the class-room, he can do nothing by correspondence; and if a student lacking the qualities just named undertake work by correspondence, one of two things will happen: either he will acquire these qualities, and succeed; or he will remain as he was at the beginning, and fail. The man who does the work at all, must do it well.

II. THE DISADVANTAGES UNDER WHICH THE CORRESPONDENCE-STUDENT WORKS.

"There are, I frankly confess, some disadvantages under which the correspondence-student works, and it is only fair to consider them.

"1. The personal magnetism of an instructor is often felt by pupils for years after they have ceased to come in contact with him. Some teachers — and it is an occasion of regret that the number of such is not larger — exert upon the students an influence for good which cannot be estimated. Such influence the correspondence-student does not feel; such stimulus he does not receive.

"2. In the recitation-room, there is a certain class-spirit, and a certain spirit of emulation, which tend to elevate the student, to quicken and to dignify him. This, of course, is for the most part lacking in the correspondence-work.

"3. An earnest, conscientious teacher, in whatever department he may work, will unconsciously furnish information, impart methods of work, let drop sugges-tions, which are not to be found in text-books. Under the inspiration of the class-room he will lead his pupils by paths which he himself never trod before. All this, the correspondence-student loses.

"4. Ordinarily the student makes one hundred and sixty to one hundred and eighty recitations in a given study during the year. The correspondence-student makes but forty.

"5. There is a drudgery in the work of writing out long lessons, which some regard as almost unendur-able. This is in sharp contrast with the freedom and pleasure with which others make an oral recitation.

"6. There is necessarily a large amount of irreg-ularity in the correspondence-work. The interrup-tions are, in the very nature of the case, quite numer-ous; and after such interruptions there inevitably comes discouragement. This is a most serious dif-ficulty.

"7. The correspondence-student is not under the eye of an instructor; the temptation to be dishonest is always at hand. He is more likely to use illegiti-mate helps, and to misuse legitimate ones, than is he who must produce the results of his work in the presence of his comrades and at a moment's notice.

"8. Whatever the common opinion may be, the re-quirements of the correspondence-system are of so exacting and rigid a nature as to prevent some from completing the work, who would certainly be able to pass through the course of study in many of our so-called colleges. This may or may not be a disadvantage of the correspondence-system, according to the point of view taken.

"These difficulties, it is true, exist; but some things may be said, which will, at least slightly, modify their force.

" 1. If personal stimulus furnished by the teacher is absolutely necessary to good results on the part of the student, then two-thirds of the oral instruction given is valueless; for it is safe to assert that two out of three teachers exert no such influence upon their pupils, their work being purely mechanical.

" 2. Is it true that this personal magnetism, this personal influence, cannot be conveyed by writing? Have words spoken, or words written, produced the greater effect? Have not many of us received greater inspiration from personal letters than from words uttered by mouth? Are there not among our best friends those whom we have never seen, whose voice we have never heard, whose words have reached us only by letter?

"In my experience with students by correspondence, brief as it has been, I can refer to hundreds of men who have acknowledged the stimulus and inspiration received by letters in the course of their study.

" 3. Class-spirit is not wholly lacking. The student knows that he is a member of a class which probably numbers hundreds, the members of which live in every State and Territory and even in foreign lands. Is there not inspiration in this fact? He knows, also, that every recitation-paper is graded, that his progress is very closely watched, that his classmates are pushing on notwithstanding difficulties and obstacles as great as he is called to meet. Is there not stimulus in all this?

"4. Only forty recitations a year are required; yet each of these forty demands the preparation and the work of three or four oral recitations; and were the number less than forty, and the amount accomplished less, the fact that the student prepares his lesson knowing that he must *recite the whole of it*, and that he must recite it by writing, goes far to make up in quality what perhaps in quantity might be lacking.

"5. The drudgery is very great, but not so great as many imagine. Besides, those to whom the work seems so onerous are those of whom such work as a matter of discipline should be required.

"6. While in correspondence-work it is true that interruptions and consequent discouragements are more likely to occur, it is equally true, (*a*) that this evil is largely mitigated by the fact that the average correspondence-student is thirty years of age, and therefore old enough to overcome the bad effect of such interruptions; (*b*) that a rigid system of reviews helps greatly, also, to counterbalance this evil; and (*c*) that, while work lost from sickness or other cause is never really made up in the ordinary class, in the correspondence-class no work is lost, the student being required to begin at the point reached when the interruption took place.

"7. After all, dishonesty in correspondence-work is more easily detected than in an oral recitation. And, besides, what is easier than so to construct the examination-paper, in each case, that at least in a large portion of the work no direct aid may possibly be obtained?

" 8. It is proper in this connection to consider the following points : (*a*) No one has ever thought of sub- stituting the correspondence-system for the oral ; the latter is conceded to be superior, and only those are advised to study by correspondence who cannot in any way obtain oral instruction. (*b*) The fact that the large proportion of correspondence-students are vol- untary workers removes many difficulties which under other circumstances might exist. (*c*) What the stu- dent loses in his correspondence-work, he may easily gain by attending the Summer Schools, which, in- deed, are intended to supplement the correspondence- work.

III. WHAT ADVANTAGES DOES THE CORRESPONDENCE- SYSTEM HAVE ?

"While it is freely conceded that there are disad- vantages attending the correspondence-system, it is confidently claimed that this system has some advan- tages over other systems Our space will scarcely permit any thing more than a bare mention of these : —

" 1. By the correspondence-student, compelled to express every thought *in writing,* there is gained what the student reciting orally does not so easily acquire, — the habit of *exact statement.*

" 2. Of the correspondence-student, compelled to state *in writing* his conception of a principle, or his translation of a· paragraph, there is demanded a greater *accuracy of knowledge* than is necessary for an ordinary oral recitation.

" 3. While each student, in an oral recitation, recites only one-tenth, one-thirtieth, or one-sixtieth of the lesson assigned, each correspondence-student recites the entire lesson, however long it may be. In four oral recitations, each student in a class of thirty recites eight minutes : in the preparation of a single recitation-paper, the correspondence-student spends at least two hours, aside from the previous work of preparing the lesson. The oral student must recite rapidly, often hurriedly : the correspondence-student works out his recitation-paper slowly, thoughtfully.

" 4. The correspondence-student, given all *necessary* assistance, but compelled to obtain every thing else for himself, or write out his questions and wait for the written answer, is led to investigate, to be independent in his study, and to have a confidence in the results of his own investigation which the student who has constant recourse to his instructor does not have.

" 5. If a written examination is a more thorough test of a student's knowledge of a given subject, surely a written recitation is not, in respect to *thoroughness*, inferior to an oral one. The correspondence-system requires of its students more thorough preparation of the lesson assigned, a more thorough recitation of it, and, in a word, a more thorough knowledge of the subject treated of in that lesson.

" 6 A prime requisite in good teaching is the ability to assign the proper lesson. Many excellent teachers fail at this point. The lesson is too long,

or too short; the ground to be covered is not defi-
nitely indicated; the method of work is not clearly
stated, etc., etc. The correspondence-lesson, since
it is generally in printed form, is prepared with the
greatest care. No part of it is given out hurriedly.
It is the result of hours of careful study and calcu-
lation. If it is too long to be prepared within six
days, the student is allowed a longer time; if it can
be prepared within a less time, the student can take
up the next lesson Nothing could be more definite
than this lesson, for it is assigned with a minuteness
of detail which to some doubtless seems superfluous,
but which in the case of others is absolutely essential.

"7. Finally, whatever may be the relative merits
of the two systems, it is clear to every one who
thinks, that there are thousands of men and women
unable to avail themselves of oral assistance, who,
nevertheless, are eager to study. It is surely an
advantage of the correspondence-system, that it can
aid this large class, who otherwise would have no
help, and would make no progress.

"These are some of the advantages of the correspondence-system. But is any one to suppose that
there exists, in the mind of those especially interested in this system, a desire to have it take the place
of oral instruction? Is the one in any sense a rival
of the other? I wish here to record, in answer to
these questions, a most emphatic *No.* What is the
fact? *Only those persons are encouraged to study by
correspondence, or, indeed, admitted to such study, who
because of age, poverty, occupation, situation, or some*

other good reason, cannot avail themselves of oral instruction. Away, therefore, with all baseless and foolish prejudice in this matter! The correspondence-system would not, if it could, supplant oral instruction, or be regarded as its substitute. There is a field for each which the other cannot fill. Let each do its proper work.

IV. WHAT HAS BEEN ACCOMPLISHED THUS FAR IN THE LINE OF CORRESPONDENCE-WORK?

"In the strict sense of the term, the correspondence-system has been in use only four or five years. This time has been sufficient, however, to enable us to note a few practical results : —

"1. It has already helped thousands of men toward a knowledge of certain subjects, which otherwise they would not have had.

"2. There are to-day many thousands of men already convinced of the feasibility of the system, who are but waiting for the moment to arrive at which they shall begin. Educators in all lines are beginning to appreciate the possibilities of this system.

"3. Institutions have been established, chief among which stands the CHAUTAUQUA COLLEGE OF LIBERAL ARTS, through whose influence the system will be more fully developed, and rendered capable of accomplishing still greater good.

"I venture, in closing this very brief and imperfect presentation, to make two statements ; one an assertion based on large experience, the other a prediction based on strong conviction: —

"1. The student who has prepared a certain number of lessons in the correspondence-school knows more of the subject treated in those lessons, and knows it better, than the student who has covered the same ground in the class-room.

"2. The day is coming when the work done by correspondence will be greater in amount than that done in the class-rooms of our academies and colleges, when the students who shall recite by correspondence will far outnumber those who make oral recitations."

From all that I have said, it will be easily seen that "The Chautauqua College of Liberal Arts" is not a rival of other colleges, competing for students, presenting inducements to persons who want college honors, on abridged courses of study, by the way of "easy" examinations, or at greatly reduced expense. Our college requirements are as rigid, the examinations as thorough, as those of any college in America. And there are institutions where a full college course may require less money than will be necessary to complete the studies of the "Chautauqua College of Liberal Arts." Indeed, it is a regulation of our institution, that we will not receive a student who can enter a resident school of the highest grade. Chautauqua deserves the heartiest co-operation of all college men.

"The Chautauqua Literary and Scientific Circle" by enlisting sixty or seventy thousand people (many of whom are parents) in a course of English reading which embraces the subjects of the college course, makes them familiar with the college world, and thus prepares them to insist that their own children shall enter that world as college students.

By providing a variety of reading courses, Chautauqua also supplements the college, and encourages graduates to continue reading and study at home and in connection with business; thus giving added value to college privileges, and showing graduates how they may continue to grow, and, while they themselves grow, to help others in the pursuit of knowledge, and in the attainment of the power which knowledge and the pursuit of it give.

CHAPTER IX.

THE SCHOOL OF THEOLOGY.

"His preaching much, but more his practice wrought,
A living sermon of the truths he taught." — DRYDEN

THE CHAUTAUQUA SCHOOL OF THEOLOGY, anticipated by the various provisions on the Chautauqua programme for the benefit of ministers visiting the
place during the summer sessions, was duly organized
and chartered in the winter of 1880–81. The objects
of the school are thus set forth in the charter granted
by the Legislature of the State of New York : " 1. To
instruct its patrons in the departments of biblical, theological, ecclesiastical, historical, and philosophical learning which are usually taught in seminaries devoted to
the training of candidates for the clerical profession,
and in such other subjects as in the judgment of its
instructors shall conduce to the efficiency of the candidates. 2. To provide an archæological library and
museum for the illustration of biblical and Oriental research, and the collection of books, manuscripts, charts,
plans, casts, relics, etc., designed to assist the biblical
student in his investigation of the evidences and contents of the Holy Scriptures

Although, in the language of the Charter, "the place
of business of said corporation shall be at Chautauqua,
in the town of Chautauqua, county of Chautauqua, New

York," the work of the school is performed by ministers at their homes; all their biblical, theological, and
sermonic studies to be recognized, under certain conditions and regulations, in the curriculum prescribed. It
is not necessary that the student of the Chautauqua
School of Theology should ever visit Chautauqua itself;
annual examinations being provided for, in centres easily
accessible to all students.

Two departments in the Chautauqua School of Theology have been announced. First, "The Chautauqua
School of Theology," the "student" of which, paying
the required fees and passing the examinations, will be
entitled to the diploma and other honors of the institution. Second, "The Jerusalem Chamber of Theology,"
the "members" of which, paying the fees and adopting
the regular course of reading, study, and reports, shall
be entitled to all printed documents sent out by the
Faculty.

The "Jerusalem Chamber" in Westminster Abbey,
London, in the time of Richard II. was hung with tapes-
try which represented the story of the siege of Jerusalem. Over the chimney-piece may now be seen these
texts: "O pray for the peace of Jerusalem;" "Build
thou the walls of Jerusalem;" and, "Jerusalem which is
above is free." Here King Henry IV died. Here, also,
the Westminster Assembly of Divines held many of
their sessions. Here, too, the revised Prayer Book of the
Church of England was drawn up, and in this historic
hall the English committee when engaged in the revis-
ion of the Holy Bible held their meetings. This memorial centre has given the name to the department of
the Chautauqua School of Theology, that proffers what-

ever advantages it may devise to ministers in regular
standing, who, having been fully inducted into the office
and work of the Christian ministry, desire the benefits
of our movement without being subjected to the examinations required of students ; to advanced lay-workers
in Sunday schools and Y. M. C A , and to candidates
for the home and foreign mission field.

The C S T. aims to promote the independent study
of the Holy Scriptures. Attention is given to the study
of Hebrew, Hellenistic Greek, and Ecclesiastical Latin.
It is impossible for the average minister to be an original investigator in linguistic lines. The scholarship of
the ages has provided tools for the work of exegesis.
The theological student should be able to read Greek
and Hebrew at least sufficiently well to enable him to
read English expositions of the word of God in which
Greek and Hebrew words occur, that he may verify the
references of the expositors, examine the constructions
emphasized, and thus corroborate to his own satisfaction
the interpretations of eminent scholars. At the same
time, he should constantly aim at thoroughness in linguistic skill and acquisition.

It is one thing to know all that is knowable about a
subject ; and another thing, and in many cases quite as
good a thing, *to know where one can find all that is
known about a subject*, scientifically classified and in-
stantly available. There are thousands of details in the
domain of the knowable, which are as serviceable on the
shelf awaiting command, as in the memory, burdening
and overtaxing it, and diverting energies and activities
from fresher and more practical pursuits. One may
spend too much time in the study of historical theology,

and of ecclesiastical discussions between schools long since, or well-nigh, extinct; in mere talk about words and "endless genealogies, which minister questions rather than godly edifying." It is foolish to commit the contents of the Rosetta Stone to memory, but it is well to be able to find it if one needs to consult it. The Chautauqua School of Theology aims to give in condensed outlines the facts of Church history, the historical development of doctrine and form ; and places within easy reach of its members whatever they may care to find out concerning the multiplied unfoldings of historical, systematic, and comparative theology.

The various schools of the Church, ecclesiastical and doctrinal, are reported to all students of the Chautauqua School of Theology by their respective representatives. The Calvinist defines Calvinism; the Arminian, Arminianism ; a Baptist gives the distinctive views of his branch of the Church ; and thus the Chautauqua School of Theology is strictly denominational, in that it guarantees to each member not only a course of doctrinal studies prepared by men authorized to speak for his Church, but it enables him to test the soundness of such statement by a careful reading of the positions taken by other or rival schools. There is a sense in which this may be called "union," but it is in the highest and best sense denominational.

The C. S. T. insists upon the study of human nature. It carefully searches into the social phenomena of our times. It seeks the haunts and homes of men, studies their trades, sorrows, wrongs, and necessities. It studies sociology — domestic, commercial, political — from the Christian point of view. It secures for its members

counsels from eminent merchants, manufacturers, educators, statesmen, and especially from distinguished
jurists, who, dealing with society as it is, understand
men, — how to approach and manage them, how to expose the devices by which dishonesty violates the spirit
while it keeps within the letter of the law, how to weigh
evidence, and how to plead with men

Especial attention is given to the study of human
nature as set forth by the distinguished students of
human nature, such as Shakspere, Addison, Thackeray, Dickens, George Eliot, Hawthorne, etc. We
study in our theological schools the specialists who
study God . why not study also the specialists who study
man ? This is all the more important because of the
false philosophy which often gains currency in an insidi-
ous way, and which should be held up to careful scrutiny in the light of the Holy Scriptures. Upon no class
of men does this responsibility so immediately and
heavily rest as upon Christian pastors.

No part of the Chautauqua work has received more
hearty words of approval from the persons for whose
benefit it was designed, than the C. S. T. No part
of the work has met with so many obstacles, or so
constantly tested the faith of its projectors. The department of Hebrew under Dr W. R. Harper, and that
of New-Testament Greek under Prof. A. A. Wright,
have been very successful. Other departments have
done excellent work, and with patience and experience
the whole scheme will soon demonstrate its practical
value. More than four hundred names are enrolled ;
and these are names of ministers in pastoral work at
present, — men who could not be in any other theologi-

cal seminary. When the "ships come in," and chairs
of correspondence are endowed, the C. S. T. will do
work that will surprise the Church.

In the study of human nature the Chautauqua School
of Theology does not forget the intimate relation between body and soul From diseased nerves often come
gloom and despondency, or a delirium of joy There
are people, too, who perpetually sin against the body,
and then wonder at their spiritual bondage and depres-
sion Every minister needs to know the laws of physical, mental, and spiritual interaction. A distinguished
physiologist and physician, Dr. J. S. Jewell of Chicago,
has prepared for students of the C. S. T. a series of
papers on "What Anatomy and Physiology have to say
to Young Ministers."

Annual *praxes* in the study of human nature are
required. Each student is furnished with blanks and
"character-questions," by the guidance of which he is
expected to study a given number of individuals in his
church or community, making reports every year ; thus
collecting valuable scientific data, and at the same time
cultivating in himself the habit of studying human
nature.

The Chautauqua School of Theology also gives attention to natural science. For his own sake as a thinker,
as a lover of wisdom and the works of God, and as a
creature made for high enjoyment, the minister should
be a student of natural science. How much more for
the sake of those whom he serves, — the young, whose
faith is threatened by the scepticism of the age ; the
studious, whose delights lie in regions of thought, seri-
ously needing the religious element with its moral stand-

ards, its bold appeals, and its corrective provisions !
The latest thought of natural science in its varied departments will be, from time to time, submitted to the
members of the C. S. T.

The minister, as a representative of the learned
profession, must keep in sympathy with the advanced
literary taste and achievements of his time.   In our
country neighborhoods, and in all of our towns and
cities (even on the frontier), with their superior schools
and with public sentiment in favor of reading and study,
there is a growing culture which the minister must not
allow to outgrow himself.   He should keep up with this
in order to understand the peculiar perils to which
youth and age are exposed from dangerous philosophies
which insidiously creep into our communities and house-
holds, undermining the faith of the people in the pure
word of God. We need not answer the utterances of
such as Ingersoll ; but when young people inquire of us
concerning his statements, we must have argument for
reply rather than anathema, and be able to put facts
over against his falsifications.   The minister must understand the literary elements which quietly antagonize
his gospel; and with taste and ability so deal with them,
that his matter and manner will command the respect
of the most highly cultivated in his community.   In the
C. S. T. the modern antagonisms of Christianity —
social, scientific, doctrinal, ecclesiastical, and political
— are conscientiously considered.

Careful attention is given to the subject of education,
secular and religious, in its relation to the pastoral
office, — the Jewish family school ; the synagogue ; the
early catechetical and theological schools ; the Sunday

school; the rise and progress of modern secular education; the relation of the Church to culture.

A museum of Sacred Archæology was opened at Chautauqua, Aug. 16, 1881, under the direction of the Chautauqua archæological department of the "Chautauqua School of Theology," Rev. J. E. Kittredge, D.D., Secretary. It is the design of this society to collate and report the results of the latest explorations in Bible lands; to form a library and museum for the collection of maps, books, relics, casts, etc., illustrating this department of research; and to provide for an annual lecture or report bringing into available form the latest thought in this field of biblical study. A gentleman of wealth has erected a building at Chautauqua which already contains several plaster *fac-similes* of the Rosetta Stone, the Black Obelisk of Shalmaneser, the Moabite Stone, the winged bull and lion from Nineveh, the famous panel of the Arch of Titus, the Hamath inscriptions, copies of the three great Codices, — *Vaticanus, Sinaiticus, Alexandrinus;* also, biblical objects, relics, coins, maps, charts, etc.

Several plans are gradually maturing, from which much good must come to members of the school; such as, a system of co-operative work for reading of a large number of authorities on a given topic; frequent syllabi of the latest review articles, and a course on biblical, theological, and ecclesiastical themes in Europe and America; the actual study of homiletical science as revealed by the observations of friendly critics, lay and clerical; the giving of incidental attention by students of the C. S. T. to mechanical pursuits, in order that they may become familiar with the varied operations of industrial life, for the sake of bringing ministers into closer sympathy with the people, and of collecting illustrations which may be employed in the application and enforcement of truth.

More than four hundred ministers are enrolled in the Chautauqua School of Theology, and are pursuing its courses of study.

CHAPTER X.

THE CHAUTAUQUA PRESS.

" When the press is the echo of sages and reformers, it works well." —
LAMARTINE.

CHAUTAUQUA at the very beginning made wise
and extensive use of the "press," in order to
arrest public attention to the work attempted.   The
"Superintendent of Instruction," in full charge of the
programme, was also editor of the Sunday-school publications of the "Methodist Book Concern;" and as the
Assembly was begun under the auspices of the "Union"
of which he was Corresponding Secretary, he was justified in making a free use of the periodicals under his
control.   And this he did   The "Sunday-school Journal" with a circulation of over a hundred thousand
copies monthly, the "Normal Class" and "Chautauqua
Bulletin," in large editions, gave notice to the world
of the coming Assembly; and through a thorough system of announcements in the general press, religious
and secular, the first meeting on "the first Tuesday
of August," 1874, was looked forward to by hundreds of
thousands of Sunday-school and church workers   Its
proceedings were as widely reported   A special secretary was employed, who prepared an elaborate account
of the proceedings in a pamphlet of three hundred
pages, more than twelve thousand copies of which were

circulated. The daily and weekly press gave lengthy reports of the proceedings. Never since then has the press been more effectively utilized than in the anticipation and report of the first Chautauqua Assembly.

It was the desire and effort of the management at the very beginning, to publish a daily paper on the grounds. But the Chautauqua meeting was an experiment, and it was feared that the expense might be too great. The Assembly with its heavy burdens hesitated about assuming this responsibility, and delayed the matter, depending upon the general press and upon the excellent facilities which it already controlled. It again and again offered the privilege, and guaranteed indorsement and assistance, to private parties who might be willing to assume the responsibility of publishing a paper. At last this offer was accepted by Rev T. L. Flood, Jamestown, N.Y., who undertook the work, and with Milton Bailey, Esq., of Jamestown, N.Y., as business manager, issued in 1876, by permission of the Chautauqua Board, the first number of "The Chautauqua Assembly Daily Herald." In course of time Dr. Flood purchased from Mr. Bailey his right in the Assembly paper, and later on entered into contract with the Board to publish both "The Assembly Daily Herald" and the monthly magazine known as "The Chautauquan." The Assembly was fortunate in this arrangement, because of the remarkable business ability, enterprise, and editorial wisdom of Dr. Flood ; who, in turn, was also fortunate in finding an institution that demanded an organ, and a reading circle so large as to guarantee an immense and profitable circulation at the very outset. "The Chautauqua Assembly Daily Herald" as the organ of the Summer

Meeting, and "The Chautauquan" (published at Meadville, Penn) as the organ of the C. L. S. C., have been
of great advantage to the Chautauqua cause. The
magazine has reached a circulation of nearly fifty thousand copies monthly.

Serious difficulties were early encountered in supply-
ing books to the members of the C. L. S. C. The
demand for the required works was so great as to
embarrass the various publishers from whose lists the
selections had been made. They were not willing to
issue large editions, lest the unprecedented and to them
inexplicable demand should suddenly cease, and they
be left with unmarketable stock on hand. Many persons joining the circle, and unable to procure the
books, dropped the whole enterprise with thoughtless
and unfair denunciation of the management. It became
necessary therefore to control the publication of books
in the interest of the Assembly and of its constituency;
and after careful deliberation "The Chautauqua Press"
was established with these objects : To supervise all
publications containing required readings, or for which
Chautauqua is in any way responsible in any of its
departments ; and to make sure that the books selected
by the Counsellors are published at low rates, and in
sufficient quantities to meet the demands of the circle.

The Chautauqua Young Folks' Reading Union has
for its organ "The Chautauqua Young Folks' Journal,"
a department of the "Wide Awake," published by D.
Lothrop & Co. in Boston. The books and apparatus
employed by the "Chautauqua Society of Fine Arts" are
supplied by Cassell & Co., London and New York. The
required books of the "Chautauqua Literary and Scien-

tific Circle" are selected from various publishers, and issued under the auspices of the "Chautauqua Press, C. L. S. C. Department, New York" Other books, and the various circulars and communications to members of the circle (including the "Alma Mater"), are printed by the Chautauqua Press, Boston About one-half of the required reading is published in "The Chautauquan," which is the official organ of the C. L. S C "The Chautauqua Assembly Daily Herald" is, as already stated, the organ of the Summer Meetings

For several years the Children's Department at Chautauqua was supplied during the season with a morning lesson paper, produced by the papyrograph process, and edited by Rev B T Vincent. For two years past Dr Flood has published a neat and attractive children's daily during the Assembly.

"The Director of the Chautauqua Press" is an officer of the University, who has general supervision of its work, promoting unity, co-operation, and improvement. It is a part of his duty to study pedagogical literature and apparatus, and to aid the Faculty and Counsellors as they may require in the selection and production of the literature required by the various departments of the University.

CHAPTER XI.

OBJECTIONS.

" Get your enemies to read your works, in order to mend them." — POPE.

ADVERSE criticism is far better than invariable and
unqualified commendation.   It is likely to rest on
truth — at least, on a part of the truth — somewhere ; and
it sets a sensible man in quest of that truth.   The wise
man welcomes the strictures of friends and foes.   If
cavils do no more than indicate possible evils, he is glad
to be forewarned.   Prudence finds help in every hint,
and gets some good out of the most ungracious growl.
Praise may paralyze effort, while the goad of the critic
is likely to stimulate both ingenuity and resolution.

Chautauqua has been criticised.   Good things have
been written concerning it, — words full of praise, —
extravagant praise.   And other things have been said,
— strongly said, — into which no word of commendation has slipped   Chautauqua has been too much glorified by some, and by some "damned with faint praise ;"
while by others it has been ridiculed on its weak side,
and denounced with a degree of ferociousness on its
strong side, until those of us who know and love Chautauqua are almost indifferent to words of praise or blame.
Almost, I say, not wholly ; for from friendly and from
unfriendly criticism we may still gain much wisdom in

developing the Chautauqua that is to be. We are still simply learners, and are eager to know.

It is not surprising that eminent scholars and representative educators should look with jealous eye on any "new departure" which professes to be an attempted reform in educational methods. It is a part of their professional function to watch with care and conscientiousness the theories and systems which aim to modify existing institutions and methods. The leaders of Chautauqua are not afraid of the closest scrutiny by these great educators; for if we cannot re-assure them as to our aims and the value of our plans, we certainly shall elicit suggestion and advice, and thus out of their wisdom there shall come to us — wisdom.

The charge of "superficiality" is the one most familiar, and the one which is always named first when the Chautauqua "summer school" and the Chautauqua home "reading courses" are mentioned. Then the scholars ask you if you "teach your French perfectly in ten or eleven lessons?" They "forget the exact number." They hint that "humbugs" are not all dead. With knitted brow and wise look they quote from Pope:

> "A little learning is a dangerous thing,
> Drink deep, or taste not the Pierian spring"

In reference to the C. L. S. C., they have something to say about "the danger of superficiality in the attempt to cover so broad a field;" of trying to give "a simple taste of a hundred alluring forms of knowledge;" of securing only "a misty conception of a thousand things."

In defending the Chautauqua movement against these

complaints of the "scholars," the "college men," and the
newspaper-editors, I do not turn for justification to the
"Concord School of Philosophy," nor to the "Summer
School in Chemistry" held during July and August in
the Harvard laboratory ; nor do I cite the average daily
or weekly paper with its "simple taste of a hundred
alluring forms of knowledge," leaving in the minds of
most who read them "a misty conception of a thousand
things." That scholars, colleges, and editors do the
very things Chautauqua is doing, will not justify Chautauqua if the things we all do are unwise and injurious.
I prefer to concede at once the point at issue, and
confess to the charge of "superficiality" in the work
we attempt. There *is* danger — *great* danger — of superficiality. And Chautauqua may not be alone in the
condemnation

The sources of knowledge are limited, — on some
subjects very much so. At his best, the student can
get only surface-knowledge What, for example, does
the most learned astronomer KNOW about the sun ?

The student's capacity and power are limited. He
may lack taste and aptitude for certain departments.
He may be purblind. He may be unable to entertain
hypotheses, or make generalizations. A blind-asylum
has no need of an astronomical observatory.

The student's time may be restricted. Time is an
important factor in mental operations. If this be already
occupied, the new appointments cannot receive attention.

Peculiar mental tastes and habits may promote superficiality. Versatility may foster fickleness A mind
generously endowed may covet sweets from many and
diverse flowers. Ambition may tempt one to seek too

wide a range, and the pleasures of persistent study may
be sacrificed Facility in acquisition may discourage
concentration and perseverance.

We live, moreover, in an age of "action." A premium is put upon "executive force," "business," and
"success." Men want some knowledge, — as much as
they can get, as wide a range as possible, — but not so
as to keep them back in its attainment from early readi-
ness for the sphere of life they have selected. Boys
and girls are crowded and hurried through the schools,
to secure an "early start for themselves," to "get established in life," and to "make a fortune." The
same eager haste is apparent among the lowest grades
of pupils. Poverty at home claims the early services of
young muscles. To read a little, write a little, cipher
a little, — that is enough ; and poorly enough do the
youngsters fare in their rapid drive, often under the
teacher's lash and frown, through the meagre course
of the primary and lower grammar grades. Then, above
the primary and grammar schools, are the higher grades,
with college and university beyond. A small number
of pupils pass into the high school ; a surprisingly small
number, into the greater institutions.

The educators of a past age in family, day-school,
and pulpit, have done too little to correct the shallow
doctrines concerning college education. We find
melancholy result in the neglect of these institutions.
There has been superficiality outside of Chautauqua.

But let us consider this charge of "superficiality."
What does it mean as applied to our work, — to the
summer work, for example ? Simply this : The time of
the annual sessions of the summer school is so short,

—three weeks, six weeks at most,—that it is impossible to give any large amount of instruction, to go into any thing like a deep and thorough investigation of any subject, to drill to any perceptible degree of perfection the pupils we enroll. What can one do toward the mastery of any science, philosophy, rhetoric, elocution, geography, psychology, music, or how can one become familiar with French or German or Latin, in six weeks? The proposal is absurd. The attempt promotes sciolism. It violates laws of intellectual growth, which demand time and rest as conditions of success.

It is, of course, well known that the summer schools do not limit to three or six weeks the educational facilities of the whole year. It is not to save time or money and labor by substituting a few weeks schooling for the older and longer processes of school training. The summer schools do not say to students: "Accept our new method, and save time. Work in the field or shop forty-six weeks in the year, and pack six weeks full of intellectual effort." This is not the idea of the summer school, as all who know any thing about the summer meetings very well understand.

We *do* say: Make a break in the routine of school and home duties. Change air, diet, scenery, associations. Come into new fellowships. Meet living exponents of great educational, scientific, and linguistic ideas. Come into conditions of soul-quickening. Watch living methods which are the outgrowths of living principles, held and illustrated by living teachers. Bring your old knowledges with you. Bring your life-long experiences with you. Bring your professional hinderances and vexations with you. Bring with you the

friendly heart that wins friends. Bring with you the purposes and longings that have cast their anchors out
into the future. Come for suggestions, inspirations, recreations, resolutions. You are making a long pilgrimage through the years. You pass over weary plains,
and into deep valleys, and through surging waters. The
way is dark sometimes, and very much hedged in. Come
now a little while to a mountain-top where the air is
pure, and the fellowship restful, and the prospect far-
reaching. Come with kindred souls, and meet kingly
souls. Come where those who know the way can show
you the mistakes you have made during the past ten
years, and the possible mistakes of the next ten, and
the really better and safer way over the hills that reach
out beyond you. Come where leaders assemble who
have thought down and thought up and thought through
the mountains and difficulties that shut you in.

All this, which the forty-six weeks of the year do not
supply, we may find in six — or less. Experience of
years prepares people for sudden movements fraught
with power. The shortness of the time is not an argument against the depth and stability of the work. How
long does it require to awaken a mind to a worthy aim?
One book will do it. One letter will do it. The touch
of a hand and the gleaming of an eye will sometimes
do it. How long does it require to summon faith in
one's power and in a plan for its development? How
long does it require to kindle enthusiasm? A biography,
one life experience, a personal appeal, may kindle a fire
by burning words that nothing can ever extinguish.
How long does it require to put a good example before
a susceptible life? How long does it take to announce

one radical principle out of which methods start as water-courses on the plain from a stream let loose on the mountain? How long does it take to give a systematic outline of work, in the presence of which all details acquire a relation and a real value, and by which all details come into order for service? How long does it require to give practical ideas of a *method* by which the tact and individuality of a teacher are made to suggest a variety of methods determinable by the individuality of the person receiving the suggestion? How long does it take to sow a handful of seed, to hoist a sail, to cross a Rubicon, to drop a vote, to watch with scientific eye the boiling of a kettle or the fall of an apple, to take an oath of office, to make a pledge of love? Life is full of pivotal opportunities, in the midst of which one may by a moment's act determine the character and influence of a decade College life (the full four years, with all their advantages), after all, only puts its candidates into direct contact with the living teachers about three hours a day, and for only thirty-seven weeks of the year.

The power of the summer school is not in the knowledge communicated. No one pretends that it is. The power is primarily in the creation and control of rare opportunity for intellectual quickening; for moral and spiritual culture; for the grasp of radical principles; for the influence of great souls, — specialists in educational philosophy and life, who have won power and position and renown, who have knowledge and intensity and tact by which they easily kindle in others a coveting of knowledge and of the power to cause others to covet and secure it. Such souls are rarer than great saints. They are like the loftiest summits of the great mountain ranges seen from afar and crowned with glory. These men make opportunity, and put into small measures of time possibilities of power. The results of an important legal case are not to be estimated by the time spent in its consideration, but by the personal power and official position of the men who manage it.

Happy the educational institution that is able to command men of like power as instructors and inspirers in the tutorial realm !

The summer school turns summer resorts into splendid academies, rivalling the best of Athens in her brightest days. I have seen native forests which had been transformed into royal parks about palaces. Trees from many climes are transplanted — rare and graceful. The Chautauqua summer-school is a royal grove Here are planted goodly trees, oak and palm and cedar, olive, elm, and sequoia. Hither let students come to sit under their shadows, catch the dewdrops that fall from them, hear the birds sing in their branches, look up at their quivering leaves and beyond to the blue sky, all the more beautiful because of the movements — half revealing, half concealing — of the swaying foliage.

Indeed, the best work of these great men may be performed in a short time. It is no reflection upon a teacher or a preacher, that his individuality — the mightiest force in him — may soon be discovered, and early and easily communicated

When the aim and methods of the summer school are considered, the charge of "superficiality" speedily falls to the ground

And when the field, which we of the summer schools

are set to cultivate, is surveyed, the prevalence of superficiality in other departments of education calls for
words of warning and reproof and direction And we,
too, may cry out to our accusers, "Beware of 'superficiality' — for the correction of which we are set
apart."

Superficiality is a fault manifest in primary education
at home and in schools. It is discoverable in the theories which limit education to the school term of life;
in the rapid and careless preparation of boys and girls
for college; in the lack of rigid examination; in the
imperfect training of college life; and is manifest in
multitudes of college graduates who are unable to read
Greek and Latin at sight, unable to speak and write
English accurately, unable to think closely and logically.

There is superficiality in the educational processes
which so generally make intellectual training — the
training of memory, perception, reason — the essential
thing of the school life, instead of going *down* to the
more important elements of culture, — conscience, will,
faith, love. These processes overlook the true aims of
life, which touch the divine capacities within us, and
train the soul after the divine ideals above us. Against
all this the Chautauqua Summer School enters solemn
and emphatic protest.

How shallow is the average citizen's estimate of the
teacher's office! The schoolmaster is only "a child's
man," a sort of "nurse," a dealer in rudiments, a man
of mere routine, an ordinary man who *cannot* be any
thing else, and therefore is — teacher; who need not be
much of a scholar, if only he keep ahead of his pupils;
who himself expects to be something else better and

higher up a little later on, — a lawyer, perhaps, or a physician, or a preacher. Against this damaging mis-conception of the tutorial profession, Chautauqua enters protest.

There is another shallow notion to which I have already called attention. It is the notion that confines education to the few years of so-called "school life." Education is to be received at school. Church and Sun-day for religion, shop and farm for business, school and college for education. The work of culture is confined to place, time, and a set of circumstances. It must have hours, text-books, teachers, recitations, examina-tions, promotions. It begins when school begins. It ends when school ends There is no education in baby-hood. Babes do not go to school There is no educa-tion in out-of-door sports, or in vacations, or after school is over. People may now travel and work, and go into society and into business, but education is over Against this irrational repression of the natural and universal longing after education, Chautauqua protests.

The summer schools thus avoid, and also rebuke, and will help to correct, the superficiality of the age, as we exalt principles above methods, emphasize the true philosophy of education, study and obey the laws of the economy of force in culture, bring living students into quickening contact with living teachers, and exalt power, intellectual and spiritual, above the getting and the keeping of mere knowledge Knowledge is not much if it be the end and the all Knowledge is best that comes by hard effort; and it is best because of the effort, and not because of the knowledge. Effort that has a right motive in connection with it is best; and it is best, not because of the effort, but because of the motive. Knowledge that comes hard and aims high, — this is valuable knowledge.

The teacher is not the giver of knowledge. He is not the full reservoir from which the pupils are to draw supplies of fact and theory at will. He is the awakener and quickener of the knowledge-getting faculties in his pupils. He is the artesian-well driver, connecting the power of the pupil with the resources of the world beneath and above; not giving and getting, but drilling and getting; they, because of the drilling, getting. He does not accumulate that they may accumulate: he sets them at work accumulating from every source but himself.

The summer school, by circulating widely the latest educational theories, shows that study may be made a delight, not by being turned into a "game" or "play," not by a sugar-coating of "fun," not by incentives of prize and reward; but by an adjustment of it to real or imagined conditions of actual life in which the imagination is kindled, personal aptitudes employed; the pleasure of observation, travel, conversation, business, utilized; and school life associated with every-day life in its varied manifestations. The task assigned becomes the duty voluntarily and heroically discharged.

In primary education the scientific methods may be employed. And this once done, a dangerous superficiality ceases. The world of fact lies all around the little learners. You may train children to pick up things, and study them, and find out other things about them; to watch and report incorrect expressions; to spell ordinary and unusual words; to study local geography ; to learn what a given science is, by seeing and sorting and explaining facts belonging to it. You may train them to keep eyes, fingers, and thoughts busy about flowers, trees, stones, and animals ; to write out the results of their observations ; to estimate measurements, distances, values, in connection with every-day life ; to go back from facts of to-day to corresponding facts in the past ; to connect the little schoolhouse in which they sit with continents and seas and stars, with sages and warriors and saints. You may run out lines of thought from events of the present to actual events of centuries past, from stones by the road to glacial periods, from base-ball to the Anabasis and great battles ; from the boy that dared to do right to-day on the playground, to the heroism of the ancient times when great men did a like thing in a more public way, and made a wider fame.

The very conditions under which the work is done in the summer schools at Chautauqua conduce to strength, solidity, and breadth. It is a place of inspirations. A temple is there, beautiful and sacred ; columns of gray and brown ; mosaics of shade and sunlight under foot ; frescoes of leaves and branches, blue sky, and tinted cloud, overhead; through all these rustic halls and recesses and corridors, sweeps the free air of heaven. There are living trees that are living teachers. The winds bless them, and the birds sing for them. There are plants and flowers full of speech ; stones ready to open their hearts, and reveal secrets that would make you marvel ; fish, insects, birds, that have lessons in hiding for your search and enjoyment

Above you in the Chautauqua Summer School, stars shine and throb and float in the darkness. These same stars shoot their arrows of light into the deep lake below. Waves break on the shore in sob and whisper. The night answers to the day, the tree to the zephyrs, the lake to the heavens. Voices of children in merry sport, voices of singers in vesper and jubilee, voices of stringed instruments and organ,—all these greet you and offer you delight. Delight may turn into memory, or bloom in hope. Hope may settle into resolve, and resolve into action, action pass into history and into character. So the summers go by, and all the seasons, and the end finally comes. May the end be the blessed beginning of an endless blessedness!

At Chautauqua, Nature is our text-book, Nature our laboratory, Nature our teacher. We study Nature in her material manifestations, in her mental and moral manifestations. We study man in Nature. We study God in Nature, for from Nature it is not far to the FATHER. All things visible are from HIM,—the invisible. The forms and forces about us speak of His presence and power and wisdom. His grace is only faintly taught in the physical realm. His goodness is shadowed there, but cyclones and earthquakes and lightning do not seem especial ministrants of mercy. The BOOK supplements Nature with added lessons, and partial explanations of Divine purposes; so that after a cyclone, earth seems less substantial, and heaven worth more, and "things which remain," and which "cannot be shaken," more worthy of human search.

"He builds too low who builds beneath the skies."

I conclude, therefore, that the aims, methods, and conditions of the Chautauqua Summer School save it from the charge of harmful superficiality, and render it rather a promoter of symmetry and soundness in the work of true culture.

The charge of superficiality against the C L S C and its prescribed courses is substantially answered by the considerations already offered. It gives general views; but these views are taken by mature minds, who desire to know, who are sure to find both pleasure and profit in apprehending the relations of knowledge, and who, discovering by that general survey some department of thought which satisfies their tastes, and for which they have natural aptitude, will be likely to apply themselves to that particular field with avidity. The best result of the C. L. S. C. is its awakening power. A distinguished metaphysician said to me, "I received the *twist* that made me a philosopher, in one week, and that from two lectures to which I listened in Germany." The C. L S C. reading gives the "twist," and it is a "twist" that lifts.

The "diploma" given to a graduate of the Circle, after four years of reading, contains a pyramid, on the steps and base of which are blank spaces for seals. There are thirty-one of these spaces. The holder of a diploma, having by four years' reading taken his general survey of the world of knowledge, and become a member of the "Society of the Hall in the Grove," applies himself to special studies. Having completed one of these, he receives a seal. Four seals place him in "The Order of the White Seal." Three more seals give him a membership in the "League of the Round Table." Seven more entitle him to a place in the "Guild of the Seven Seals," with degree after degree

to be achieved This simple desire is a perpetual incentive to diligence. Is it slight or "foolish"? Then
address your wisdom to the great universities, who
have faith in promotions and sheepskins and seals and
titles, and never think of abandoning them.

There have been objections to the text-books employed by our Circle. It could not be otherwise. The
aims of the C L. S. C. are unique The provision of
lesson-books precisely adapted to these unique aims has
been one of the ever-present problems. If our readers
were children in the schoolroom, and daily recitations
were practicable, it would be easy to find suitable lesson-
books on every subject in the curriculum. If these
readers were chiefly high-school or college graduates
desiring advanced courses of reading, it would be comparatively easy to provide standard works written by
specialists for specialists, and assuming on every page
a large measure of knowledge already possessed by the
reader. If it were the aim of the C. L. S. C. to study
one subject at a time, and that for a long time, exhaus-
tively, from its alphabet to its "last word," it would not
be difficult to find numerous text-books on that subject
adapted to every variety of capacity and attainment.

The C. L. S. C. is not, however, designed for school-
children, nor for advanced readers, nor for specialists.
It has enrolled but few names of members under eighteen years of age Its members are "out of school."
It rejoices in thousands of college graduates ; but these
take up its readings not for advanced study as post-
graduates, but to review under favorable conditions the
scholastic studies of former years, and in some cases,
perchance, to make amends for carelessness and super-

ficiality during those years of unappreciated opportunity.

Here lies the chief cause of our embarrassment. It
is difficult to provide books precisely adapted to the
needs of our peculiar constituency. The Superintendent of Instruction and the Counsellors have felt this
from the beginning. Heavy and elaborate books discourage a class which we are anxious to lure into the
love of literature. Books too much abridged fail to
satisfy more mature minds. Old books may be behind
the times, or, although acknowledged to be standards,
may not for the reasons above given be fully adapted to
our readers. As for new books, every one knows how
hard it is to secure them, and how easily a flippant
criticism may destroy the confidence of the uninitiated
in them. Notwithstanding these embarrassments we
have tried to do our best, providing old books where
the council could agree upon them, and new books
where they seemed to be absolutely necessary.

It is not to be expected that any book, especially any
new book, will meet with universal approval. As for
criticism — well, who knoweth the ways of critics with
the new books? Did not Samuel Taylor Coleridge say
of Burke's essay on "The Sublime and the Beautiful,"
"It seems to me a poor thing"? Did not Horace
Walpole call Goldsmith "an inspired idiot"? Did not
Dr Johnson pronounce Fielding "a blockhead"? Does
not Hume affirm that "no page of Shakspere is without glaring faults"? Was not the manuscript of Thackeray's "Vanity Fair" rejected because the critic to
whom it was submitted pronounced it "without interest"? As a distinguished writer has said : "Good books

have always been criticised upon some points adversely. Plato freely criticises Homer. Quintilian criticises Cicero. Cicero criticises Demosthenes. Addison criticises Milton. And in each instance no doubt real faults were pointed out. The most enlightened French critics used to pooh-pooh Shakspere. They did likewise with Dante."

Some books of the C. L. S. C. have excited unfavorable criticism, — religious books by those who do not care to read religious books at all, and think it an impertinence to obtrude them upon the general reader; certain scientific books, because "not up to the times," or the critic, being himself a scientific specialist, is certain that the views of our specialist are "unsound."

A recent scholarly criticism of a series of C. L. S C. books — the series most nearly reaching my ideal — appeared in one of the foremost quarterlies of the United States. And because it so well states the object of the C. L S. C. movement, I venture to reproduce it here : —

It is not possible to praise too highly Dr Wilkinson's "After School Series," of which this is the fourth and concluding volume. It is a series remarkable for comprehensiveness, accurate scholarship, critical acumen, and literary skill. It is the work of a man who can tolerate no slipshod work, who never lets any thing leave his hands until he has made it as good as he knows how to make it. It is not often that a writer with so sensitive a conscience, and so exceptional qualifications for the task, undertakes the labor of writing a popular text-book.

The book before us, with its three companions,

takes the reader over a much fuller course of the classical authors than is to be had in any college curriculum. Dr. Wilkinson would be the last to claim that the reading of his books is a satisfactory substitute for a thorough classical training. No encouragement of superficial knowledge will be drawn from these books : on the contrary, the taste here gained of classical literature will doubtless stimulate not a few to "drink deeply of the Pierian spring." But there is a large class of intelligent persons, young and old, to whom the acquisition of Latin and Greek is impracticable. Why should they therefore be shut out from all knowledge of the rich literatures of Greece and Rome, and the life mirrored in those literatures? It is true that translations, even the best, are imperfect representations of an original: the peculiar aroma is lost, the delicate bloom is rubbed off in the process. Homer is not Homer in the verses of Pope or Bryant, or even of Chapman. But it is also true that the ordinary student of the classics never gains sufficient freedom from his grammar and lexicon to appreciate this flavor of the original. The college student, we fear, knows his classics chiefly through translations, — known to the initiated as "ponies," — some of them atrociously bad. The student spends his time in learning the niceties of Greek and Latin grammar, rather than in becoming familiar with Greek and Latin literature. The careful reader of these volumes, therefore, though he will by no means be a classical scholar, will be almost if not quite equal in real knowledge of classical literature to the average graduate of a college.

Will saying these things discourage classical learning? Not a whit   But we hope they will discourage
the excessive teaching of philology, and encourage
the teaching of the classics as literature, in our colleges.   As things have been, a classical education
has been an education in every thing but the classics.

It is charged against this movement in behalf of
popular education, that by it we shall unfit people in
the humbler walks of life for the work we need from
them.   What shall we do for servants?   What shall
the dear girls of our homes do for subordinates to follow their bidding?   And how, if people acquire taste,
and begin to aspire after personal refinement, and to
respect themselves, shall we be able to keep them in
their places?   What unendurable airs they will put on!
And how we shall be at the mercy of our inferiors!

So let it be, — that our children shall be compelled
to treat other people with respect; to recollect that
servants have souls and rights; that people who do
lowly service with true motive are worthy of honor;
that true refinement is as courteous and thoughtful
when servant-girls are concerned as when one meets
a favorite of fortune or a princess of royal blood

So let it be, — that our spoiled and petted girls shall
come to know that there are science and art and taste
in kitchen ministries, and that the ignorant, white-
fingered, indolent little simpleton who despises honest
labor and the people who earn their living by honest
labor is herself beneath a servant-girl's contempt

I hope that we shall educate the people, and all the
people, — the poorest and the meanest of them, — until
in lordly way, worthy of royal blood, they refuse to be

trodden upon or ordered about by the impertinent and
arrogant pretenders of modern society.

I hope that we shall educate the people until the
cultivated poor shall have more power than the ignorant rich; until the votes of the humblest cannot be
bought by the bribes of the highest, until a man's
rights as a citizen, though he be poor as poverty, shall
command all the resources of the nation in his defence
and protection; until the gates of the nation shall fly
open on the sides of the east and of the west to welcome strangers from afar; until the comers-in at the
east shall not dare to close the gates against the comers-
in at the west, until parties and their leaders that discriminate between foreign classes, and cater to low race
prejudices, shall be punished unto purification, or, if
necessary, annihilated.

I hope that we shall educate the people until a soul's
inheritance as an immortal being, with the universe of
God at his feet, shall count for more in the thought
of his heart than all the gold and all the glory of the
world.

I hope that we shall train people to understand that
manual labor is a degradation when brain-power and
taste and heart are all sacrificed at the shrine of toil
and bread and money.

Looking at a farm from which by years of toil the
stumps have been dragged out, the stones picked up
and put into substantial wall-fences, and the ground
cultivated until it yields a rich harvest, I ask: Who did
all this good work? Whose sweat moistened this soil?
Whose hands piled up these fences? Whose feet trod
these furrows? Was it a boor or a scholar, — a machine

or a MAN? If muscle without brain, and mercenary motive without heart or sympathy, did it all ; if it were merely for bread and lodging and the prolongation of physical life, and the laying-up of money for a rainy day, that a used-up body might be fed and warmed until death gave it to the dust, — then I see no charm, no beauty in the scene, above the mere products of utilitarian nature.   But if this farm were cultivated by a man, a husband, a father, a saint, a thinker, it becomes a new bit of scenery to me, with beauty everywhere, a most delicate tone pervading the landscape.   I all at once see flowers among the grass, and rainbows in the heaven.   I hear psalms among the trees, and see ladders let down from heaven resting on every stone.

It is the mission of the true reformer, the true patriot, the true Christian, to offer Knowledge and Liberty and Refinement, Science, Literature, Art, and Religious life, to all the people — everywhere.

CHAPTER XII.

THE HALL IN THE GROVE.

" Heaven touches earth as onwards now I go,
Hasting to reach the city of the blest." — HENRY BURTON.

"THE Hall in the Grove" is the centre of our charmed Circle. Towards this spot all loyal Chautauquans turn, coveting the privilege, if they have never been there, of "seeing it some day" with their own eyes ; or recalling with strange delight the hours they have spent under the shadow of its white columns and in the fellowship of the Circle.

Here the "early lectures" are delivered by the magnates, — the philosophers and the theologians, who love to "discourse on lofty themes " At eight o'clock they and their disciples come, sometimes crowding the hall even on a rainy morning, and "many women are among them." Profound and learned lectures, followed by close and animated conversations, all packed with rich and weighty thought, give the "Hall of Philosophy" a peculiar attractiveness to great and cultivated brains who come to Chautauqua. The "elect" are they, who make their way through St. Paul's Grove, morning after morning, for these "early lectures."

Here at five o'clock in the afternoon the "Round Tables" are held. Then all the "C. L. S. C.s" are present. They come in unformed processions and hurrying crowds, from Normal Hall and Temple, from

cottage and hotel, from Museum and Park of Palestine,
from boats on the lake and from gymnasium.   Every
chair is soon occupied, — often even before peal or
chime rings in the hour.   Rude benches are pulled up
to the mounds that rise just outside of the Hall.   Shawls
are spread, and scores of people seated on the ground.
Many stand.   It is a beautiful sight, — this closely
woven and fringed mass of human beings in and about
the white hall, among the green trees, the lake a little
way beyond, the rays from the setting sun reflected
from quivering leaves, or touching with their beauty
the gray and brown trunks of trees and the fair columns of the hall, and illuminating faces of singers and
speakers and people.

The "Round Table" exercises are begun by a song,
a word of greeting, "uplifted hands" or "standing up"
to report the classes represented, or to answer the
question, "What C. L. S. C. members are here for the
first time?" and then a vigorous expression of welcome
from the rest by the clapping of hands, that the new-
comers may feel "at home"   Then comes a very short
lecture on some C. L. S. C topic; or a "conversation" in
which one or more educational themes are discussed by
a question or series of questions from the conductor and
by concise answers from the Circle, these answers being
taken down, and read and re-read in the hearing of all.

The "Question Drawer" may be opened; and on
slips of paper passed up from every part of the hall to
the desk, come questions relating to the C. L. S. C., —
Why such a "book was put on the list;" whether one
or another "book may be used as a substitute;" what
is the standing of a member who "read the books of

three years, but dropped out of the Circle for one year," what is required in order to win the "white seal;" the difference between the white and the "white crystal;" the "duties and privileges of those who belong to the 'League of the Round Table,'" the various "grades of the 'Guild of the Seven Seals;'" "how to reconcile a statement in one of the required books with a statement in another," "why we cannot have more 'drills' at the Round Table;" "what is the color of the badge for '86" or "'89" or some other year; "who is president of the Class of '89," etc. Sometimes the questions are asked orally, and somebody answers before the conductor has a chance to speak. Questions and answers are sometimes so good or so simple, so odd or so ill-timed, as to cause a ringing laugh from one end of the hall to the other.

The Round Table is now and then resolved into "A Conference on Blunders of Speech at Chautauqua." Everybody is at liberty to report remarks, pronunciations, violations of grammar, etc, heard at Chautauqua on the street, in the cottages, or from speakers on the platform. Oral and written questions now fly thick and fast: "How do you, Mr. Conductor, pronounce ——?" Perhaps the conductor has just mispronounced it. On the platform sit two or more professors with copies of Webster, Worcester, and other authorities, to whom appeal is from time to time made. This is, on the whole, one of the most amusing and useful of the Round-Table exercises.

Now and then we listen to reports from C. L. S. C. work in various sections of the country, to statements of difficulty, to a proposal of new plans, to an illustration of method in local-circle review of current studies, to an account of some special programme on a memorial day. There is scarcely any limit to the possible and useful exercises of a "Chautauqua Round Table."

As the hour draws near its close, the *Song of Evening Praise* — "Day is dying in the west" — is invariably given out or called for.[1] It is always sung. Once it

was omitted, and a part of the audience had left. Some one reminded the conductor; and the Hall was soon filled again, and the hymn was announced and sung. It is a beautiful hymn. Mary A. Lathbury was inspired when she wrote it. No one can hear it sung at the close of a Round Table or Vesper Service at Chautauqua, without feeling its power. All Chautauquans are supposed to know and often to sing it.

The classes of the several years usually hold brief business meetings at the close of the Round Table. It is interesting to watch the groups in each corner of the Hall, one at the centre and one or two under the trees outside, attending to the business of their respective classes, electing officers, arranging for special meetings, an excursion, a reception, a song-service perhaps, or something else designed to bring them together and to foster the class-spirit.

The "Vesper Hour" is at five o'clock on Sabbath. It is never omitted during the season; and the resident Chautuaquans have for one or two years kept it up through the entire year, gathering on the stormiest evening in the Hall, to sing the evening hymn and to pray for "all members of the Circle all over the world."

The Sabbath "Vesper Hour" at Chautauqua, especially during the Assembly, is the most impressive of all the Chautauqua services. There seems to be a brooding Presence which invests the place and hour with most solemn and tender influences. Hymns are sung, one of the prescribed vesper services rendered responsively, and remarks made, usually by the Chancellor and one of his associates. The greatness of God our

Father as revealed in Jesus Christ, in the Word, and in
Nature, is emphasized, — His patience, His mother-like
gentleness, the "wideness in His mercy," His delight
in forgiving and forgetting, His loathing of sin, His
love of righteousness, His pity, His providence which
although hidden in its processes is most beneficent in
its aim and end The way to meet the sorrows and
bear the burdens of life is tenderly presented ; the value
of high aims ; the reflex influence of self-sacrifice ; of
silence when one wants most to speak ; of speech when
silence would compromise us ; the dignity of lowly
duties ; the glorious opportunities of motherhood, even
in very humble homes where children catch inspirations
and where they form ideals of heroic character, ideals
which they forever associate with mother and father
and home.   Really the key-note of the Vesper Hour is
found in those matchless words of Paul, "Whatsoever
things are true, whatsoever things are honest, whatsoever things are just, whatsoever things are pure, whatsoever things are lovely, whatsoever things are of good
report ; if there be any virtue, and if there be any
praise, think on these things."

I cannot better give my feelings towards the " Hall "
and its services, than to reproduce a few passages from
my letters in " The Chautauquan "   These express my
confidence in the radical work which is being wrought
under the blessing of the infinite Spirit of Wisdom and
Love, through the whole Chautauqua work, and especially through the services which hallow to all Chautauquans the dear old " Hall in the Grove."   And they
contain some old counsels which are not too old to be
repeated.

The season is over. The crowds have gone. The classic groves are again quiet. The silent lake lies by a silent shore, reflecting the lovely verdure of trees and terraces, and the deep blue of over-arching heavens. The Temple, busy scene for all these weeks, is solitary now as a deserted abbey. The huge amphitheatre with its capacious concave, its chairless orchestra and sealed-up organ, seems awful in its vast emptiness, and sacred with haunting memories of eloquence and song, and of surging, enraptured, applauding multitudes. Palestine is deserted Jerusalem is solitary. The waters of the Dead Sea have backed up until Jordan has far over-flowed its banks. The fountains have ceased their play, the electric light no more vies with moon and stars, the walks are well-nigh forsaken, and again in the prime-val forest one walks alone, and undisturbed meditates in the temple of nature. One spot is doubly sacred since the crowds have gone It is the Hall of Philoso-phy. In impressive majesty it crowns the hill. Its white columns present a fine contrast with the brown and gray trunks, and the now changing foliage of the trees, in St. Paul's Grove. The vesper-song has ceased. The voices of query and counsel, raillery, jest and mel-ody, are no more heard. The earnest souls who hither came with love and zeal, with hope and desire, have passed forth into a busy world, with memories not soon to be forgotten, joys never to be wholly extinguished, and resolutions which reach out towards the higher, larger plane of human aspiration, to find their end and crown in God.

There is to me an ineffable charm about this dear old hall. In it nature dwells, and God reigns. In it

many a burdened soul has found, in earnest thoughtfulness, freedom and rest. Many an unsyllabled vow,
without human sign to mark it, has here brought peace
and strength out of the silent but all-encompassing
heavens, to prepare human souls for human and divine
service in far-away homes, and in coming days of struggle and sorrow. The most sacred centre of the whole
Chautauqua world is the "Hall in the Grove." It is
not far thence to heaven

As I linger a few days in these silent and sacred
sanctuaries after the multitudes have gone, to rest myself and prepare for severer duties out in the world, I
think, of course, of the great and goodly company of
readers and students in the C L S C., over this and
other lands, and I know you will receive a few words
of advice that spring from the grasses and drop from
the trees, and steal out of the silences as enthusiasm
turns a listening ear to what the unembodied spirit of
Chautauqua may say to the sons and daughters of Chautauqua everywhere.

First of all, let me say that enthusiasm, enkindled by
solemn services such as we have here enjoyed, needs to
be incarnated and exercised in plain, straightforward,
every-day doing through the whole year. Songs and
raptures, longings and covenants, must be transformed
into heroisms of a plain and practical type, in the
unsentimental and homely fields to which stern duty
may lead us. The Chautauqua fervor must become fidelity. The Hall of Philosophy must help shop, kitchen,
schoolroom, and parlor. Emotion must go into motive
and muscle. Songs in August must make sinews for
October and May.

After the grand review — dress-parade, oratory, music, flags, and fireworks — comes the common, every-day routine, — plough, pen, needle, and nursery. Farewell to the holiday! All hail to the working-day! Between the two there is a vast difference ; and both are good.

There is a difference between the peal of morning bells rolling over lake and through forest-trees, with the warble of wild-wood birds, waking one up to a day of music and eloquence, Sunday clothes, and good society ; and the gruff call or dissonant bell-ring of somebody whose business it is to tell you to be up and at it, at once and for all day, whether you feel like it or not.

There is a difference between sitting down to a breakfast that was prepared for you by servants ; and getting up to build a fire, and boil a kettle, and broil a steak, and wait for all the household to come down and in, and get through, and give you a chance to do something else before a half-dozen other things claim your time and thought, and thus make way for a dozen and one additional things that fill up the unprinted programme of your own domestic or official "assembly" at home.

There is a difference between a precious Bible-reading at eight o'clock, with all the sweetest texts in the book put into lines or clusters or circles like gems in royal treasure plate ; and the care of a "mussed-up" table, a pile of soiled dishes, or a naughty, nervous, or afflicted child.

There is a difference between one of dear brother Adams's devotional conferences at nine o'clock, with the fresh experiences of many hearts (who for the time forget crying children and crowded kitchen) full of joy and peace and triumph, with the ingenious interpretations of old or difficult or out-of-the-way texts, with the sweet and fervent prayers that sound as if heaven were near and not afar off, and as if all the people one saw filling the Amphitheatre were saints of God who had left the "exceeding glory" for an hour to give Chautauqua a taste of the celestial life; there is, I say, a difference between all this, and the sweeping and dusting, the stewing and sweating, the clerking and teaching, the hammering and ploughing, and all the rest of the indoor and outdoor exercises that usurp the blessed nine-o'clock devotional conference hour, for which at home no bell rings, and to which no organ or solo welcomes.

There is a difference between the eleven-o'clock lecture about life, science, and philosophy, full of wit and wisdom ; and the planning and toiling for a dinner in which something will scorch or spoil, and concerning which peevish and fault-finding words are sure to be spoken by those who ought to be, but are not, considerate and sympathetic.

There is a difference between a two-o'clock afternoon concert of gifted voices, stringed instruments, and organs ; and an aching head and quivering nerves, where rest is refused you, and the hard, straining, dragging work *must* go on, whether you like or loathe it.

There is a difference between the four-o'clock "specialties," full of help and instruction ; and the insipid, fashionable call that wastes your time, disturbs your conscience, and makes you wish " society" to the dogs.

There is a difference between the precious five-o'clock Round Table or Vesper Hour, with its free conversations (like a family chat) about simple things connected with our beloved Circle, with its broad thoughts, its sweet friendships, its holy prayers, its soothing and uplifting "Day is dying in the west," when the sunlight seems like a veritable revelation of the shechinah, and the air is vibrant with divinest sympathies; there *is* a difference between the Chautauqua five o'clock, and the average five o'clock at home, in field, in street, in shop.

There is a difference between a Chautauqua evening of lectures, songs, burlesque, boat-ride, camp-fire, reception, illuminated fleet, and gorgeous fireworks; and the weariness of a routine life evening, — the physical energy gone, the children out of sorts, misunderstandings in home, neighborhood, or church, the prospect of a sleepless night, and of an enervating and irritating to-morrow.

A difference, to be sure. But then remember that these every-days should be glorified by the Chautauqua days. And remember that they test the sentiments enkindled and resolutions formed in the pleasurable excitements, devotional services, splendid processions, and great audiences of the more favored season.

Fellow-students, let the charm of the Chautauqua days be felt through all the intervening days By strong resolve, put high thoughts, tender sympathies, devout aspirations, unwearying patience, into the most unsentimental, uncomfortable, and vexatious experiences and emergencies of home and business life, and thus diminish the difference in real value between Chautauqua days and other days.

Remember well that worthier than the head is the heart, — the heart, with its sympathies, emotions, affections, and conscience, and will. I put these all in

one, — HEART. Without heart, students and teachers
are as worthless as terraced gardens on the slopes of
an iceberg.   Concerning a promising but passionless
cantatrice, a musician said, "She sings well, but she
wants something, and in that something every thing.
If I were single I would court her; I would marry
her; I would maltreat her; I would break her heart:
and in six months she would be the greatest singer in
Europe."

   Does God deal in some such ways with his children,
— his teachers among men?   Is the whole of life a
normal school for our training?   The best lessons we
receive are not those given from rostrum, blackboard,
or laboratory.   Nor are they always in the lines of
literary and scientific thought   They come through
petty vexations, pricking thorns, defeats of ambitions,
stings of gossip, desertion by friends, open graves, and
hushed voices without whose melody we did not think
we could live.   Out of such grief, and in such grief,
God's grace is given   Adelaide Procter has sung a
song of comfort for God's students : —

> "I think, if thou couldst know,
>   O soul that will complain,
> What lies concealed below
>   Our burden and our pain, —
> How just our anguish brings
> Nearer those longed-for things
>   We seek for now in vain, —
> I think thou wouldst rejoice, and not complain.

> "I think, if thou couldst see
>   With thy dim mortal sight
> How meanings, dark to thee,
>   Are shadows, hiding light;

Truth's efforts crossed and vexed,
Life's purpose all perplexed, —
    If thou couldst see them right,
I think that they would seem all clear, and wise, and bright.

    " And yet thou canst not know,
        And yet thou canst not see;
    Wisdom and sight are slow
        In poor humanity
    If thou couldst trust, poor soul,
    In Him who rules the whole,
    Thou wouldst find peace and rest:
Wisdom and sight are well, but trust is best."

" Day is dying in the west," and it is time for closing words. Very soon autumn leaves will strew the ground, and very soon the glory of autumn will be hidden by the crystal splendors of winter. The blessed re-unions of this summer will have passed into history, and our scattered fraternity be engaged in the conflicts of this weary and busy, but, after all, glorious world. In the strife and the weariness and the work, let us remember every inspiring service of the past, and gather strength also from our look of faith into the future, — the future that is nearest, and the future that is very far off; a future in which we shall be the glad children of a good Father; that Father a great King, and that King immortal, invisible, eternal, who has wonderful things for us which one day he will give to us when he gives to us himself.

CHAPTER XIII.

THE FUTURE OF CHAUTAUQUA.

" No perspective, no ambition." — VICTOR HUGO.

HOWEVER comprehensive may have been the original conceptions of our honored president and his associates when they began the summer movement in the groves at Chautauqua, the gradual unfolding of the scheme has been a source of surprise and delight to the world of curious and interested observers. And there must be "more to follow." As long as people love to listen to music and lectures, and as long as men and women have genius, scholarship, and power to please, the summer meetings at Chautauqua will be patronized. As long as people love to read for personal improvement, the Circles which provide useful and attractive reading will enroll members, and give them direction. Chautauqua is an institution for to-morrow.

Twenty-five years from now, the old trees by the lake will canopy multitudes of loyal hearts assembled at the shrine of Alma Mater. Men and women who saw the beginnings in 1874, and who passed the "Golden Gate" in 1882, will be there. Comparatively young then, they will by that time be numbered among the old. And they will remember the rude beginnings of the movement, — the narrow quarters, hard beds, and poor fare.

And they will remember, as associated with those rough and rural surroundings, the eloquence, brilliancy, and scholarship of the first programme. New names will shine on the lists announced, new orators and new singers hold new multitudes by the spell of speech and song; but no eloquence will excel some of the earliest performances under the trees of the Chautauqua auditorium. Shall I speak of Simpson, Gough, Bidwell, Baird, — and others whose voices still sound in our memories?

At the opening meeting of each Assembly, on the "first Tuesday evening in August," the question has always been asked, "Who are here to-night who were present at the first meeting in 1874?" Many arise at this call. Another question is asked: "Who have been present at every meeting from the beginning?" Those who are able to arise in response to this question are proud of their record. If they can be at Chautauqua on only one occasion, it must be on "the first evening."

The time is coming, when to the old question, "Who are here to-night who were present in 1874?" there will be no response, — a hush, a sudden turning to see if no one is there, and then a solemn silence as the leader on that evening announces: "Not one." What year will that be? It must be a long time hence; for there were children in that auditorium on the first night in 1874, who were but six years old, and who in 1944 will be seventy-six, and one or more of them may be present that season. Long may loving representatives of the first Chautauqua linger to appear at the annual openings, to rejoice in the progress made, and to be living links between these widely separated dates!

What shall those blessed old eyes see when that day comes? Will the Chautauqua of 1944 bear any resemblance to the Chautauqua of 1874? Many of the trees will still be standing, — different and yet identical, — having shed the leaves of more than seventy summers, and borne the blasts of as many winters. The lake will still be there, shining, darkening, rippling, sleeping, leaping into white-crested waves, breaking against the shore in whisper or shout, reflecting the blue heaven by day and the stars by night, bearing on its bosom great boats whose keels yet grow in forests or rest in unsmelted ore in the heart of the earth. Men now unborn will stand at the wheel, pace the deck, manage the engine, — the electric engine, — of that day. New generations of men, women, and children will drink in the health and gladness that sweep on the air of Chautauqua; and as they listen to the "old Chautauqua chimes" that date from the season of '85, and look at the kind old face of the "Seth Thomas clock" to see the hour, will land at the great dock with its crowded balconies of watching Chautauquans, and linger for a day or longer to study the institution which began so long ago, and which has never ceased to grow in wealth of treasure, attractiveness of programme, and loyalty of devotion on the part of those who are proud to call Chautauqua "Alma Mater."

What will be the attractions of A.D. 1944, at Chautauqua, who the singers, and who the orators of that season, no prophet has told us. They are not yet in their cradles Who shall sit as president in that delightful office? Who shall stand as chancellor on that ample platform, under the dome of the new amphitheatre with its seating capacity and acoustic possibility for twenty thousand people? Who shall preside at the huge organ, — the Chautauqua organ that will outrival the historic instrument in Music Hall, Boston? Who shall wield the baton that shall direct five thousand voices in music such as Sydenham Palace never heard? Who, as superintendent of grounds, shall travel about, now in his *coupé*, now on the electric-belt railway that is to bring into close neighborship the remotest parts of this university town by the lakeside?

To these questions, the future makes no reply. The blood that is to throb in the veins of these men of 1944 is even now burning with Chautauqua enthusiasm somewhere, — perhaps in homes where the Chautauqua inspiration has come like a gift from heaven, but where there is little thought of that possible future. So that the spirit of Divine Wisdom guide, and the spirit of Divine Love possess, we care little about the *personnel* or antecedents of the men and women of the Chautauqua that is to be!

What of the Chautauqua buildings of that coming time? what of the groves and parks and pathways? what of the places of concourse, and the schools, and the cottages? what of the courses of study, and the sessions, the teachers, the laboratories, and the museum?

Chautauqua began with a two-weeks' session. Now, twelve years later, "Teachers' Retreat," "Schools of Language," "Assembly," "Preliminary Week," and "After-Week" fill up two full months of the summer. We are urged to linger still later, and among the scarlet and gold and crimson leaves hold an "Autumnal Meeting " The want of suitable buildings is the only reason for not responding to still another call, and arranging for a mid-winter as well as an autumnal session, for the " Farmers' Institute " with snow and ice carnival ; with evening lectures in comfortable and well-lighted halls that would allure young people by the hundred to entertainments in science and art, adding to the bracing power of the sleigh-ride through frosty air the stimulating influence of foreign travel and historic study, by the lecture and stereopticon, thus neutralizing the temptations of town and country life through the long winter evenings.

What marvels will be achieved by that time, through electricity, in macrophone, microphone, phonograph, telephone, and in locomotion ; in photography, which has not reached the third hour of its day of wonders ; and in every department of discovery and invention ! For these will yield greater results during the coming half-century than during the last. Will a tower two hundred feet high send a light, tenfold the brightness of the present electric light, over every part of Chautauqua Lake ? And will a human voice, magnified by the new instrument, reach every part of the lake with its daily announcements ?

What wonders in the department of entertainment ! Music in the air, among the trees, and on the lake, from bells, bars of steel, from chords of Æolian harps, moved into melody by the touch of the electric fire ! Lights appearing and disappearing as by magic, changing place and color ; now on the lake, now in the heavens, filling the place with weird beauty ! Fountains of water, crimson and gold and blue, rising in unlooked-for places, at unexpected times ; now shooting up from the bosom of the lake, now dropping as out of the heavens !

A museum, substantially built, will furnish miles of treasure and surprise to students in every line. Teachers will find models of schoolrooms from all countries on the globe, and apparatus of every variety. Geologist, botanist, zoologist, antiquarian, will resort to the Chautauqua museums for treasures provided nowhere else. In picture-galleries the history of art will be illustrated, and by the power of the copyist the masterpieces will be accessible to the humblest student. Aquaria, dens, and cages will give to the student of natural history perpetual delight.

I am not a prophet, nor do I claim to be a seer; but in my dreams I catch glimpses of the Chautauqua University of the future. And if, elated by the successes of the past, my dreams are naught but dreams, generous Chautauquans who read these pages will attribute to sanguine temperament and Chautauqua enthusiasm what their more sober judgment pronounces chimerical and impossible.

I see among the trees of our groves stately halls, grand museums, lofty observatory, and delightful homes.

A park extends along the lower level by the lake, with winding walks, pleasant arbors, whispering fountains, climbing vines, snow-white statuary, parterres ablaze with blossoms. The world of history from the very beginning is in this park represented. Here are symbolic illustrations, memorial columns and arches, marble busts of distinguished men in history, arranged in chronological order. One can travel from the Tower of Babel to the Bartholdi Statue, or some later monument erected fifty years hence in honor of a decree by a universal congress of nations that "war is to be forever abolished on the planet." By a guide-book of history, biography, literature, and art, even a child may make a pilgrimage which will be better to him than a score of text-book lessons in history.

In my vision I see also the great world-park, covering an extended area, with mountains and valleys, and with artificial ponds representing oceans, seas, and lakes ; with small and accurate models, properly located, to represent the principal cities on the planet, — making it possible for tourists on foot to study the physical geography as, in the park by the lake, they have passed through all the centuries of history.

The old model of Palestine will by that time have been repaired. Returning merchant-ships from the Levant will have brought quantities of rock, earth, and timber from Syria itself, these will be transferred to Chautauqua, become a part of our own model of Palestine, and people may tread the sacred soil without crossing the sea.

In my vision I see another admirable teaching provision : A Hall of Geography, octagonal in form, with lofty walls, has in its centre a colossal globe indicating in bas-relief the continents and mountain ranges. One hemisphere is hidden under the floor, but a child's touch will turn the globe, and bring at once any desired region into the light. On the eight walls are arranged huge maps presenting the details of physical geography. Near each map I find a library of choice books relating to the continent to which the wall is devoted. In a huge portfolio resting on an easel are pictures, engravings, and photographs by the hundred, illustrating the architecture and natural scenery of the same continent, with smaller stereoscopic views by the thousand, all these helps furnishing the best facilities in the world for the thorough study of geography.

The illustration of language-teaching, by the natural method at its perfection, will be given. The student may live for weeks in German quarters, where all the conversation will be conducted in German, and where the habits of German social life are reproduced. He may listen to lectures, and study the literature of the language, as though he were himself in Germany. French, Latin, and Hebrew quarters will give the same rare opportunities to the students of these several languages.

One of the best features of the "Chautauqua that is to be" will be found in the "After-school,"—a session of from four to six weeks, devoted to specialties ; the most distinguished lecturers which the world can furnish being present for from two to four weeks, so that the student in any specialty may listen to lectures from the greatest living authorities on the planet, and receive instructions for a short space of time from the best teachers, using the new "After-school Series" of text-books yet to be provided The advantages of the four to six weeks' "After-school" of specialties will be so great that no teacher or student can well afford to be absent from their privileges.

Schools of music, schools of art, schools of science, schools of medicine, of theology, of law, and of general handicraft, will be organized and conducted by competent leaders.

Models of cottages and farmhouses will illustrate architectural possibilities within the reach of the humblest people.

Especial attention will be given to the department of humanity; to modes of preventing pauperism, and of making honest poverty respectable; to ways of reform, of honest living, of training childhood, and of industrial life in all of its demands and possibilities.

A "Foreign Tour" in that coming time will prove an almost perfect preparation for an actual journey. Whatever art, literature, and the living voice can do, will be found in connection with the "Teachers' Retreat;" and people expecting to travel abroad will avail themselves of this annual opportunity for preparation.

In my vision I see the "Hall of Philosophy," more than double its present size, built of snow-white marble, standing among the trees of St Paul's Grove. Multitudes tread its pavements, joining in Chautauqua songs, observing "memorial days" with solemn service, keeping the "vesper hour," and under the blaze of the "Athenian watch-fires" joining in the "night vigil;" holding "round-table" discussions and "students' sessions," and listening to scholarly lectures delivered by the foremost thinkers of that coming time.

Resident professors will devote themselves all the year to the work of correspondence, and ten thousand students in all parts of the world will be directed in reading and study from that central office. University examinations will take place during every month of the year, and candidates will come for such examination from many lands.

A "Ministers' Retreat" will at that time have been

erected. For a nominal sum ministers may bring their families to Chautauqua, and find comfortable quarters while they listen to courses of lectures in literature and science bearing upon their professional duties.

The Chautauqua Press will have provided ample libraries in all departments of literature, in cheap or more expensive form, according to the taste and ability of the readers.

There will be "high days" in Chautauqua, — "Memorial Days," when names precious to all Chautauquans will be tenderly spoken; "Recognition Day," when the golden gate shall be opened, and children with their baskets of flowers, conforming to custom from time immemorial, will strew with blossoms the pathway of pilgrims under the arches to the "Hall on the Hill." There will be the great "Commencement Day," when diplomas are given and degrees conferred by the chancellor of that time, and representatives from all parts of the world will come to receive the rewards of diligence, fidelity, and perseverance.

There will be ample means provided for the Chautauqua of the future. Men and women who have directly or through their parents received from Chautauqua awakening and inspiration, and who have thereby accumulated property, will contribute liberally of their ample resources to the building-up of "Alma Mater." I dare not name the sums which in my dream I see placed on the altar at Chautauqua, — sums which will in 1950 A.D. constitute her munificent endowment.

There will be at Chautauqua a "Holy Catholic Church," where no denomination that names the name of Christ will be rejected, and where all denominations may bend at a common altar, in unity of spirit, with the freedom of truth and charity. In the service of that church, all that is great, venerable, and precious in the liturgies of the ages shall be connected with the liberty of extemporaneous service. However diverse the denominational relations of Chautauquans, believing souls shall be one at that sacred shrine, where the Christ of humanity is exalted, and his Spirit imparted. Their motto shall be: "In the freedom of truth, and the spirit of Jesus Christ, we unite for the worship of God and the service of men."

In my visions I behold in the centre of the grove a sacred temple to which few have access; lofty, strong-built, crowned with ivy; only those go beyond its well-barred portals who know the sacred pass-words. Blessed shall they be who are then members of that "Guild of Chautauqua;" a "guild" we call it, although but few know its real name, — a "guild" in existence to-day, very sacred, and membership in it very honorable, and further revelation concerning it impossible.

But what if those dreams of place and circumstance turn out to be "naught but idle dreams"? The real "Chautauqua" is not dependent longer upon locality. The grove may be cut down, the buildings consumed by fire, the golden gate broken into fragments, the Hall of Philosophy remain only in memory, all visitors cease to tread the sacred paths of the old resort, and the Summer Meetings be forever abolished, — yet CHAUTAUQUA remains, and must remain. The Chautauqua of ideas and inspirations is not dependent upon the literal and local Chautauqua. May they long remain united, and each minister to the strength and glory of the other!

APPENDIX.

I.

CONDENSED PROGRAMMES.

"From dusty cities, and from hamlets rude,
Are men of every name and sect and mould,
Making a garden of this solitude." —C. D. ANGELL, 1874.

THE first Chautauqua Assembly opened on Tuesday evening, Aug. 4, 1874, and closed on the morning of Tuesday, Aug. 18.

The Assembly was pronounced by "everybody" a great success. The attendance was larger, the weather finer, the interest greater, the work more radical, the entertainments more agreeable, the lectures on the whole more able, and the final results more satisfactory, than the dreams of its projectors had dared to promise.

For a whole year efficient committees had been hard at work. The official letter from the Secretary of the Chautauqua Lake Camp-meeting Association is now before me. It speaks of the "Berean Assembly," and reports the ratification by the lot-owners of the action taken by the Board of Trustees. This letter bears date Aug. 16, 1873.

For economy and effectiveness, the work of the Assembly had been distributed among six departments, — Instruction, Entertainment, Supplies, Order, Recreation, Sanitary. The Department of Instruction had charge of the devotional and instructional exercises of the Assembly, J. H. Vincent in charge. The Department of Entertainment provided hotel and tent accommodation for permanent and temporary members, for the invited guests of the Assembly, and for visitors, and also had charge of tents and other places devoted to public service, Rev H. W. Leslie in charge. The Department of Supplies was appointed to provide and superintend markets for the supply of provisions, and to have general supervision of hotels and restaurants controlled by the Assembly, Mr. J. E. Wesener in charge. The Department of Order was required to enforce the rules of order adopted by the Executive Board, to have charge of the lights, and in every possible way to promote the peace and quiet of the Assembly during its entire session, Rev. R. M. Warren in charge. The Department of Recreation was to provide and control the recreations allowed by the Assembly, Rev. W. W. Wythe, M.D., in charge. The Sanitary Department was required to provide and enforce such sanitary measures as shall promote the health and convenience of the Assembly, J. E. Stubbs, M.D., in charge. All these departments were subject to the direction and approval of the Executive Board. Lewis Miller, Esq., was chairman of the Assembly, and *ex-officio* chairman of the Executive Board.

The first Sunday-school Assembly was widely advertised. "The Sunday-school Times," and leading Sunday-school papers of all denominations, seconded the efforts of "The Sunday-school Journal" and other publications of the Methodist-Episcopal Church in announcing the Assembly and in publishing its programme in advance.

"Chautauqua Extras" of "The Sunday-school Journal" were issued in large numbers, giving ample answers to the questions: "Where is Chautauqua?" "How to reach Chautauqua," "What is to be done at Chautauqua?" with the course of study to be pursued at the Assembly, the list of speakers, teachers, and singers expected, announcing months beforehand the books which candidates for the Normal Department were expected to read in advance.

The following are some items in Chautauqua Extra No. 1: —

— "It is spelled with three *u*'s, — Cha*u*tau*qu*a "

— "It has been known to rain at Chautauqua Lake."

— "Are you afraid of little discomforts? Stay at home."

— "That delightful singer, P. P. Bliss of Chicago, calls the Assembly 'a *chat-talk-away* affair.' He will be there."

— "No recreations during lecture and institute hours. Persons who are not willing to observe this law will please stay at home."

— "The Department of Order will organize the best boys on the ground into a police-page corps. The shield badges are ready."

— "Bring your biggest shawl. Chautauqua Lake is twelve hundred feet above the Atlantic Ocean, and it is sometimes comparatively cool there even in August."

— "The gates will be closed on Saturday evening, and kept closed until Monday morning. No steamers will be allowed to land at Fair Point on Sundays."

— "Persons attending the Assembly must be prepared for the usual discomforts of out-door and camp life. The weather may not always be propitious. The accommodations will not equal those of the city hotels. The Board of Managers will do their best to render all who visit Fair Point as comfortable as possible, and yet, at the best, they may need patience and forbearance on the part of guests and members of the Assembly."

The wide announcements of the programme brought letters of inquiry in great numbers and from many places. Looking over the files of letters which I carefully preserved, I am myself surprised to see how far the news had spread, and how general an interest had been created in the new Sunday-school movement. Here are letters from men who have heard of the Assembly, and who cannot come; from men who will come; from men whose friends want them to come; from men who would like to come, especially if they could have a place on the programme and have their expenses paid. Letters are on file from Pictou, N.S., from many other parts of the Dominion of Canada, from Iowa, Rhode Island, Missouri, Ohio, Pennsylvania, Massachusetts; from Presbyterian, Congregational, Baptist, and other ministers; and inquiries by railway men. Here on my table is a letter from the General Agent of the New-York Associated Press, asking for daily telegrams. Here are letters from dear old Stephen Paxson of St. Louis, from Bishop E. O. Haven, then Chancellor of Syracuse University; from Bishop Simpson, from Dr. Perrine of Michigan; from A. O. Van Lennep, from the beloved F. A. Goodwin, whose music on the cornet will never be forgotten by those who heard him at the first Assembly; from John B. Gough. Here are letters from Henry P. Haven of Connecticut, from Gen. Fisk, B. F. Jacobs, Dr. Talmage, and a score of others still living. A telegram lies before me, received on the 8th of August:—

"Hold the fort, for we are coming. Expect us to-morrow. — BLISS AND WIFE."

Several bright letters relating to the Assembly are on file from P. P. Bliss. Telegrams were received from the Illinois State Y. M. C. A. in session at Aurora, Ill., giving greetings; and from the Geneva District Sunday-school Convention, in session at Phelps, N.Y., Aug. 6. On the morning of the Opening Day, a telegram was received from Pike's Peak, Col., sent by Bishop Thomas Bowman: "The Colorado Conference sends sunrise greetings to the Chautauqua-Lake Assembly."

The opening meeting on Tuesday evening, Aug. 4, was a good beginning of a great work. The stars were out, and looked down through trembling leaves upon a goodly, well-wrapped company who sat in the grove, filled with wonder and hope. No electric light brought platform and people face to face that night. The old-fashioned pine fires on rude four-legged stands, like tall tables covered with earth, burned with unsteady, flickering flame ; now and then breaking into temporary brilliancy by the contact of a resinous knot of pine or a vigorous stirring-up by the stick of the rustic fireman who knew how to snuff candles and how to turn light on the crowd of campers-out. The white tents were very beautiful in that evening light.

The Assembly opened with the reading of Zech. iv. 1–6, and a prayer; after which the International Lesson for the following Sabbath, Mark iv. 35–41, was read. Singing and prayer followed, with brief addresses by the representatives of the Baptist, Congregational, Presbyterian, and Methodist-Episcopal Churches. The following Vesper Service was used almost daily during the first Assembly, and, since then, at the opening session of every Assembly " on the first Tuesday evening in August :" —

Leader. — The day goeth away. (Jer. 6: 4.)
Congregation. — The shadows of the evening are stretched out. (Jer. 6: 4.)
L. — Praise waiteth for thee, O God, in Zion ;
C —And unto thee shall the vow be performed. (Ps. 65: 1)
L. — Thou makest the outgoings of the morning and evening to rejoice. (Ps. 65 8.)
C. — Evening and morning, and at noon, will I pray and cry aloud. (Ps. 55 : 17.)

Communion with God   4 lines, 7s.

Softly now the light of day
Fades upon our sight away ;
Free from care, from labor free,
Lord, we would commune with thee.

L. — And they heard the voice of the Lord God walking in the garden in the cool of the day,
C. — And Adam and his wife hid themselves from the presence of the Lord God, amongst the trees of the garden   (Gen. 3: 8)
L. — Draw nigh to God, and he will draw nigh to you. (Jas. 4: 8.)

Bethany. 6s and 4s.

Nearer, my God, to thee,
Nearer to thee !
E'en though it be a cross
That raiseth me ;
Still all my song shall be, —
Nearer, my God, to thee,
Nearer to thee.

L. — And Jacob went out from Beersheba, and went toward Haran. And he lighted upon a certain place, and tarried there all night, because the sun was set;

C. — And he took of the stones of that place, and put them for his pillow, and lay down in that place to sleep.

L. — And he dreamed, and behold, a ladder set up on the earth, and the top of it reached to heaven:

C. — And behold the angels of God ascending and descending on it. (Gen. 28: 10-12.)

> Though like a wanderer,
>   The sun gone down,
> Darkness comes over me,
>   My rest a stone,
> Yet in my dreams I'd be
> Nearer, my God, to thee,
>   Nearer to thee!
>
> There let my way appear
>   Steps unto heaven;
> All that thou sendest me
>   In mercy given;
> Angels to beckon me
> Nearer, my God, to thee,
>   Nearer to thee!

L. — And it came to pass, when the Lord would take up Elijah into heaven by a whirlwind, that Elijah went with Elisha from Gilgal. (2 Kings 2 : 1.)

C. — And it came to pass, as they still went on and talked, that behold, there appeared a chariot of fire, and horses of fire, and parted them both asunder;

L. — And Elijah went up by a whirlwind into heaven.

C. — And Elisha saw it, and he cried, My father, my father! the chariot of Israel and the horsemen thereof. (2 Kings 2: 11, 12.)

> Or, if on joyful wing,
>   Cleaving the sky,
> Sun, moon and stars forgot,
>   Upward I fly,
> Still all my song shall be, —
> Nearer, my God, to thee,
>   Nearer to thee.

Prayer.

An Evening Song. L. M.

> Glory to thee, my God, this night,
> For all the blessings of the light:
> Keep me, O keep me, King of kings,
> Beneath the shadow of thy wings.

Forgive me, Lord, for thy dear Son,
The ill which I this day have done;
That with the world, myself and thee,
I, ere I sleep, at peace may be

Teach me to live that I may dread
The grave as little as my bed;
Teach me to die that so I may
Rise glorious at the judgment-day.

L. — The Lord bless thee, and keep thee;
C. — The Lord make his face shine upon thee, and be gracious unto thee.
L. — The Lord lift up his countenance upon thee, and give thee peace.
(Num. 6 : 24–26.)

Closing Verse. C. M.

Thus when life's toilsome day is o'er,
　　May its departing ray
Be calm as this impressive hour,
　　And lead to endless day.

The programme was divided into three terms. The following report published by the author in "The Sunday-school Journal" for Nov. 18, 1874, will give an idea of the *first* Assembly : —

The following *résumé* of work for the three "terms" into which the fourteen days were divided will show how much was accomplished.

First Term : Aug. 4–9.

I Lectures on Practical Sunday-school Work. 1 "The Superintendent in the Desk," by Rev. H Clay Trumbull 2. "The Power of Sympathy in Sunday-school Teaching," by Bishop Janes 3. "Temperance and the Sunday School," by Mis. J F. Willing 4 "The Foes we Fight," by John B Gough. 5 "The True Training of Children," by Rev George A Peltz

II Lectures on the Bible. 1. On Bible Evidences: "The Sunday School and the Scientists," by Dr. L. T. Townsend 2 On Bible Biography "Moses," by Dr C H Fowler 3 On Bible Geography "Palestine and its Topography," by Dr W. W. Wythe; "Palestine and its Scenery," by Dr. W H Perrine

III. Four Conductors' *Conversazioni*, discussing the work of Sunday-school institute and normal-class conductors; J H. Vincent.

IV Practical Sessions Four meetings of primary teachers, Mrs. Dr. Knox of Elmira, N Y, leader One of the meetings, in Mrs Knox's absence, Mrs. George Partridge of St Louis led Four of pastors and superintendents; J. H. Vincent, Dr. F. H Marling, Dr. J. H Castle, Rev. H Clay Trumbull. Three of intermediate-class teachers; Mr Peltz, J. H. Vincent, H. C. Trumbull. One of senior-class teachers, C. P. Hard leader.

V Eleven Specimen Meetings. 1. Two teachers' meetings; J. B. Tyler (perhaps also J S Ostrander). 2 A Sunday-school session, Dr P. Gillett, Superintendent. 3 Four Bible-readings; Rev Mr Norton of Erie Conference, Rev Isaac Crook, Rev. C. P Hard, Rev. J. S Ostrander. 4 A praise service; Philip Phillips. 5. A caricature lecture; Frank Beard. 6. Stereopticon exhibition; Dr. W H Perrine (illustrations furnished by McAllister, of New York). 7. A children's meeting; addresses by J. S. Ostrander, Mrs. J. F. Willing, Rev. W F Crafts, and F Beard.

VI. Two Sermons Rev. F. H. Marling and Rev. W. C. Willing

SECOND TERM · Aug 10–13.

I. Lectures on Sunday-school Work. 1. "How to Utilize the Sunday School," by J. B. Tyler, Esq. 2. "Language and Illustration in Teaching," by Rev. J. M. Buckley. 3 "Dynamics of the Sunday School," by Dr. E. O Haven. 4. "Helps of Science in Religious Teaching," by Dr. H. W Warren. 5. "The Teacher and his Bible," by Ralph Wells, Esq 6 "The Use of the Imagination in Bible Teaching," by Dr J F Hurst. 7. "The Study of Childhood," by Rev. W. F. Crafts 8. "The Growth of Moral Ideas," by Dr. C. H. Fowler. 9. "The Sunday School and Our Country," by Dr A L. Chapin. 10. "The Sunday-school Teachers' Decalogue," by Dr E. O. Haven.

II. Lectures on the Bible 1 Two on Bible Institutions: "The Tabernacle and its Furniture," by Rev Wolcott Calkins 2. Bible Geography "Palestine and its Scenery," by Dr. W H Perrine.

III Four Conductors' *Conversazioni*, J H Vincent.

IV Practical Sessions. Four meetings of primary teachers; Mrs W. F. Crafts, leader Two of intermediate teachers; Miss H. N Morris, leader. One of Sunday-school superintendents, Rev. H. C Trumbull.

V. Meetings of Sections A, B, C, and D,—four each Subjects of drill: The Books of the Bible; Bible History and Chronology; Bible Geography. J. S. Ostrander, C. P Hard, J. A Worden, W. F. Crafts, H. R Miller, J B Tyler, John Pearson, Dr Niles

VI. Five Specimen Meetings 1 The Blackboard Hour; 2. A Tabernacle Talk on Entertainments, 3 A Stereopticon Exhibition; 4 Two Praise Services,—W F Sherwin, W. F Crafts

VII Two Sermons. Rev. T. De Witt Talmage, D.D., and Rev. Dr. C. F. Deems.

THIRD TERM: Aug. 14–18.

I Lectures on Sunday-school Work. "The Church Sunday School," by Rev. Dr. D. Curry 2. "The Ideal Sunday School," by Rev. W. F. Crafts. 3 "How to Handle the Boys in Sunday School and at Home," by Dr. J. H. Vincent. 4 "Sunday-school Literature," by Mrs. Emily Huntington Miller. 5. "The Sunday School a Training School for the Ministry," by Rev. Dr T. M. Eddy 6 "Children at Preaching," by Bishop Peck 7. "The Church of the Future in the Sunday School of the Present," by Bishop Simpson

II. Practical Sessions. One for a Primary-Teachers' Question Drawer; questions answered by Mrs Knox, Mrs Partridge, Mrs Crafts, and Miss Hattie N. Morris. One for a Miscellaneous Sunday-school Question Drawer, questions answered by Rev J M Freeman of New York, Prof. P. G Gillett, LL.D, of Illinois, Rev C P Hard, Rev S. McGerald, Rev W. A. Niles, D D, Rev. J S Ostrander, and J. H. Vincent.

III Meetings for Sections A, B, C, and D, — two each Subjects of drill: The Christian Evidences, Rules for Bible Interpretation

IV. 'Six Specimen Meetings: 1. A Children's Meeting; Dr. J. M. Freeman on "The Invisible Blackboard," Frank Beard on "The Visible Blackboard," Bishop Peck on "Things Visible and Invisible." 2. Teachers' Meeting; 3 A Sunday-school Session; J S Ostrander, superintendent; 4. Teachers' Prayer-Meeting; 5 Missionary Meeting,[1] Rev C P Hard, Rev J H Messmore, and Bishop Simpson; 6 Competitive Examination

V. Four Sermons. Bishop Simpson, Bishop Peck, Dr. T M. Eddy, Dr. W. X. Ninde

SUMMARY OF WORK

Twenty-two lectures on the Sunday-school work, — theory and practice. Seven lectures on Bible history, geography, evidences, etc. Sectional Meetings nine primary; six intermediate; one senior; one superintendents', four pastors' and superintendents' Eight normal-class and institute-conductors' *conversazioni.* Normal sections A, B, C, and D, six each. Three teachers' meetings for the preparation of the lesson; two specimen Sunday-school sessions, four Bible-readings; three praise services; two children's meetings, and six sermons.

All the leading Protestant denominations were represented Persons were present from twenty-five States; also from Ontario, Montreal, Nova Scotia, Ireland, Scotland, and India.

---

[1] Largely as a result of this meeting, Rev. F. A. Goodwin the young cornetist and Rev. John E. Robinson offered themselves as missionaries, and sailed for India, Oct 20, 1874.

We do not attempt here to mention the names of all who assisted in this great enterprise. Our thanks are due to a host of men and women whose names are in our heart, and with whom we hope to work for years to come in this noble cause, and whose fellowship in our Father's kingdom we expect to enjoy forever. The meetings were all well attended. The occasional showers did not seem to abate the general enthusiasm. Then we must confess that these showers came just at the right times. But one lecture was postponed on account of the weather. The evenings and mornings were cool, and only on one day did we suffer from the heat.

The marvels of the museum, the novelty and sacred associations of our tiny bit of "Holy Land," the beautiful park on the Point, with its fountain and statuary and rustic seats, the grand old forest-trees, the lovely lake, the songs of the multitudes, the inspiring lectures and sermons, the instructive class-exercises, and the sweet fraternal fellowships, — all these, and a host of unmentioned delights besides, made the days pass so swiftly and so sweetly by that we could scarcely credit the old almanac when the final Tuesday dawned upon us.

Successful as the Assembly was, it is understood to have been but a tentative movement, and one could not expect the thoroughness of organization and work which we trust to realize in some future meeting of the same general character. Its results satisfy us, and at the same time quicken us to another and a better effort. We had too many lectures at Chautauqua, and too little normal-class work, and this because we feared that the latter would fail if too strongly pressed. We are now certain that two hours a day of actual drill will be acceptable to the majority of our teachers, and that two popular lectures a day will be sufficient to attract the masses. Besides the class-drills, much more time may be spent in what we call the "practical sessions."

The conductors of all normal-class sessions should be prepared beforehand for their work. This we have always required in local and temporary institutes. At Chautauqua we at first depended upon the Sunday-school leaders whose experience in the work rendered them ready at a moment's notice for the management of a section. On the first day of the second term, we called a meeting in our tent of these conductors, and spent two hours in arrangements for the remaining sectional sessions. Every man knew his work for five days in advance. Should another Assembly be held, we trust that the managers will provide leaders long before the meeting for these practical and normal sections. The "Bible-readings" may be made more of at another Assembly. "Praise-meetings" should be held daily. More emphasis should be placed upon the conversational method in the conduct of sectional or department meetings   The "Vesper Service" was one of the most beautiful and impressive features of the occasion

The "Department of Entertainment," under the ingenious direction of Dr Wythe, deserves mention.   Its contributions to the pleasures of the Assembly cannot be too warmly commended   The day's labor was lighter for the delights and recreations afforded by the genial doctor.   The fireworks and balloons and music, the "views" and panoramas, and promenades, and Park of Palestine all helped in the heavier service of normal-class and lecture hours.   •

The Park of Palestine was laid out on the grounds of the Sunday-school Assembly, in order to provide a large map or model of the Holy Land for the instruction of teachers and young people interested in Bible history, and who desired to see the topography which gives to that history such vividness and power   The model in stones and earth was not, of course, a true representation of the geology, the fauna, or the flora of the Hóly Land.   It is hoped that one of these days we shall have such a complete reproduction, on a small scale, of all the characteristics of Canaan, as shall render a visit to it second only to a vision of the land itself.   The Park of Palestine was an attempt to present the general outline of the country, — the principal hills and valleys, the water-courses, the cities, etc   In this particular the Park was accurate and invaluable   One could get from it a general idea of the leading features of the country   A distinguished geographer, who honored it with a visit, remarked, "A study of this Park at Chautauqua, and Dr Perrine's 'Chromo of Palestine,' are almost equivalent to an actual tour of the Holy Land."   The Park of Palestine was the work of Dr. Wythe of Meadville, Penn., chairman of the Department of Recreation, for the Assembly   To him was committed the idea, and most admirably he carried it out.   Personal surveys, personal labor, prosecuted through weeks of discouragement and not a little ridicule, were crowned with most gratifying success   He brought to the work a thorough knowledge of his subject, rare resources of device, invention, and a persistency which nothing could discourage.

Palestine is but a small portion of the Bible world.   Its superior importance, however, as the great centre of Bible history, justifies us in giving it a prominent place in our studies.   Were we to represent the whole of Bible geography on the same scale as that adopted for the Park of Palestine, we should cover an area seven thousand feet from east to west and five thousand from north to south   We limited ourselves, however, and on a plat of ground about seventy-five by one hundred and twenty feet we presented the salient features of the sacred land, where lived and flourished Abraham, Isaac, Jacob, Joseph, Samuel, Saul, David, Solomon, and, above all and greater than all, the Lord Jesus, who became man and lived on our earth and died for our sins

The "Museum" was a success. It was rich in curiosities and in practical helps.

The worthiest exercise of the Assembly was the competitive examination on the last Monday morning. Two hundred persons entered the tabernacle on the hill, to pass a written examination Fifty questions were placed in the hands of each competitor. Twenty or more candidates dropped out before an hour A hundred remained for more than two hours and a half, while some lingered for three, some four, and a few nearly five hours One hundred and seventy-five papers were finally submitted for examination. We have not yet finished the inspection of these papers, but hope to do so before this number of the "Journal" is out of our hands A prize will be awarded to the three most perfect competitors,[1] and a diploma from our Normal Department to all whose examination papers will justify it This is but the beginning of a new movement which will spread over our country, and awaken a new interest in Bible study among our teachers.

Who will say that this attention to the intellectual part of the work can interfere with the spiritual aims of the Sunday-school teacher? We do not believe that there is any such tendency in the normal work Without the Spirit of God to inspire us, the highest human training will be vain. Having the Spirit, we shall do our work the better for knowing well the Word of God. Let us not decry training; but, seeking it in perfection, let us trust implicitly and pray ardently for the life and power of the Holy Ghost

I take the liberty of republishing from "The Western Christian Advocate" a pleasant picture of the first competitive examination at Chautauqua : —

"The tent is a very large one, and was plentifully supplied with benches, chairs, camp-stools, etc The spectacle was very imposing. The ladies seemed to be a little in the majority There were two girls under fifteen, and one boy in his fourteenth year. Each was provided with paper and pencil, and each wore a more or less silent and thoughtful air There was no shuffling, no listlessness, no whispering The conductor, with a big stump for his table, occupied a somewhat central position, ready to respond to the call of any uplifted hand We stood just back of Dr. Vincent, with the scene in full view To our right, but a

---

[1] The three candidates receiving the honors were Rev C. P. Hard, Mr. Caleb Sadler, and Rev. S. McGerald.

little on the outside of the tent, were Bishop Simpson and Dr Eddy, who remained only a few moments, as the latter was compelled to take the ten o'clock train for New York. On the same side, and a little nearer to us, were groups of visitors, mostly from the country adjacent, who gazed in rapt astonishment at the sight before them, not daring to inquire the meaning of all this mute array of paper and pencil A little to our left was a lawyer of large experience and almost national fame, who had removed his hat, cravat, collar, coat, and cuffs ; just by his side was an ex-State-senator; and a little farther on was a boy from Iowa. He had improvised for his table a small round log, and had gathered together, for the better resting of his knees, a good-sized pile of dry beech-leaves. This lad, we learned, had been studying the normal course during the last year ; and we further discovered that he succeeded in answering accurately all except ten or twelve of the fifty questions, one of the to him insolvable and incomprehensible ones being this, ' What is the relation of the church to the Sunday school ? ' Nearly in front of the conductor were two veteran spectacled sisters, who at no time whispered to each other, but kept up a strong thinking and a frequent use of the pencil Near these sat a mother and daughter from Evanston, Ill , silent and confident. Every now and then the knit brow would relax, and the dimple in the cheek and the fire in the eye showed that victory in a hard cause had been achieved On the outer row of seats we observed three doctors of divinity, a theological student, a president of an Ohio college, a gentleman connected with the internal revenue, and a lady principal of a young ladies' seminary, all with their thinking-caps admirably adjusted.

"At the end of an hour and forty minutes, a New-York brother, who had been specially active in sectional work, held up his hand in token of success, and his paper was passed up to Dr Vincent Shortly afterward another made a similar signal ; but nearly all occupied over three hours in the work Over one-half attained to seventy-five or eighty per cent "

It is difficult to give in short space a satisfactory report of that first Assembly. This life in the woods was a novel experience to so many; and a novel experience as well, to those accustomed to the old camp-meeting, was this blending of instruction and recreation Many unique and charming pictures are recalled by the Chautauquans of 1874 We all remember the first appearance of Mr Van Lennep as an Eastern shepherd in full Oriental costume, with his long shepherd's crook in hand, a thousand people climbing upon the mountains east of the Jordan to hear his lecture about "The Land and its People." There is a picture, too, of the little yacht with its burden of melody, steaming out into the lake, amidst a blaze of fireworks. On that boat were Professor Sherwin; the itinerant Trio from Wyoming, — Rev Messrs W. B. Westlake, J B Sumner, J. C. Lacock; there, too, was the beloved Goodwin with his cornet, which always seemed to have a Christian tone; and his associate, the Rev. John E. Robinson; together with Mr. Van Lennep, who, when the time came, sang his Turkish song, followed as it was by thunderous applause from the thousands on the shore. The first night of pyrotechnic display is memorable, when Capt Whitney turned over his steamer, the "Colonel Phillips," to Dr. Wythe, and a great company of singers mounted the deck of the illuminated steamer, and, under the leadership of Prof. T. C. O'Kane and Rev F A Goodwin, delighted the crowds with music from the grand chorus Meanwhile Dr. Wythe sent off rockets, balloons, and elaborate pieces of fireworks There was rest in that recreation. Who will forget the days of rain, especially the shower that came flooding all the lower parts of the encampment? As a correspondent said, "The Jordan overflowed its banks, and became a swelling flood" How heartily everybody laughed! How soon the storm was over! How soon the water subsided! The sun came out, and the memory of the shower gives pleasure even to this day "It sometimes rains at Chautauqua."

1875.

The Assembly of 1875 was in every respect an improvement upon that of 1874 The speaker's platform of the auditorium had been rebuilt. A Jewish Tabernacle, an exact imitation (half-size) of the original, and a section of the Pyramid of Gizeh, had been erected under the skilful direction of Dr. W W Wythe, Superintendent of the Department of Recreation Instead of one bell, the Clinton H. Meneely Company of Troy, N.Y. (at that time Meneely & Kimberly) gave us a peal of three bells The Oriental House, and a miniature model of modern Jerusalem, added to the attractions of the lower park. I copy from the announcements of the programmes published in advance in "The Chautauqua Assembly Bulletin," beautifully illustrated and printed, a copy of which is before me. —

    — Last year, one bell
    — This year, a chime of bells, musical bells.
    — Think of the evening concerts on the lake
    — We will not positively promise, but we expect a pipe-organ of great power to be set up at Fair Point
    — It is probable that the grounds will be illuminated with the calcium lights, flooding the place with brightness.

— The division tents of the lower grounds will be seated, provided with platforms, blackboards, maps, bell, etc   There are four of these tents

— Furniture to a certain extent may be rented on the ground, but persons coming to the Assembly should provide themselves with towels, pillow, spoon, napkin, etc. Do not forget a good, warm woollen shawl Even in midsummer it is sometimes cool fourteen hundred feet above the Atlantic Besides the shawl, bring a waterproof, rubbers, and umbrella. It once rained at Chautauqua; it may rain again.

— The Division Sessions are those in which the several classes of workers, pastors, superintendents, infant-class teachers, etc., meet in separate session to discuss the topics especially interesting to them.   They will state difficulties, discuss principles, illustrate methods, exhibit appliances, etc

— The Drill Sessions are those in which all grades of the workers meet in classes for drills in the Normal-Class themes : Bible history, geography, chronology, evidences, interpretation, etc. ; also, for practice in whatever pertains to the work of teaching, illustration, questioning, reviewing, etc.

— Our dear brother F A Goodwin, whose cornet gave us so much delight at Chautauqua, last summer, writes us from Kurrachee : " Here I am in the Bombay and Bengal Mission, about a thousand miles from our main work in the Oudh, and several hundred miles from any other Methodist organization. But Brother Taylor called for ‘ men willing to go anywhere,’ and I came. So they sent me to the borders of Afghanistan, at the mouth of the Indus."

— The subjects for the normal course at Chautauqua in 1875 will be : 1. The text-book of the Sunday school, its divine origin, mission, and classification and division of its several books, etc   2. The true theory of the Sunday school, as to its place, purpose, and relations, etc   3. The teacher and the teaching work in Sunday school ; the teacher's office, its place and power, etc.

The promise in 1875 of a chime of bells was not realized until 1885 The great organ was erected by George H. Ryder of Boston, and dedicated in 1882.

In addition to the normal work, classes in map-drawing, blackboard sketching and lettering, were organized under the direction of Professor Frank Beard. A class in Hebrew was held daily, taught by the Rev. S M Vail, D D., the number of regular attendants being about forty, eight of whom were ladies. The kindergarten scheme was explained and illustrated in a series of admirable lessons by Madam Kriege of New York Instruction in Sunday-school singing was given by Dr. Eben Tourjée, Prof. P. P. Bliss, and Prof W F Sherwin " The Tennesseeans " spent several days at Fair Point, and gave pleasure to the people. The " Erie District Trio " sang with good effect Professor Tingley of Alleghany College, Meadville, Penn., took charge of the stereopticon projections upon the screen, and gave several scientific lectures. Mr. George

A Ford gave eighteen talks on the model of Jerusalem. Mr A O Van Lennep gave sixteen lectures on Palestine Park. Old Chautauquans will never forget the Orientalist as he marched over Palestine, describing the sacred sites, and recalling historic events which give them their charm

During the fourteen days of three "terms," the following work was accomplished at the Assembly of 1875: in addition to the Hebrew lessons, lectures on the Park of Palestine, and model of Jerusalem, we reported fifty normal-class sessions, five praise-services, twenty-two general Sunday-school addresses, eleven lectures on miscellaneous topics, four sermons, three children's meetings, five primary-teachers' conventions, seven prayer-meetings, two teachers'-meetings, two blackboard meetings, three illustrated lectures on Oriental customs, twelve stereopticon exhibitions, two lake concerts.

In 1874, two hundred students attended the competitive examination; to 152 of them, diplomas were sent In 1875, 190 students attended the examination; 130 papers were sent in, of which 123 attained the standard required, and thus 123 names were enrolled as members for 1875 of the Chautauqua Normal Alumni, which organization was effected this year, Otis F Presbrey being appointed *president;* Rev. J S. Ostrander of New York, Mrs W. E. Knox of Elmira, N Y, George H Babcock, Esq, of Plainfield, N J., *vice-presidents;* and Rev J A Worden of Steubenville, O, *secretary*

The "hymn of greeting" by Miss Mary A. Lathbury, "The Flush of Morn," was sung for the first time this season, and also the song of 1875 by Miss Lathbury, "The Winds are Whispering to the Trees," with music by Miss Lucy J. Rider.

The opening of the Assembly on the first Tuesday evening in August was memorable from the heavy rain which drove a large audience from the auditorium to the great tabernacle on the hill. The usual vesper-service was used Prof. W F Sherwin conducted the singing; Mr J. C. Howard of New York played the cornet. Addresses were delivered by President Lewis Miller, Dr Presbrey, Professor Sherwin, Dr A Alexander Hodge (then of Alleghany, Penn). Professor P. P Bliss sang "It winna be for long;" and Rev Mr Princell, of the Swedish Church of New York, spoke; also Dr Edward Eggleston of Brooklyn, Mr. C M Nichols of Ohio, Rev. H M Parsons of Boston, Dr Warren Randolph of Philadelphia, Dr. W. W Wythe, Dr R M Hatfield, then of Philadelphia. The music on the lake was dispensed with ("The lake is wet to-night"), and the bells rang out the call to rest at ten o'clock.

The normal workers for the season of 1875 were Rev J A. Worden, Rev. J. S Ostrander, Rev. R. S. Greene, Rev. J. L. Hurlbut, Rev. Alfred

Taylor, S. W. Clark, Esq., Prof W F Sherwin, A O Van Lennep, S. McGerald, Rev J M. Freeman, Rev. H M. Parsons, Miss Hattie N. Morris, Dr. W. A. Niles, Rev. G. A. Peltz, Dr. S. M. Vail, J. B. Tyler, Esq., George H Babcock, Esq.

Lectures and addresses were delivered by Dr Edward Eggleston, "The Paradise of Childhood," Dr. Walcott Calkins, "Socrates," Dr. S M. Vail, "The Study of Hebrew," Dr H M Parsons, "The Whole Church in the Sunday School," Rev. Alfred Taylor, "The Child and his Companions;" Mr J Bennet Tyler, "Church Training and Work in Sunday School;" Dr. J. M. Freeman, "Country Schools," Dr. Warren Randolph, "The International Lesson System," Dr. W. W. Wythe, "The Wonders of Canaan," with stereopticon illustrations in the hands of Prof J Tingley; Dr. J. M. Walden, "The Press and the Sunday School;" Mrs. Emily Huntington Miller, "A Parish in Fairhaven;" Professor Frank Beard, "Chalk Studies in Character;" Dr Justin D. Fulton, "The Force that Wins;" Dr. Theodore L Cuyler, "Some Talks I have had with Great Men;" Rev. T. L. Flood, "Temperance," Dr J. W. Armstrong of Fredonia Normal College, "Processes of Nature;" Dr. W. H Perrine, "Christian Art," Dr J. M Reid, "The Sunday School and the Missionary Cause;" Miss Frances E Willard, "Temperance," Dr. R. M. Hatfield, "The Perils of our Youth;" Rev. J S Ostrander, "Oriental Illustrations," Dr. J. M. Buckley, "Questioning;" Miss Hattie N. Morris, "Character-building;" Dr. William E. Knox, "Unity of the Protestant Church," Rev J. L. Hurlbut, "John Knox," M. C. Hazard, Esq., "The Child in the Midst;" Dr W L Niles, "The Teacher's Needs;" Dr. C F Deems, "The Sunday-school Teacher and his Book of Nature;" Dr Richard Newton of Philadelphia, "The Elements of Success in Sunday-school Teaching;" Dr Eben Tourjée, "Music." Sermons were preached by Dr B K. Peirce of Boston, Dr Richard Newton of Philadelphia, Dr. C F. Deems, and Dr. C H Fowler The Assembly Sunday school, Aug 8, reported a total attendance of 2,997, and Aug 15, of 3,348.

The most important event of the season of 1875 was a visit from President U. S. GRANT. He arrived on Saturday, Aug 14, accompanied by his son Ulysses, Gen. Babcock, and Oliver Hoyt, Esq., of Connecticut The President lunched at the residence of Alonzo Kent, Esq., of Jamestown, and came to the grounds in the afternoon, on the yacht "Josie Belle," accompanied by Miss Lilla Kent, Rev T. L. Flood, President Miller, Hon W L Sessions, Judge Lakin, and Alonzo Kent, Esq When the President was presented by the Superintendent of Instruction to the immense audience in the auditorium, the enthusiasm surpassed any thing that had ever been seen at Chautauqua. The "Song of Welcome" composed by Miss Mary A. Lathbury for the occasion was sung to the tune "Hold the Fort," and was as follows : —

> "Like the surge of hidden waters,
>   Like a wordless song,
> Deep and strong the breath of welcome
>   Stirs the waiting throng.

> "*Chorus.* — Heart and voice, awake to greet him
>   Who our hosts has led !
> Let the true heart of the nation
>   Greet the nation's head !

> "Earnest hearts that love and labor,
>   Christian hearts that pray,
> Builders of the nation's future,
>   Greet our chief to-day !

> " Not in royal garments stand we,
>   Not in jewels rare ,
> But the children of the nation,
>   ' These our jewels are.'

> "Greet him ! Let the air around him
>   Benedictions bear :
> Let the hearts of all the people
>   Circle him with prayer."

Addresses were then delivered by Dr. Fowler, Hon. Oliver Hoyt, and Dr. Deems The grounds were brilliantly illuminated in the evening. The President attended service on Sunday. At the close of the sermon in the morning by Dr. C. F. Deems, from Luke xxiii. 33, a copy of the Bagster Bible, and also a copy of the new Teacher's Bible published by the American Tract Society, were presented to the President In the evening Dr. Fowler preached on "The Exaltation of Christ."

1876.

The Chautauqua movement this season introduced some new features. Among the announcements in the "Normal Class Bulletin" were the following : —

— Chautauqua in 1876, of course.

— Chautauqua would be a good substitute for the Centennial.

— The old steamers on the lake have been refitted, and one new one has been built.

— Chautauqua will be a centennial exhibition in itself. Let all who go to Philadelphia, come to Chautauqua. Let all who cannot go to Philadelphia, come to Chautauqua.

— The bells, the Tabernacle, the model of Palestine, the model of Jerusalem, the Orientals, the fountain, the statuary, the Oriental House, the museum, the Pyramid, the boats, the bathing, the music, the normal-class lessons, the re-unions, the delightful prayer-meetings, the alumni association, the vesper services, the cornet, the piano, the songsters of the South, the great praise-meetings, the night-concerts on the lake, the bells at ten and the bells at six, and the RAIN, — who would not be a Chautauquan?

— "The Chautauqua Assembly Herald" will be published at Fair Point from Wednesday morning, July 26, to Friday morning, Aug 18, Sundays excepted. It will be a thirty-two-column paper, folio, and will contain full stenographic reports of lectures, sermons, and speeches, a column of personal items, local news, and able editorials on Sunday-school and church work

The work for the summer at Chautauqua was divided into four parts · 1. The *Scientific Conference* for all Bible students interested in the present state of natural science, and its relations to the Bible; beginning Wednesday morning, July 26, and lasting for three days 2. The Chautauqua *Temperance Convention*, for two days, July 29 and 30. 3. The *Sunday-school Assembly*, Aug 1-15. 4. The *Church Congress*, Aug. 16-18.

At the *Scientific Congress*, lectures were delivered by Rev. Dr. James M Buckley, on "The Circle of the Sciences;" Dr. E O Haven, chancellor of Syracuse University, "The Relation of Material Science to Mind and Spirit;" Dr R. Ogden Doremus of New York, "Heat, its Sources and Effects," "Heat converted into Light," "Heat and Electricity;" Prof. S A. Lattimore of Rochester University, "The Physical Forces," "The Wonders of the Sun," Dr E. F. Burr of Lyme, Conn., "Celestial Magnitudes," Dr. Alexander Winchell, "Rocks," "The Geological Structure of Chautauqua Lake," "Words in the Rocks;" Dr. A. A. Hodge, "Bible Miracles and Modern Science;" Dr L. T. Townsend of Boston, "Latest Results of Scientific Investigation, and their Bearing upon the Bible Idea of Heaven." Professor Doremus's lectures were most brilliantly illustrated. Scientific *conversazioni* were held on the following subjects "Alleged Discrepancies between Science and the Bible;" "The Importance of Science to the Religious Thinker;" "The Best Methods of familiarizing the People with Scientific Subjects."

Hymns for the Chautauqua Scientific Conference were printed on separate slips, and the devotional spirit of the Conference was very remarkable. Three burlesque bills of fare for Wednesday, Thursday, and Friday, July 26–28, were prepared by a distinguished scientist, — the first "astronomical and gastronomical," the second "geological and evolutional," the third "chemically prepared in the laboratory." I am sorry I do not have room for them. The Scientific Conference was in every way successful.

The Chautauqua *Temperance Conference* opened July 29. Addresses were made during the session, on "Scientific Certainties, not Opinions, about Alcohol," by Dr. H. W. Warren; by Miss Julia Colman, on "Methods of Work;" by Rev. Thomas Graham, "General Aspects of the Cause;" Miss Frances E. Willard, "Work before us." Practical conferences were held, in which the following persons participated: Rev. Dr. G. B. Jocelyn of Michigan, Mr. J N Stearns of New York, "Mother" Stewart of Ohio, Miss F. E. Willard of Illinois, Miss Julia Colman of New York, Mrs. Sessions, Mrs Dawson, Dr. E. F. Burr, Dr James Strong, and the Superintendent of Instruction. A sermon was preached by Rev Dr. Jocelyn, on Isa. xxviii 14–19. The "North-Carolinian" band of jubilee singers was in attendance.

The third Assembly opened on Tuesday evening, Aug 1. Profs. W. F Sherwin and P. P. Bliss led the singing. The vesper-service of 1874 was used. Brief addresses were delivered by Dr. Warren Randolph of Philadelphia; Dr. O. F. Presbrey of Washington, D C.; Prof A F. Townsend of Iowa, who spoke for the Assembly at Clear Lake; Rev. T. L Flood of Jamestown, representing "The Daily Assembly Herald;" Rev H. M. Sanders of Yonkers, N Y; Mr John D Wattles of "The Sunday-School Times," Philadelphia; Mr. A. O. Van Lennep made a short speech in Arabic, and another in English; and Mr. W. Aver Duncan of London, Eng, spoke of Old England to Young America Addresses were also delivered by Dr. W. E Knox, Dr Lyman Abbott, Frank Beard, Professor Sherwin, Rev Dr Burr, H W. Warren, Mr. C M Nichols

The "Superintendent of Instruction" was assisted in the normal work by Rev. J. A. Worden, Rev. J L Hurlbut, A. O. Van Lennep, J. S. Ostrander, Dr. Lyman Abbott, Dr S. M. Vail, Rev. R S. Greene, Mrs Dr Knox, Rev. S. McGerald, Lewis Miller, Frank Beard, Lucy J. Rider, C. B. Stout, Dr. H. S Osborn of Lafayette College, Rev. Dr. Walcott Calkins. Each department of normal-class study was under the care of a director who chose his own helpers for the simultaneous lessons in each of the section tents, and reviewed the work afterward in the pavilion. The subjects were again brought forward in their order by four public platform reviews conducted by the "Superintendent of Instruction," when the outlines of the whole work were passed over once more.

Monday afternoon, Aug. 7, at a normal-class *conversazione* held in the pavilion, a committee of seven was appointed to consider the practicability of preparing a "Chautauqua Normal Course of Study." This committee met, and on Tuesday, Aug. 8, made a report recommending the appointment of a committee of nine for the preparing of this list of lessons. The report was adopted, and eleven persons appointed. For the substance of their report, see pp. 57, 58 of this volume. On Friday, Aug. 11, the annual address was delivered before the Chautauqua Alumni, by Rev. Dr. O. H. Tiffany. On Monday, Aug. 14, ninety-eight persons presented themselves for examination, eighty-four of whom passed successfully, and received diplomas, and became members of the "Chautauqua Alumni."

The children's meeting was inaugurated this season. The first meeting was held on Wednesday morning, Aug. 2, Rev. J. S. Ostrander in charge; and addresses were delivered by Rev. J. L. Hurlbut, Rev. B. T. Vincent, and others. Later on, the children's meeting (now called "The Boys' and Girls' Class") was placed in charge of the Rev. B. T. Vincent and Frank Beard.

Lectures and addresses were delivered during the Assembly of '76 as follows: Dr. W. E. Knox, "The Old-Testament Severities;" Dr. Warren Randolph, "Hopeful Aspects of the Sunday-school Cause," Rev. Dr. Lyman Abbott, "Biblical Interpretation;" Dr. George P. Hays, "How to Reason," Dr. R. M. Hargrove of Tennessee, "Childhood and the Sunday-school Work;" Frank Beard, "Our School" (caricature lecture), "The Beautiful;" "The Use of the Blackboard;" Rev. J. S. Ostrander, "Illustrations of Oriental Life," Rev. Dr. A. N. Cowles, "Primitive Christians in Rome;" Rev. Dr. G. W. Woodruff, "Bright Days in Foreign Lands," Rev. Alfred Taylor, "Good Health for Sunday-school Teachers," Rev. Dr. A. J. Baird of Tennessee, "Going Fishing with Peter;" Rev. J. A. Worden, "What a Presbyterian thinks of John Wesley," Professor William Wells, LL.D., "Bismarck and the Pope;" Prof. L. T. Townsend, "Paul's Cloak left at Troas," Dr. Richard Newton, "The Sunday-school Teacher's Work, How to do it;" C. B. Stout, Esq., "Common-sense in Crayon;" Bishop J. T. Peck, "The Transcendental in Theology," Rev. Walcott Calkins, "The Fast Young Man;" M. C. Hazard, Esq., "The Dynamics of Sunday-school Teaching," Rev. Thomas K. Beecher, "Thoughts for Advanced Sunday school Workers," Rev. Dr. W. A. Niles, "The Pastor and the Little Children;" Rev. Walter Condict, "The Sabbath."

Professor James Strong, S T.D., of Drew Theological Seminary, conducted a class in New-Testament Greek, and Dr S. M. Vail a class in Hebrew. Mr A. O Van Lennep gave peripatetic lectures on the Park of Palestine; and Rev. S. McGerald, on the Model of Jerusalem Two or three impressive "eventide conferences" were held in the Pavilion.

The musical programme for the season of 1876 contains the names of Prof. W. F. Sherwin, P. P. Bliss, the North Carolinians, the Wyoming Conference Itinerant Trio, with instrumental accompaniment, piano, cabinet-organs, cornet, and the Mayville Brass Band. On the afternoon of Aug 11 a very fine Old-Folks' Concert was given by singers of Westfield and Ripley, N Y.

A unique exercise was a Specimen Sunday School held in the Auditorium on Friday, Aug 4, Lewis Miller as superintendent, with a full corps of officers and teachers, and a regular working-session of a model school.

The Centennial of our American Independence was observed at Chautauqua. A centennial service was held on Saturday, Aug 5 Bishop Simpson, who had consented to deliver the oration, was unable on account of illness to be present; and addresses were delivered by Dr. George P. Hays of Pennsylvania; Mr. James M'Nab of Toronto, Ont ; Rev. Dr. A J Baird of Nashville, Tenn ; Mr W Aver Duncan of London, England; and Dr. W. E. Knox of Elmira, N Y. A "Children's Centennial" meeting was held in the afternoon of the same day, with addresses by Dr J. L. Hurlbut and Mr Frank Beard In the evening an impressive Bible-service, "The Voice of the Sea," was conducted on the shore of the lake by Prof. W F. Sherwin, after which the North Carolinians gave a concert of slave-songs Late in the evening, an "illuminated fleet" of vessels large and small, decorated with lanterns, moved about on the lake, closing the entertainment with a grand display of fireworks, which appropriately completed the exercises of "Centennial Day." A centennial service was also held on Saturday, Aug 12, when an address was delivered on "The Century," by Dr. O. H Tiffany A "Centennial Tree-planting" was observed with appropriate ceremonies on the same day.

Sermons were preached during the Assembly by the Rev Dr H. M. Sanders of Yonkers, N.Y., Dr A J Baird of Nashville, Tenn.; Dr George P Hays of Washington, Penn ; Dr Hargrove of Nashville; Dr. C. H Payne and the Rev. Dr. Walcott Calkins of Buffalo

The old "Guest House," known for years as "The Ark" ("Knower's Ark," as Frank Beard called it), for the accommodation of distinguished guests, was opened in 1876 One is not able to tell all the stories of misery, mirth, and music, which are associated with "*The Ark.*" It was removed a year or two ago, to another part of the grounds. Many old Chautauquans still cling to it in spite of its rustic character and insufficient accommodations.

The Sunday school on Aug. 6 reported a grand total of 1,549; and Sunday, Aug. 13, of 1,403.

The farewell meeting was held on Tuesday, Aug. 15, at eight o'clock. Addresses were delivered by Lewis Miller and Dr. Wythe. Prof. P. P. Bliss sang a song; and the Superintendent of Instruction, after a few remarks, announced the close of the *Third Annual Sunday-school Assembly.*

The Church Congress opened on Tuesday evening, Aug. 15, with a service of praise and prayer conducted by Prof. P. P. Bliss, and a sermon by Rev Dr C. N. Sims on "The Vicarious Sacrifice of Christ." On Wednesday morning an address was delivered by the Superintendent of Instruction, on "The Place for the Book." A conference on "The Laity and Church Activities" was held at 2 P.M.; and at 3 P.M. Dr. T. De Witt Talmage of Brooklyn gave a lecture on "People we meet." Dr. Sims lectured in the evening, on "Church Leadership." On Thursday morning, Aug. 17, a conference of church-workers was held by Rev. Dr. D P. Kidder, on "The Pastor's Work" Bishop R. S. Foster spoke at eleven o'clock on "The Elements of Power in Church and Pulpit." At the close of the Bishop's address, Dr Talmage gave a brief address on "How to Start Preaching." At 2 P.M. Dr Payne lectured on "How to secure a Revival." At 4 P.M. Rev George A. Hall delivered an address on the Young Men's Christian Association. He was followed with remarks by Mr. Cree and Dr Presbrey. At 7 P M. the Assembly Chapel, built for the use of the residents upon the grounds, was dedicated with appropriate services, Bishop Foster preaching in the evening from Isa. ix. 6.

On Friday morning at eight o'clock Prof. W. C. Wilkinson delivered a lecture on "Maxims for Pulpit and Pew." A discussion followed, participated in by Bishop Foster, T P Warner, Dr. O. F. Presbrey, and others. The doxology was sung, and Bishop Foster pronounced the benediction.

The Chautauqua Song of 1876, "Arise and Shine," beginning, "Lift up, lift up thy voice with singing," was written by Miss Mary A. Lathbury, and the music by P P. Bliss.

1877.

During this year the name "Fair Point" was transformed to "Chautauqua." There were two or three reasons for this change. Many letters addressed to "Fair Point" went to "Fairport," another post-office in

New-York State. The Managers of the Assembly thought it but just that the movement which had done so much towards giving Chautauqua Lake and the word "Chautauqua" a world-wide reputation should have the honor and advantage of the name itself. The use of the word in the advertising of other centres on the lake made it a business necessity that the Assembly should retain and emphasize what was practically its legitimate trade-mark. Application was therefore made to the United-States authorities to call our place simply "Chautauqua." The request was promptly granted ; and since that time the site of the Assembly has been called, and will for all time be called, "Chautauqua."

The meetings for 1877 covered twenty days, — Aug. 4-23 The programme was distributed into seven departments : 1. The *Council of Reform*, discussing in lectures and conferences the work of the Societies for the Suppression of Vice, Prevention of Cruelty to Animals, Prevention of Cruelty to Children, Prison Reform, and Temperance. 2. The *Church Congress*, discussing in lectures, sermons, and conferences the work of the preacher, the pastor, the laity, the Y. M. C. A., etc. 3. *Biblical*, providing daily lessons in the Greek Testament by Dr. James Strong and in Hebrew by Dr. S. M Vail ; conferences, class-drills, Bible-readings, lectures, and other biblical studies formed a large part of the programme for this season. 4. *Sabbath school Work*, including catechetical drills, conversations, lectures, children's meetings, with conferences on home and primary class-work. 5. *Normal Work*, which in 1877 was of the most thorough character. Every subject of study was opened in a preparatory treatment by the Superintendent of Instruction; after that came the catechetical drills in the section-tents, under wise instructors; followed by the third stage, which was that of review, in which all the sections were united and the knowledge of the students tested by questions upon the portion of the course pursued. After this each instructor stated before all the classes and his fellow-teachers his own methods of teaching, and then profited by the written criticisms of the normal members themselves. The fourth step was that of the final review, where the whole work was again examined, the student's attainments measured, and he thus prepared for the final examination Normal conductors' meetings were also held 6. *Scientific*, with lectures and scientific *conversazioni*. 7. *Recreative*, including all the entertainments of the Chautauqua programme desired to prove restful and inspiring.

Among the distinguished lecturers of the season were the following : Mr. Anthony Comstock of New York, who lectured on the "Society for the Prevention of Vice," Dr. J. P. Newman of Washington, D.C., on "The Peculiar Christian Reformatory Forces," and on "The Far East;"

Francis Murphy, on "Temperance," Frank Beard, "Crayon Sketches
illustrating Reform;" Rev Dr W W Ramsey, "The Church and Tem-
perance;" Rev Dr H. W. Warren, "The Forces in a Sunbeam;" John
B Gough, on "Eloquence and Orators;" Rev W. F. Crafts, on "Relish
for Bible-reading," "Methods of Bible Study," "Use of your Bible;"
Rev Joseph Cook, on "Certainties in Religion," "God in Natural Law,"
"New-England Scepticism," "The Decline of Rationalism in the German
Universities," Rev. J. S Ostrander, "Oriental Illustrations," Bishop
J T Peck, "Science and the Spirit World," James L. Hughes, Esq., of
Toronto, Ont, "True Object Teaching," Dr. George P. Hays, "Plain
Answers to Flippant Questions," Prof R N Greene, of Ontario, deaf-
mute, in a pantomimic lecture, Dr. Ira G Bidwell, "The Conflict of
Ages," Dr. J. M Buckley, "Studies in Human Nature," and "Imitation
and Emulation;" Dr. P S Henson, "Fools," Rev. Dr C E Felton,
"Palestine as seen through the Eyes of the Bible," A O. Van Lennep,
"Bible Orientalisms," Mrs G. R. Alden ("Pansy"), on "What not to
do," also "Three Sunday Schools," Philip Phillips, "Sunday-school
Music," Dr R Ogden Doremus, "The Spirits of the Air," "The Spirit
of Spirits," also "Divers Spirits," Frank Beard, "People who come
and Some who do not come to Chautauqua;" Dr. Lyman Abbott, "Why
I teach in the Sunday School," Dr C. F Deems, "The Bible and Modern
Science;" Dr E F Buir, "Telescopes and the Wonders they tell;"
Prof S A Lattimore, "The Microscope and its Uses," also "Electricity;"
Prof B P Bowne, "The Foundations: a Philosophical Lecture," also
"The Postulates of Scientific Knowledge;" Dr W W. Wythe, "Na-
ture's Mechanics," Professor Lacroix, "The Literature of Science," Dr
A T Pierson, "Scientific Thinking."

In the normal work, the Superintendent of Instruction was assisted by
Mrs Emily Huntington Miller, of Evanston, Ill, who gave a number of
delightful papers on "The Relations of Home to Sunday-school Work;"
and by Rev. W. F. Crafts and wife In addition to the normal assistants
of other years, Rev B T Vincent, Rev Charles Rhoades, Rev A D.
Morton, Rev. J. B Atchison, and James Hughes gave valuable help

The "Chautauqua Salute" was introduced for the first time on the
occasion of the charming pantomimic lecture delivered at the old auditorium The waving of white handkerchiefs by the people, in expression
to the deaf man of the high appreciation of his silent lecture, was remarkable, brilliant, and effective. The "Chautauqua Salute" (the "blooming
of the white lilies ") has been given since then on special occasions, and,
by an unwritten law of the Assembly, only at the suggestion and under
the direction of the Superintendent of Instruction.

The children's meeting every morning, under the direction of Rev B. T. Vincent and Frank Beard, was this season fully established, and the " Minutes of the Children's Hour" published by the papyrograph process It was edited by both Mr Vincent and Mr. Beard.

Two competitive examinations were held in August, — one Tuesday, Aug 14, to accommodate persons who were not able to remain until the close of the Assembly; the other on the morning of Tuesday, Aug 21. Fifty persons presented themselves as candidates for the first examination, and about three hundred for the second.

There were twenty-five members of the class in Hebrew during the season of 1877 Ten lectures were given on the Palestine Park A daily microscopical exhibition was given by Professor Lattimore and his cultivated and amiable daughters Miss Rose and Miss Lida.

"The Assembly Daily Herald" continued to give reports of every day's proceedings The speaker's stand had been raised and enlarged, and moved forward some twenty feet. The calcium lights were placed this year upon raised platforms, which greatly increased their effectiveness. The pavilion was removed from the stumpy centre on the hill to the natural amphitheatre south of the dining-hall and west of the great tent (where the amphitheatre now stands). The bells were this year moved from the dock to the hill between the Chapel and the Pavilion.

The music was under the direction of Prof. W. F. Sherwin and Philip Phillips The "Apollo Club" (boy choir), of New York, gave several concerts The alumni banquet annual meeting was held on Thursday evening, Aug 16 On Friday evening, Aug 10, was held a memorial service in memory of the "dead of Chautauqua," — Bishop E. S. Janes, Dr. T M Eddy, Dr G B Jocelyn, and P P Bliss and wife The service was very impressive. A song composed by Miss Lathbury beginning "O where is the shrine of the singer?" with music by Prof. W F Sherwin, was sung on this occasion

The season of 1877 gave us several new Chautauqua songs, words by Miss Mary A Lathbury, and music by Prof. W. F. Sherwin, as follows : "When the day is high and clear," the *Morning song of praise*, beginning, "Incense from dews of the morning," *Evening song of praise*, beginning, "Day is dying in the west," *Alumni song*, beginning, "Join, O friends, in a memory song;" *Study song*, beginning, "Break Thou the bread of life."

1878

The Chautauqua meetings for 1878 opened on Saturday, Aug 3, and closed on Thursday, Aug 22 The principal events of this year at Chautauqua were the dedication of the children's temple, and the organization of the "Chautauqua Literary and Scientific Circle." The children's temple was dedicated on the opening day, with addresses by Dr. W. E. Knox, Bishop R. S. Foster, Lewis Miller, Esq., Rev. Dr. Cooper, Rev. B. T. Vincent, and Prof. W. F. Sherwin.

The "C. L. S. C." was organized on Saturday, Aug. 10, at 10.30 A.M. For a full account of this opening, see pp. 79–112.

On Saturday afternoon, Aug. 17, at four o'clock, St. Paul's Grove was dedicated. The Superintendent of Instruction gave an address explaining the design of the management in providing a grove for the "C. L. S. C." He was followed by Gov. Colquitt. Bishop Foster delivered the dedicatory prayer, and a dedicatory hymn written by Dr. Hyde was sung by Professor Sherwin and his choir.

This was "the year of the telescopes" at Chautauqua. One instrument was generously loaned by Mount Union College, and superintended by Professor Clark of that institution. A smaller instrument was used by Mr. White of Castile, N.Y. The Department of Microscopy was also held under the direction of the Misses Lattimore.

The following were the principal speakers of 1878: Hon. Horace Bemis, on "Temperance;" Dr. R. M. Hatfield, Prof. William Mason Evans; Dr. J. M. Reid, on "Missionary Work," Rev. R. B. Hull, on "The Minister in the Pulpit," Rev. R. G. Seymour, "A Week of Work in my Church;" Bishop R. S. Foster, on "The Minister in his Study," and "Beyond the Grave;" Rev. Dr. Alfred Wheeler, "Religion and Politics;" Dr. C. H. Fowler, "The Bible the Prophet of Science;" Rev. J. S. Ostrander, "Bible Manners and Customs illustrated;" Dr. Ira G. Bidwell, "Studies among the Shadows and Sources of English Literature;" Frank Beard, "A Chalk Talk," "The Telephone, Phonograph, and Some Other Things;" Dr. J. F. Hurst, "How England became a Protestant Nation," Dr. John Lord, "Queen Elizabeth," "Cromwell," "Burke;" Rev. Joseph Cook, "Lost Souls under Natural Law," "Saved Souls under Natural Law," Rev. J. G. Townsend, "John Milton," Rev. Alfred Taylor, "Oddest People;" Dr. H. W. Warren, "The Heavens Visible at Chautauqua," "The Significance of the Universe," Rev. C. W. Cushing, "The World without the Bible," Professor William North Rice, "The Conflict of Science and Religion;" Dr. L. H. Bugbee, "The Intuitive in Christianity;" Dr. T. DeWitt Talmage, "Big Blunders;" Dr. C. F. Deems, "The Superstitions of Science."

There were four Reform Councils; four Church Colloquies; four "C. L. S. C." Students' Sessions (devoted to English history); six lectures on English history, four "C. L. S. C." astronomical lessons conducted by Dr. H. W. Warren, on "Measurements of Celestial Movements," "The Sun," "Our Neighbors the Planets," and "The Universe Beyond."

On Tuesday, Aug 6, the interesting meeting reported on pp. 26, 27, was held in the Temple, when Baptist, Congregational, Methodist-Episcopal, and Presbyterian brethren reported the distinctive organization, doctrine, and customs of their respective churches Prof. B. P. Bowne conducted scientific *conversazioni* on the "Relation of Ethics to Atheism, or, Is there Morality without God?" "Relation of the Doctrine of Efficient Causes to Belief in Purpose;" "Present Aspects of Materialism." Miss Rosa Lattimore conducted a scientific *conversazione* on "An Hour with the Microscope," Dr. Strong, another hour on "How to promote the Popular Study of Science" There were this year several superior concerts under the direction of Prof. C. C Case and Prof W. F. Sherwin, assisted by Miss Belle McClintock of Meadville, Penn.; elocutionary readings by Professor Lowell Mason; lectures on the Park of Palestine and the Model of Jerusalem; platform-meetings especially devoted to Sunday-school work; vesper services, even-songs, Sunday-school sessions; sermons by Dr. W. E. Knox, Dr. R. M. Hatfield, Dr. A. N. Craft, and Dr. Ira G. Bidwell, a question-drawer lecture by Rev. Joseph Cook, the pilgrimage of the children through Palestine, under the direction of Mr. McGerald; the alumni re-union and annual illuminated fleet; and entertainments in magic by Professor Coville.

One of the most important events of the season was the visit of a distinguished guest,— Gov A H Colquitt of Georgia, President of the International Sunday-school Convention. There was a public reception given him on Thursday, Aug. 15.

On Thursday, Aug. 22, the closing day, there was a brilliant Chautauqua Procession, a custom observed for several years.

Our excellent Dr. W W Wythe was absent this year for the first time since the organization of Chautauqua

In the Normal Department there was a special examination on the morning of Aug 14, when twenty persons presented themselves as candidates The regular examination took place on Wednesday, Aug 21, more than one hundred and forty persons passing the examination, and becoming members of the Chautauqua Normal Alumni Association

1879.

1879 was an eventful year at Chautauqua. It was the first year of the Chautauqua Normal School of Languages, which opened July 17, and closed Aug. 28, the Chautauqua Teachers' Retreat, holding from July 17 to Aug 1; the Chautauqua Foreign Missionary Institute, from Aug. 2 to Aug 5; the Sixth Annual Sunday-school Assembly, from Aug 5 to Aug 21

This year the great Amphitheatre, and also the Hall of Philosophy, were dedicated In every respect the programme was richer and stronger than ever before It is impossible from this time forward to give a complete list of the lecturers and their lectures during the entire Chautauqua season, and a full programme of Chautauqua meetings would itself require a large volume

Among our distinguished lecturers were Bishop Harris, Bishop Simpson, Rev W O Simpson of England, Dr. R L Dashiell, Dr. N. G. Clark, Dr. H. W Warren, Rev. Dr. Peddie, Dr J M Buckley, Frank Beard, Dr Daniel Curry, Prof J W. Churchill, Dr James Strong, Dr. C H Fowler, Joseph Cook, Bishop Foster, Dr John Lord, Dr. J. P Newman, Hon J. W Wendling, Dr C H. Payne, Dr. J. T. Cooper, Prof B. P. Bowne, Dr Archibald Alexander Hodge, Dr George Dana Boardman, Dr G D. B. Pepper, Dr E O Haven

The Chautauqua Normal Scheme embraced lessons on the Text-Book, its contents, its study, the school of the Book, the teachers of the Book, and special studies in the Book, together with afternoon lessons in Bible geography The music was under the direction of Prof. C. C Case and Prof W F. Sherwin Round-tables were held in the Hall of Philosophy, for conversation on the work of the C. L S. C., for criticisms, and for students' sessions. The anniversary of the C L S C and of the dedication of St Paul's Grove, and the usual alumni re-union, were held. Denominational congresses were held on Wednesday and Thursday, Aug. 13 and 14. The following denominations were represented: Baptist, Congregational, Lutheran, Methodist-Episcopal, Presbyterian, Protestant-Episcopal, United Presbyterian.

A the philosophical and theological lectures, at eight o'clock every morning, ministers of the following denominations were present Baptist, Free-Will Baptist, Congregational, Methodist-Episcopal, Presbyterian, Protestant-Episcopal, Disciple, Evangelical Association, United Presbyterian, Friends, Wesleyan Methodist, Methodist-Episcopal South, United Brethren, Methodist Protestant, Christian, Reformed

About one hundred persons entered the competitive examinations of the children's class, about twenty-five the intermediate, and about one hundred and seventy-five the regular normal

The Misses Lattimore conducted classes in microscopy; and Mrs E. Seymour of New York, the Primary Department Miss Parloa gave lessons in cookery.

1880.

Fifty acres were this year added to the grounds of Chautauqua, making in all between one hundred and thirty and one hundred and forty acres. The new hotel was projected and begun. Devotional conferences were made a part of the regular programme, and Rev W W Ramsay appointed to take charge. Madame Kraus-Boelte, assisted by her husband, conducted the kindergarten work. An experiment was made in tonic sol-fa, under the direction of Professor Seward. A course of brilliant lectures in English literature was delivered by Prof J. II. Gilmore of Rochester University Ram Chandra Bose of India gave several scientific and popular lectures. The Fisk Jubilees visited Chautauqua for the first time, and they, with the North-western Band, and the great chorus led by Professors Sherwin and Case, made the musical attractions of 1880 superior to those of any previous year.

Mrs. G R Alden ("Pansy") took charge of the primary work, Prof. E. A. Spring, of clay-modelling A series of philosophical lectures were delivered by Prof. B P Bowne, and of scientific lectures by W. W. Keen of Philadelphia. The National Woman's Christian Temperance Union held its sixth anniversary at Chautauqua in August The National Education Association met there between July 13 and 16 The Christian Commission Re-union was also held. Aug 1 was observed as Y M C. A. Day.

Gen Garfield, then candidate for President of the United States, spent a sabbath with us. The Hon. Schuyler Colfax during the session delivered his famous lecture on "Abraham Lincoln." The camp-fire of the C. L. S C was inaugurated on Tuesday evening, Aug 17. Aug 19 was observed as Processional Day The Missionary Institute was the best that had ever been held at Chautauqua; and all were delighted with the presence of our old friend Dr H W. Warren, who had in May of this year been made Bishop by the General Conference of his Church.

Among our new lecturers were. Dr S J. Wilson of Alleghany City, Penn, Dr J O Means of the A B C F M, Dr L D McCabe of Delaware, O , Dr. Sheldon Jackson, Professor Holman of Philadelphia, Dr R. R. Meredith of Boston, Prof. Stuckenberg of Springfield, O., Dr W W. Patton of Washington, Dr C. L Goodell of St Louis, Mo Miss M F. Boice of Philadelphia gave a very successful course of lessons in elocution Thursday night, Aug 19, the "Arkites" made their night-march, — a unique and laughable feature of the closing days of the season.

In the Normal Department, including the Intermediate and children, there were nearly two hundred and fifty graduates

1881.

Chautauqua in 1881 began Thursday, July 7, and closed Monday, Aug. 22 The Department of Phonography, under the direction of Prof W D. Bridge, was inaugurated this year Calisthenics were taught Among the special attractions were the old-fashioned singing-school, the old-fashioned debating-society, and the usual spelling-matches The Fisk Jubilee Singers again assisted Professors Sherwin and Case in the musical entertainments. Signor Giuseppe Vitale, the brilliant and promising young violinist, spent several weeks at Chautauqua The Christian Commission held its re-union The Chautauqua School of Theology was established. The Hotel Athenæum was finished The new museum, Newton Hall, built through the munificence of Jacob Miller, Esq, of Canton, O, was opened The Chautauqua Extension of the Buffalo, New York, and Philadelphia Railway opened Chautauqua for the first time by railway communication to the outside world Signor Alessandro Gavazzi was our distinguished foreign guest Prof S S Curry of Boston University gave daily lessons in voice-culture; Prof. W. D. McClintock of Kentucky, in Anglo-Saxon and Shakespearian literature; Nathan Sheppard, a course of lectures on Carlyle, George Eliot, Thackeray, Darwin, Dickens, Bulwer, Heine, Macaulay, Scott and Macdonald, Ruskin. The Teachers' Retreat was especially valuable. Dr. J W Dickinson of Boston gave talks on "Object Teaching," Prof S F Frost of Massachusetts lectured on "Geography outside of the Text-Books," Prof. C. F. Richardson, on "Intellectual Economy," and "The Native Element of American Literature," C. E. Bishop, Esq, read an able paper on the "Home School," and Mr Daniel H Post of Jamestown, on "What our Pupils read." An interesting discussion took place during the Retreat, on the question, "Are the schools of to-day, with their superior facilities, relatively more effective than the schools of forty years ago"?

Among the new lecturers at the Assembly for that season were Rev. Dr. D. A Goodsell of New Haven, Conn ; Prof J L Corning; Dr William Hayes Ward, editor of the New-York "Independent;" Rev. A. H. Lewis of Plainfield, N J , Rev A. E Dunning of Boston, Dr Edward Everett Hale; Dr Philip Schaff, Dr J W Hamilton of Boston, Dr. W H Withrow of Canada, Gen O O Howard of West Point; Dr. A. A Willits, and Rev. H H Moore of Erie Conference.

An impressive memorial service was held on sabbath, Aug 7; Rev. J. H Knowles speaking on Dr. S M Vail, Rev C P Hard on Bishop E. O. Haven, Rev James Hamilton on Dr W H Perrine, Rev. J L. Hurlbut on Rev W O Simpson of England

The Sunday-school Normal Department course included three lectures by the Superintendent of Instruction; six conferences; twelve Bible-drills in the children's class, under the direction of Rev. B. T. Vincent; twelve intermediate-class drills by Mr. Vincent; twelve Bible-drills and twelve normal drills conducted by Rev. J. L. Hurlbut. Lewis Miller's normal class from Akron, O., passed the examination. The "Chautauqua Young Folks' Reading Union" was formally inaugurated on Thursday, Aug. 18. In the Normal Department on Wednesday, Aug. 17, 120 children, 53 intermediate, and 115 normals entered. There was also a special primary examination.

1882.

1882 was the first graduating year in the C. L. S. C. A full account of this imposing service is given on pp. 113-126. Among the distinguishing features of this year were the lectures of Prof. W. T. Harris, Concord, Mass.; Prof. William H. Niles of Boston; Wallace Bruce, Esq.; T. De Witt Talmage; Dr. Isaac Erret; Dr. Wilkinson; Dr. Alexander Sutherland of Canada; Dr. William M. Blackburn of Cincinnati; Dr. Mark Hopkins; Rev. H. H. Moore, on "The Elements of Vital Philosophy;" Anthony Comstock; John B. Gough; Dr. B. M. Adams of Brooklyn; Chaplain C. C. McCabe; Dr. Lyman Abbott; Dr. A. D. Vail, who gave us the "Story of Our C. L. S. C. Banner;" Bishop H. W. Warren; Dr. Philip Schaff; Bishop R. S. Foster; Dr. L. T. Townsend; Dr. J. M. Buckley, etc. Readings were given by A. P. Burbank, Esq., and Prof. J. W. Churchill. The visit of "The Royal Hand Bell-Ringers and Gleemen" of London, Eng., was one of the most brilliant attractions of the season. The great organ in the Amphitheatre was formally dedicated on Saturday, July 8, and several admirable organ-concerts were given by Professor George H. Ryder. The musical department for 1882 was especially rich. In addition to "The Royal Hand Bell-Ringers and Gleemen" of London, the following names were announced: Prof. W. F. Sherwin, Prof. C. C. Case, Prof. N. Coe Stewart, Prof. E. L. Ayres, Signor Vitale, the Misses Lynnie and Minnie Becher (violinists), Miss Belle McClintock, Mrs. C. T. Westlake, Mrs. O. A. Baldwin, Miss Ethel Crippen, Mr. Leon H. Vincent, and Miss Fannie A. Compton. The "night vigil" was held for the class of 1883. Rev. B. M. Adams began that series of devotional conferences which has so intimately associated his name with Chautauqua.

A pleasant telegram was this year received from J. E. Mosely of Madison, Wis., as follows: "Monona Lake Assembly to Chautauqua, the mother Assembly in the leafy temple under Eastern skies: This, the youngest of the goodly sisterhood of daughters, between the Wisconsin lakes, sends its greetings, with a hope that we may join hands across the States in the great work of building up the cause of our common Master, Jesus Christ." To this message, the following reply was sent: "Chautauqua accepts Monona's greetings with gratitude and joy. May both institutions promote science, faith, and philanthropy, in the guidance of the gospel of Jesus Christ"

The anniversary of the C. L. S. C was held on Saturday afternoon, Aug 5. Dr Goodell of St. Louis, Dr. Leonard of Cincinnati, Bishop Simpson of Philadelphia, and Dr Mark Hopkins of Massachusetts, delivered the addresses. The Sunday school for Aug. 7 enrolled 3,127 members, and that for Aug. 14 three thousand "Recognition Day" was observed on Saturday, Aug. 12. The "Chautauqua Society of Christian Ethics" was instituted this year. The normal examinations were passed, including the children's, intermediate, primary teachers', and regular normal department, by three hundred and twenty-two persons.

1883.

The distinguishing features of 1883 were, the first "Ideal Foreign Tour through Europe," with lectures by C. E. Bolton, Esq., and "Tourists' Conferences" conducted by Mrs S K Bolton; the "Day Fireworks," under the direction of Professor Hand of Hamilton, Ont.; readings by Prof. R. L. Cumnock of Evanston, Ill.; classes in cookery, by Mrs. Emma P. Ewing of Chicago. A course of lectures was given by Professor Charles J. Little. Lectures were delivered by Dr. Julius King of Cleveland, Hon. A. W. Tourgée, Hon. Will Cumback, Prof. W. C. Richards (a brilliant series in physical science), B. F. Jacobs, Esq., of Chicago, Edward L. Wilson, Esq., of Philadelphia, Dr Everett of Harrisburg, Dr J. B Angell, Dr W. F. Mallalieu, Dr. Joseph Cummings, Rev. George H. Vibbert, Dr. P. S. Henson, Dr. Arthur Mitchell, Dr. Alexander Martin, Dr. A. G. Haygood, Dr. R. B Hull, Prof. A A. Wright, Dr. Julius H Seelye, Dr J S Jewell, Dr. Alfred Wheeler, Professor Charles A. Young of Princeton College. Profs. E S. Shumway and W R. Harper were introduced to the Chautauqua schools of language as teachers. Rev H. H. Moore lectured on "The Nihilistic Philosophy."

The annual address on "Recognition Day" was delivered by Dr Lyman Abbott of New York. Important additions were made to the Museum, among which was a magnificent cast of one of the two great panels of the Arch of Titus at Rome, containing a relief of the seven-branched golden candlestick taken from the temple by Titus at the capture of Jerusalem This was one of the purchases made for the Museum by the gift of $1,000 from Capt. J. J. Vandergrift of Pittsburgh

Several brilliant concerts were given by Professors Sherwin and Case. The "Spanish Students" gave a concert on Wednesday, Aug 1. Miss E. M. Reed taught a session of the summer school on the "Quincy" method A very interesting series of women's devotional conferences was held by Miss Fannie A. Dyer, and a series of temperance conferences by Mrs. T. B. Hoover. Memorial services were held on Tuesday, Aug 14, in honor of Rev. E J. L. Baker, one of the trustees of the Assembly; Rev L. H. Bugbee, D D, the first member of the C. L. S. C., Amos K. Warren, Esq, for years the Superintendent of Grounds. The loss of Mr Warren was a serious one to the Assembly. He was a man of remarkable executive ability and enterprise Saturday, Aug 18, was "Recognition Day" this year Mrs B. T. Vincent had charge of the primary teachers' normal department this season About two hundred and fifty persons passed in the examinations in the various departments of the Sunday-school normal work.

1884.

"The Youth's C. L. S C" paper for boys and girls was established by Dr Flood, this season, at Chautauqua It is an illustrated paper, of which twelve numbers were published "The Chautauqua Foreign Tour" this year was through England, Ireland, and Scotland, with lectures by Rev. Jesse Bowman Young, Prof H. H. Ragan, and Mr George Makepeace Towle The opening address on Saturday, July 12, before the C. T R and C. S L, was delivered by the Rev H L Hubbell, D D, of Jamestown. Music was furnished this season under the direction of Professors Sherwin and Case, with Mr. T. P. Ryder of Boston as organist, the Meigs-Underhill Combination; Donavin's famous Tennesseeans, Mrs Juvia C Hull of New York, soprano; the Yale-college Glee-club; Miss Belle McClintock; Mr. Excell and Miss Tuthill of Chicago; Miss Julia Ball of Buffalo, solo pianist, and Mr Walton N. Ellis of Brooklyn, tenor. A course of brilliant lectures on English literature, by Professor Charles J Little, was given, lectures also by Dr Henson, Miss Susan Hayes Ward, T. DeWitt Talmage, Dr R. M. Stratton, Rev. J W. Butler of Mexico, Rev. S G Smith, D D, Ram Chandra Bose of India, Rev. Dennis Osborne of India, Bishop Samuel Fallows of Chicago, Dr. William Butler, Sau Aubrah of Burmah, Rev A J. Palmer. A course of superior lectures in philosophy was given by Principal A. M. Fairbairn of England; lessons in microscopy, by W. C J. Hall, Esq, of Jamestown; lectures by Miss Frances E Willard, Mrs. M. H Hunt, Mrs. Mary T. Lathrop, Dr Herrick Johnson, Gen. J C Black, Dr O P Fitzgerald of Nashville, Dr. Daniel Curry, Dr John B Finch, Hon. George W Bain, President Julius Seelye On Saturday, Aug 23, a reception was tendered to Robert E Pattison, Governor of Pennsylvania. A memorial service was held on Sunday, Aug 10, in honor of A. O Van Lennep, Dr W. E. Knox, Dr A J Baird, and Bishop Simpson. C. L S C. Recognition Day was held on Tuesday, Aug 19 The annual oration was delivered by Dr. W. Cleaver Wilkinson Dr John Williamson conducted a series of interesting Bible-readings during the Assembly. Advanced normal examinations were conducted by Rev. Frank Russell Friday, Aug 15, was observed as decennial anniversary day of the National Woman's Christian Temperance Union. A class of young people was taught by Mrs. A. M Rice, called "The Temperance Classmates" The Rev II H. Moore conducted the "Socratic Academy."

1885.

The twelfth year of the Chautauqua Assembly opened a "Preliminary Week," July 7; beginning the regular programme of the C. T R and C. S L July 11, and closing with an "After-week," Friday, Aug 28, making the longest season since the founding of Chautauqua The records of this most recent year are so accessible that it will be hardly necessary here to reproduce more than the salient features of the programme. The studies of the "Foreign Tour" embraced Italy, Roman history, and Latin literature A series of organ-recitals by Prof. I V. Flagler attracted much attention Memorial services were held on Sunday, Aug. 9, in honor of Bishop I. W Wiley, Mrs. Victor Cournelle, Rev. Joseph Leslie, Hon Schuyler Colfax, and Gen U S. Grant The Sunday-school Normal Alumni Re-union was addressed by Rev Dr J. M. Freeman of New York The representatives of the Baptist Church held a series of special services, including a conference, a tea-meeting and sociable, and the anniversary of "The Chautauqua Baptist Reading-Circle" The baccalaureate sermon before the graduating class of the C. L S C was delivered by Dr Charles F. Deems "Recognition Day" was Wednesday, Aug 19, and the annual address was delivered by the Rev. Dr. E E. Hale of Boston A special series of "Yale University Historical Lectures" was delivered by Professor Arthur M Wheeler of Yale College The "First Rally of the Chautauqua Town and Country Club' took place on Saturday, Aug 22, with an address by Mr Charles Barnard of New York. The first meeting of the "Chautauqua Society of Fine Arts " was also held at this time. Bishop Cyrus D. Foss made his first appearance at Chautauqua, preaching on Sunday, Aug. 23. Dr. J. P. Newman delivered a lecture on Tuesday, Aug. 25, in memory of Gen U. S. Grant. The season of 1885 was closed at noon of Friday, Aug. 28.

II

OTHER ASSEMBLIES.

There are limitations upon author and publishers, and it becomes necessary to present in the most condensed way possible the reports which we hoped to be able to give in full, from the various Chautauqua centres through the country.

ACTON PARK ASSEMBLY.

"Acton Park Assembly," Indiana, on the Cincinnati, Indianapolis, St. Louis, and Chicago Railroad, twelve miles south-east of Indianapolis. Five years ago a course of literary lectures was established at the Acton Camp-ground. The name was changed from "Acton Camp-ground" to "Acton Park Assembly." Mr. James C. Pulse proposed a Chautauqua Day at Acton Park in 1885. The audience was large and enthusiastic. James C. Pulse of Greensburgh was elected president; Miss Ruby Sexton of Rushville, Ind., secretary. The officers of the Acton Park Assembly are Hon. Will Cumback, *chairman;* W. H. R. Reed, *super-intendent,* — both of Greensburgh, Ind.

ARKANSAS CHAUTAUQUA ASSEMBLY.

"The Arkansas Chautauqua Assembly," proposed at a public meeting of the citizens of Siloam Springs, Ark., by E. V. Dolgoruki, Esq., Jan. 31, 1885, has been chartered by the State. An amphitheatre a hundred by a hundred and twenty feet was built in the summer of 1885. The Arkansas Chautauqua Assembly opened its first session June 13, 1885. The programme was varied, practical, interesting. Siloam Springs has two thousand inhabitants, and is situated in the south-west corner of Benton County, Arkansas, a mile and a half from the Indian Territory. The Assembly for 1886 begins July 12. Officers: C. W. Hinds, *president;* E. V. Dolgoruki, *superintendent.*

BAY VIEW ASSEMBLY.

Bay View Assembly, near Petoskey, Mich., at the terminus of the Grand Rapids and Indiana Railway. Six hundred and fifty acres of land overlook a beautiful bay upon Lake Michigan, near the northern extremity of the lower peninsula of Michigan   The grounds are under the control of the Michigan Camp-ground Association   The first annual meeting was held Aug. 1, 1876   The location is one of rare beauty and healthfulness, the climate equable, and the pure, cool, northern lake-breezes are invigorating.   Especial facilities are furnished by the railway and steamboat companies   Nearly one hundred and fifty cottages have already been erected   There are a large hotel, an auditorium with seating capacity of twenty-five hundred, a chapel, restaurant, good dock, offices, and an excellent system of water-works supplied by inexhaustible fountains from a high point near the centre of the grounds.   There are annually held at Bay View, Sunday-school Normal Meetings, sessions of the Michigan Ministerial Association; and in the season of 1885 an educational department was organized.   The aim is to make Bay View, Mich, "a Michigan Chautauqua"   A C L S C Recognition Day, Round-table Conferences, etc , will be held   The Assembly is thoroughly catholic in spirit, and all denominations have a hearty welcome.   Watson Snyder of Ypsilanti, Mich , is *president;* Rev. S Reed of Flint *secretary;* David Preston, Detroit, *treasurer*   John M Hall has charge of the "C L S C." work; Rev. Washington Gardner, of the Normal Sunday-school Department, and President Lewis R. Fiske, D D , of Albion College, of the Ministerial Union.

CANBY, OREGON

Canby, Or., a camp-ground, on the Molalla River, midway between Portland and Salem, Or., forty acres.   Ten or twelve years ago the grounds were laid out in blocks and lots, with streets and broad avenues A tabernacle a hundred by a hundred and fifty feet was built   Rev. W. T. Chapman, having attended the annual assemblies at Chautauqua in 1875 and 1876, returned to Oregon an alumnus of the Chautauqua Sunday-school Normal Department   Arrangements have been made to hold a Chautauqua Assembly the third week of June each year, in the interest of the " C. L S C " and of normal Sunday-school work. Information concerning Canby may be received from Rev. W. T. Chapman, Hubbard, Or.

CAZENOVIA.

The Cazenovia Assembly was held for a few years on Lakeview Camp-ground, Cazenovia Lake, N Y   The meetings were quite successful for several years, under the direction of Professor Smythe, W A. Duncan, Esq., Rev. J. S Ostrander, and others. Later on the grounds were sold, and the Assembly abandoned.

CLEAR LAKE, IOWA.

Clear Lake, Io, Assembly was organized in 1876. It is nearly midway between the Mississippi and Missouri Rivers, on Clear Lake, in Northern Iowa, a beautiful sheet of water. The first session was held the centennial year, Rev. J. R Berry *superintendent.* Sessions of 1879 and 1880, superintendent Rev. J. A. Worden. The "C L. S. C." is recognized at Clear Lake. There are annually at Clear Lake a camp-meeting, a Sunday-school assembly, a musical festival, and a temperance jubilee Officers: Truman Woodford, Milwaukee, Wis, *president;* Rev. H W. Bennett, Bloomington, Ill, *secretary.*

ENCHANTED ISLAND, LAKE MINNETONKA.

Lake Minnetonka is fifteen miles west of Minneapolis, Minn, and is "the Saratoga of the West." A joint Chautauqua committee, representing the Circles of St Paul and Minneapolis, was formed in May, 1885; and on Friday, June 26, 1885, an assembly was held at Enchanted Island. About three hundred Chautauquans and friends were present, principally from St. Paul and Minneapolis, though Anoka and Duluth Circles were officially represented, and visitors were present from St. Louis, Mo, and other points. After a pleasant excursion on the lake, and a lunch, a public meeting was held; William H. Eustis of Minneapolis presiding. The question of permanent organization was discussed by a number of distinguished gentlemen. A permanent organizing committee was formed, with power to add to their number, to prepare and adopt a constitution, to elect officers for the coming year, to appoint an executive committee with power to arrange for meetings during the year. Reports were received from a large number of circles. The evening session was held around a camp-fire and on the deck of the boat. There were toasts and songs The permanent committee met in July, and elected James Surdam, Esq, of St Paul, *chairman,* and E. G Brandebury of Minneapolis, *secretary* and *treasurer* It was under the auspices of this committee that the "Recognition Service" was held at Mahtomedi, White Bear Lake. (See Mahtomedi.) In Minneapolis and St. Paul, there are more than thirty circles, with a membership of over six hundred.

FLORIDA CHAUTAUQUA.

The Florida Chautauqua, located in Western Florida, on the Pensacola and Atlantic Railway, about eighty miles from Tallahassee, and about the same distance from Pensacola. It is on a high ridge of land, three hundred feet above the level of the Gulf of Mexico, which is twenty-four miles away. Two hundred and eight acres surround a beautiful lake, a mile in circumference, and sixty feet in depth, the water being clear and pure, and the beach of hard white sand. The Southern pine, oak, magnolia, and bay grow on the grounds. There is a tabernacle which will seat twenty-five hundred persons. There are also buildings for cooking-school, kindergarten, and young people's headquarters, and a large two-story building with assembly-room and class-rooms. The "Hotel Chautauqua" is a large and comfortable house. Rev. A. H. Gillet, D.D., is Superintendent of Instruction. W. C. Chipley, Esq., vice-president of the Pensacola and Atlantic Railroad, has charge of the business department. Mr. C. C. Banfill is secretary. The first session opened February, 1885, and closed March 10, 1885. The outlay for programme reached nearly ten thousand dollars. The Florida Chautauqua holds its annual session in February and March, and offers, in addition to the delightful climate of Florida, the attractions of a first-class assembly to Northern tourists and Southern residents alike.

GENESEE COUNTY ASSEMBLY.

Genesee County Assembly, on Long Lake, Genesee County, Michigan, is a recent organization for summer meetings of the "C. L. S. C." in Genesee County; Rev. William M. Ward, Goodrich, Mich., *superintendent*, and John Western, Flint, Mich., *secretary*. The first meeting was held on Tuesday, Aug. 25, 1885. Music, lectures, "C. L. S. C.," constituted the programme, which seems to have been very enjoyable. A similar but more elaborate meeting was projected for the summer of 1886.

INTER-STATE SUNDAY-SCHOOL ASSEMBLY.

The Inter-State Sunday-school Assembly, Kansas, was organized in 1878 by Rev. J. E. Gilbert, then pastor of the first Methodist-Episcopal Church, Topeka. He conducted the meetings for two years. The third year, Dr. E. W. Schauffler of Kansas City was chosen president. In 1882 the meeting was held at Hartzell Park, near Topeka, under the presidency of George M. Stearns, Rev. J. L. Hurlbut conductor. In 1883 the fifth annual meeting was held at Forest Park, adjoining the city of Ottawa, Kan., which is now the permanent location of the Assembly. Ottawa is situated on the Southern Kansas Railway, and is the terminus of a branch of the Missouri Pacific Railway. It is fifty-one miles southwest from Kansas City, Mo. It has a population of seven thousand. Forest Park is the property of the city, and lies within its limits. It contains forty acres, and lies on the banks of the Maraise des Cygnes River. Through the liberality of the city, the Park has been provided with a large and convenient tabernacle, normal-class building, and assembly-hall. The Assembly has free use of the park during the meetings, and the people of the city and adjoining country take an earnest and active interest in the welfare of the Assembly. The Sunday-school normal work is the "heart" of the Assembly. "Chautauqua was the suggestion, and has been the ideal." For five years Professor Sherwin has had charge of the music. Rev. B. T. Vincent was an instructor one year. In 1885 Prof. R. S. Holmes taught an advanced normal class. The "C. L. S. C." round-tables, camp-fires, and "Recognition-Day" service are observed at the "Inter-State Sunday-school Assembly." It is the ambition of this organization, in the language of one of its officers, "to be known and recognized as the Chautauqua of the West." The eighth annual session, from June 22 to July 2, 1886. Rev. D. C. Milner of Atchison, Kan., *president;* Rev. Dr. J. L. Hurlbut of New York, *superintendent of instruction;* D. C. Hanes, Ottawa, Kan., *secretary.*

ISLAND PARK ASSEMBLY.

Island Park Assembly, Rome City, Ind., is on the Grand Rapids and Indiana Railway, thirty-five miles north of Fort Wayne. The Assembly is located on the shores of a lovely lake. Its banks are heavily wooded, the water is clear, and numerous islands make it exceedingly picturesque. The principal buildings are on the island, twenty acres in extent. There are wide and well-kept gravel walks, flower-beds, rustic arbors, fountains, bridges, and a forest of young oak-trees. There is a large tabernacle which will seat twenty-five hundred people, a museum building, art hall, normal-class room, and a building sheltering a beautiful model of Palestine. A bridge leads to the mainland, where the kindergarten and C. L. S. C. buildings are located. The railroad passes within a few rods of the main entrance. The grounds are brilliantly illuminated by electric lights. The Assembly was organized in 1879, at the suggestion of Rev. Dr. A. H. Gillet, who is still superintendent of instruction. C. L. S. C. recognition services and round-tables have been held annually at Island Park. In fact, the first public recognition-service ever held anywhere was held here in 1882, the meeting anticipating by a few weeks the first Recognition Day at Chautauqua. Educational work is carried on in art, kindergarten, music, schools of language, etc., at Island Park. "The Assembly Record," a sixteen-page monthly paper, is the organ of the Assembly, edited by Dr. A. H. Gillet, assisted by Prof. J. L. Shearer of Cincinnati, O.

LAKE BLUFF, ILL

Lake Bluff, Ill, thirty-five miles north of Chicago, on Lake Michigan, on the Chicago and North-western Railroad. The first Assembly was held in 1877 From 1878 to 1880 the Assembly was under the supervision of Revs John Williamson, D D, and A W Patton; from 1881 to 1882, under the care of Rev. J. E Gilbert, D.D. It is the centre of a Sunday-school training college of which Dr Gilbert is president. Session in 1886 under direction of Rev T. P. Marsh

LAKESIDE ENCAMPMENT

Lakeside Encampment, Lakeside, O., on the peninsula which forms Sandusky Bay, a little west of Sandusky, O. Distant about ten miles, may be seen "Put-in-Bay" Island, immortalized by the victories of Commodore Perry; on the north, four miles away, Kelley's Island, on the north-east, the waters of Lake Erie, the shore beyond cannot be seen. The lake-breezes make it a cool summer resort The encampment contains about a hundred and seventy-five acres The grounds are reached by a delightful steamer-ride of ten miles from Sandusky, through the bay and around the eastern end of a peninsula ; or by stage from the Danbury Station of the Michigan Southern Railroad, which is six miles away. There are at Lakeside a good hotel, and boarding-houses, restaurants, stores, beautiful cottages, a chapel, a large auditorium, and other buildings Lakeside opened as an encampment in 1873, and as a Sunday-school assembly or encampment in 1877; the Rev Dr Worden conducting the first annual meeting The Rev Dr. C W. Cushing conducted the encampment the second year, the Rev. B T Vincent, in 1879 and 1880. In 1881 the programme committee, under the direction of Dr Hartupee, chairman, managed the meetings Dr J H Vincent superintended in 1882, and since then the Rev B T Vincent has had charge. Every year are held boys' and girls' meetings, primary teachers' work, and the regular normal work The Lakeside Normal Alumni Association is large, studious, and influential In addition to the annual camp-meeting, and Sunday-school encampment, a secular normal school is held each year on the grounds, under able instructors There are also conventions on reformatory work. "C. L. S. C." recognition services, round-tables, and camp-fires find place at Lakeside

LOVELAND, O

Loveland is a camp-ground thirty-five miles from Cincinnati, where an Assembly was formed in 1876, and conducted during 1877 and 1878 under the supervision of Rev. J. E. Gilbert

MAHTOMEDI ASSEMBLY

Mahtomedi, or Great Bear Lake, is a large lake about equidistant from St Paul and Stillwater, Minn. Several cottages have been erected, and also a fine tabernacle seating about three thousand people. There have been two sessions of the Assembly. During the summer of 1885 (Aug. 12) a public recognition-service of the "C L S C" was held, at which Dr. A. H Gillet presented four diplomas to graduates from St Paul

MAINE CHAUTAUQUA ASSEMBLY

The Maine Chautauqua Assembly, Fryeburg, Me, 1884. A thorough Chautauqua Assembly, supported chiefly by the beneficence of an elect lady in Portland, loyal to the "C L S C"

MAPLEWOOD PARK ASSEMBLY.

Maplewood Park Assembly is located on Clear Lake, near the town of Waseca, Minn There are about one hundred and thirty acres, containing a promontory extending into the lake, and about seventy feet above its level The place is about a thousand feet above the sea. Sunday school, normal, and "C L S C" work receive attention The first public recognition of the "C L S C" was held at the session of 1885, conducted by Dr A H Gillet, superintendent of instruction Another feature of the Maplewood Park Assembly is a Ministers' Institute, conducted in 1885 by Dr. H. B Ridgeway of Evanston.

MONONA LAKE ASSEMBLY

The first session of the Wisconsin State Sunday-school Assembly was held in 1880, on the shores of Green Lake, Wis In 1881 it was removed to the shores of Monona Lake, near Madison In 1880 Dr Hurlbut conducted the Sunday-school normal class. In 1881 Rev. Dr C H Richards was chairman of the executive committee. In 1882 Dr Gillet was elected superintendent of the normal department During this Assembly of 1881, the first C L S C camp-fire was lighted in Wisconsin. In 1883, 1884, 1885, public Recognition Days of the "C. L S C." have been observed The Monona Lake Branch of the C. L S C was organized in 1883 Dr Gillet was made president, and Mrs William Millard secretary. The next year Rev. F S Stein was made president. A C L S. C. building was erected and dedicated during the summer of 1885 With the close of the Assembly of 1885, Dr. Gillet resigned the position of *superintendent,* and Dr. J. L. Hurlbut was appointed to take his place.

MONTEAGLE ASSEMBLY.

Monteagle Assembly is at Monteagle, on the Cumberland Mountains, Tenn. A meeting of persons interested in organizing a Southern Sunday-school Assembly was held in Tullahoma, Aug 17, 1882, at eight P.M. Representatives were present from several States A committee was appointed to select a location. This committee, after visiting several places in Tennessee, Georgia, and North Carolina, chose Monteagle, Tenn , and a charter was secured The Assembly is undenominational, unsectional, and to be managed for the pecuniary benefit of no one It is under the control of a board of trustees elected annually by the members, with an equal number from each Christian church represented in its membership. There are about a hundred acres, which have been laid out into parks, drives, and building-lots. A children's temple and large amphitheatre have been erected by the Assembly There is a good restaurant, and a large hotel. Monteagle is on the top of the Cumberland Mountains, between Nashville and Chattanooga, directly on the line of railroad owned and managed by the Tennessee Coal and Iron Railroad Company The altitude is twenty-two hundred feet above the sea. The nights are delightfully cool The Assembly grounds extend to some of the grandest mountain scenery in America Three Assemblies have been held, — 1883, 1884, 1885. In no year have there been less than twenty States represented. The Assembly work at Monteagle comprises two features, — summer-schools and the Assembly proper The people of Nashville and Memphis, Tenn , and the people of Mississippi, have erected and furnished large buildings for the free lodging of teachers in their secular schools, who will attend Monteagle These buildings contain nineteen or twenty rooms each Similar buildings are soon to be erected for the States of Georgia and Alabama. These "teachers' homes" are very popular. The course of instruction is broad and liberal The members of the "C. L. S. C." in the South have erected a Hall of Philosophy at Monteagle, in which they hold round-tables and other meetings The camp-fires have been kindled for several years at Monteagle Dr. James H Carlisle of Spartanburg, S C , was the nominee of Monteagle Branch of the "C. L S C ," and was at their request most gladly appointed one of the "counsellors" by the "C. L. S. C." authorities. The Assembly and schools open June 30, in 1886; the schools continue six weeks. The Assembly closes Aug 26 R B Reppard, Esq , of Savannah, Ga, is president; and Rev J H Warren of Murfreesborough, Tenn , chairman of the executive committee.

MONTEREY, CAL.

A State Sunday-school Convention was held in 1879 at Pacific Grove, Monterey, and the "C. L. S C." of California began its history. Rev. C. C. Stratton, D D., was made *president;* Rev. Joseph H Wythe, D D, *vice-president,* and Miss Lucy M. Washburn, *secretary* The California class of 1883 numbered six hundred members The Assembly of 1880 was largely attended The Southern Pacific Railroad Company had purchased Pacific Grove, building a commodious hotel in the grove, and so reducing railroad rates, both for passengers and baggage, that people of even limited means could attend the Assembly. Many of the notable scholars, scientists, and literary people of the coast, lent a generous hand to the Chautauquans, and brought to the Assembly the ripe products of their scholarship. Six years have gone by since the C. L S C. beginning. Dr. Stratton has continued to serve as president, but Miss Washburn was compelled to resign on account of other duties, and Miss Mary E B. Norton was her successor for two years; she was then succeeded by Mrs Mary H Field, the present efficient secretary. "Pacific Grove" has become a city of summer homes, with graded streets, bountiful water-supply, fountains, and comforts without end The good secretary writes "Nature and art have rivalled each other We challenge the world to show such another camp-ground. Each Assembly of two weeks' duration has had fresh attractions Music, art, literature, science, and religion are all represented."

MOUNTAIN GROVE, PENN.

Mountain Grove Camp-ground, Luzerne County, Penn., is on the Sunbury, Hazleton, and Wilkes Barre Railroad, thirty-seven miles from Sunbury. It embraces thirty-four acres of land. The first camp-meeting was held there in 1872, under the direction (as it was from the suggestion) of Rev. Samuel Barnes of Philadelphia. The grounds are beautiful Years ago an effort was made by Rev Hiles C Pardoe, to give the C L S C. a place at Mountain Grove, but the plan was not carried out until 1885, when the Chancellor held a C L S C. day, and organized a Chautauqua Department at Mountain Grove; W. M. Gearhart of Danville, Penn, *president;* Mrs. S. C. Jayne of Berwick, Penn, *secretary.* The meetings for 1886 open Aug 4 The officers of the ground are : E. W M. Low, Lime Ridge, Penn, *president,* Cyrus Straw of Wilkes Barre, Penn, *secretary;* C. C. Sharpless of Catawissa, Penn, *treasurer.*

MOUNTAIN LAKE PARK.

This charming place is situated in Garrett County, Maryland, on the Baltimore and Ohio Railroad. It is elevated twenty-seven hundred feet above the sea, two hundred and forty-four miles west of Baltimore, and a hundred and forty miles east of Wheeling. During the summers of 1879, 1880, and 1881, an assembly was held at Oakville Camp-ground, Penn., and was known as "the Cumberland Valley Assembly." Later on it was removed to Mountain Lake Park. The first Assembly was held there, July 26 to Aug. 1, 1882. Dr. W. Maslin Frysinger of Balti-more is *president*, and Rev. J. B. Young *secretary;* Rev John T. Judd in charge of the Chautauqua movements and plans in connection with the park In 1883 the Assembly was in session from Aug 7 to 17. It was preceded by a summer school of theology under the direction of Rev. A. A. Wright. In 1884 the Assembly held its sessions from Aug. 14 to 29, and a "summer school of amateur photography" under the direction of Professor Himes of Dickinson College was established. It was held again in 1885, and is pronounced a great success. The lessons of the Assembly Normal Union were employed in 1885 under the direction of Dr Frysinger. The place is one of rare beauty. Its atmosphere is tonic and bracing, giving relief at once to patients suffering from hay-fever The grand mountain scenery is within easy reach. It is the Chautauqua of the Alleghanies.

PINE TREE "C. L. S. C."

The Pine Tree "C. L. S. C." at Maranacook, Me., is a summer-meeting of a few circles in the vicinity of Auburn, Me., about fifty miles from Portland, on the Maine Central Railroad. It is a public ground, appro-priated for annual use during a brief season by the various circles who constitute "the Pine Tree C. L. S. C." It was organized in Auburn, March 20, 1885. There are ten circles in the Association. The leader in the "Pine Tree Association" is J. C. Haskell of Auburn, Me.

THE NEW-ENGLAND ASSEMBLY.

The New-England Assembly, held at Lakeview near South Framing-ham, Mass., was begun in 1880. It was the joint product of the Massa-chusetts State Sunday-school Teachers' Association, and Dr. William Clark of the Framingham Camp-ground. The first Assembly was held during the last ten days of August in 1880. It is a reproduction of Chautauqua, with many of the same lecturers, normal studies, teachers, and leaders in music It has its children's meetings, its devotional hours, and has a "C. L. S. C." enthusiasm quite equalling that of Chautauqua itself. The "Hall on the Hill" is a precise reproduction of the "Hall of Philosophy" at Chautauqua, and is situated on a lofty eminence, and commands a most charming view. There are at Lakeview dormitory, cottages, normal hall, dining-hall, book-stores, and a number of tents. The New-England Assembly has been under the direction of the Superinten-dent of Instruction at Chautauqua, assisted by Dr. Hurlbut, Prof. R. S. Holmes, Rev A. E Dunning, Prof W F Sherwin, and others. In the winter of 1885-86 the Assembly Board was duly constituted; H J Darling, Esq., *president,* and T P Barnefield, Esq, of Pawtucket, *secretary* The New-England Assembly meets in July, and has the strength and en-thusiasm which are characteristic of Chautauqua. The little lake near the grounds is a pleasant sheet of water.

<h4 style="text-align:center">OCEAN GROVE, N J</h4>

A camp-ground on the Atlantic coast, six miles south of Long Branch, in Monmouth County, New Jersey. The Association is composed of thirteen laymen and thirteen ministers, and was organized Dec. 22, 1869. The grounds contain over three hundred and fifty acres, three-fourths of which are covered by a thriving grove of oak and pine. There are nearly a thousand cottages or hotels upon the grounds. An inexhaustible supply of pure water is furnished by means of artesian wells. The auditorium, tabernacle, and young people's temple are located in the edge of the grove, five hundred yards from the sea. Services varying in character, educational, reformatory, evangelical, etc, are held during the summer months. The spirit of the place is thoroughly catholic. The gates are always closed on sabbath. Ardent spirits are not allowed to be sold on the grounds, and by a special law of the State the liquor traffic is pro-hibited for a distance of one mile in all directions. The Chautauqua idea is fully indorsed, and its work enthusiastically adopted. A Chautau-qua Day was held in the summer of 1885. Several graduates of that year received their diplomas. Centrally situated between the two great cities New York and Philadelphia, it furnishes an admirable field for educational and religious work.

<h4 style="text-align:center">PARK BLUFF, IOWA</h4>

Park Bluff, Io., on the shores of the Mississippi River, thirty miles below Burlington. An "Assembly" promised.

<h4 style="text-align:center">PIASA BLUFFS ASSEMBLY</h4>

Piasa (*Pi-a-saw*) Bluffs Assembly, in Illinois, not far from St. Louis. A place of unusual beauty and promise. Dr Benjamin St. James Fry of St. Louis is *president;* Morris R Locke of Jerseyville, Ill., is *secretary.* The C L. S. C. fire has been lighted at Piasa.

Several local Chautauqua circles having been organized in Washington Territory (Rev D. J. Pierce, the pastor of the Baptist Church of Seattle, having organized the first in September, 1884), it was decided to hold a summer assembly, and a point on Vashon Island, midway between Seattle and Tacoma, was selected as the place. Rev. W. H. Reeves of Seattle is *president;* Rev. D. J. Pierce *secretary.* The point where the Assembly met on Vashon Island is the property of Rev. R. B. Dilworth, for years a welcome worker at Chautauqua A series of meetings, with special days, was held in 1885, as follows Opening Day, Public-school Day, College Day, Chautauqua Day, Science Day, W. C. T. U. Day, Missionary Day, Children's Day, Y. M. C. A. Day. Camp-fires were held each evening, bringing out much latent talent to the service.

ROUND LAKE ASSEMBLY.

The Round Lake Sunday-school Assembly, on the Delaware and Hudson Canal Railway, between Troy and Saratoga, was organized July 16, 1878, under the supervision of the Superintendent of Instruction at Chautauqua The Assembly is now conducted by the Rev. H C Farrar and the Rev. B. B. Loomis. The C L. S. C. work began at Round Lake in 1880 under the direction of Rev. H C Farrar. Recognition Day was observed in 1885, and diplomas were distributed.

SOUTHERN CALIFORNIA ASSEMBLY.

"The Chautauqua of Southern California" began in 1884, when a few enthusiastic Chautauquans met for a two-days' encampment at Long Beach, Cal, one of the most delightful seaside resorts on the Pacific coast, twenty miles south of the city of Los Angeles. A meeting was held in 1885 "The Acropolis crowning that famous height of ancient Athens, overlooking the waters of the Ægean Sea, was not regarded with greater pride by the native Athenian than is our pavilion or amphitheatre by our native Chautauquans, crowning as it does the bluffs of the mighty Pacific, and overlooking the ruins and the dreamland of the Montezumas. Here as nowhere else in the United States do January and July continually smile on each other. Here at eventide the devout Chautauquan chants the hymn of his Alma Mater, —

> ' God bless the hearts that beat as one
> Though continents apart ;
> We greet you, brothers, face to face,
> We meet you heart to heart.' "

The *president* is Prof. G. R. Crow, and the *secretary* Rev. S. J. Fleming

WASHINGTON COURT-HOUSE ASSEMBLY.

On the camp-ground owned by the Methodist-Protestant Church, near Washington Court-house, O , an Assembly was established, the first meeting having been held in August, 1885, under the direction of Dr. J. E. Gilbert, now of Indianapolis.

III

THE BANNER.

THE Banner of the C. L. S. C. represents so much that is precious to the loyal members of the institution, that I take the liberty to insert the address of presentation delivered at Chautauqua on our first Recognition Day in 1882

The Banner is carried in the annual procession at Chautauqua, and the "flag" is handed under the keystone of the arch of the Golden Gate during the passage of graduates

" The banner presented to the C. L. S. C. on Commencement Day is a rich and costly thing. It is made of heavy blue silk, gold fringed and tassseled, mounted on a mahogany staff, with a metallic head and star On one side of the banner is a faithful painting of the Hall of Philosophy, and the legend, "Chautauqua Literary and Scientific Circle," with the three class-mottoes beneath. On the other side are applied two silk handkerchiefs, the souvenirs of many journeys in foreign lands, on which are painted a cross and an open Bible. It bears also the device, "C. L. S. C., organized A. D. 1878." This valuable and beautiful standard is the gift of Miss JENNIE MILLER, daughter of President LEWIS MILLER. Another item added to the long list of Miller benefactions to Chautauqua "— *Assembly Daily Herald*.

On the silk flag, which Dr A. D. VAIL presented to the C. L. S. C, are inscribed the names of the principal localities in which the flag was placed, or waved, or washed, during its long pilgrimage.

At 2 P. M., Aug. 12, 1882, the Amphitheatre was crowded to its utmost capacity ; and, after a brief devotional service, Rev A. D. VAIL, D D., was introduced, and read —

The Story of the Banner.

There was a time when the C. L. S. C was in embryo, when it lay, like another Minerva, in the uneasy brain of our great Zeus of Chautauqua. Many were the workers who were commissioned by him to weave the garments and to fashion the adornments of this yet unborn goddess. It was made my task to provide materials for a banner, to be borne on great festal days at the head of processions, and to be hung on the walls of the new Parthenon. As I was to go abroad on a long journey, four years ago, Dr. Vincent came to me with the wish that I would purchase for him some silk suitable for a banner, that I would have it inscribed with the name and mottoes of the Circle, and then made the earnest request that I would bear it with me all through Europe, Egypt, and the lands of the East. As it is no easy thing to stand against his will, I accepted his commission, and I am here to-day to tell " The Story of the Banner."

His plan for the new reading circles embraced all fields of literature and art, history and science, language and travel. And it was his fancy to have a banner that had floated over all the great historic lands and seas, that had saluted the great centres of education and philosophic thought, that had been sprinkled with sacred waters, and rested on the great shrines of religious devotion and reform, — a banner that should be as wide and varied in its associations as the course of reading he was then mapping out for your use.

In this Hall of Science it is doubtless my duty to make a clear and definite statement of certain very commonplace but quite material facts as to the origin of this banner. Failing to find in London or Paris a large piece of silk of the size desired, I adopted the happy thought of using smaller ones that I knew could be recolored and cut into letters or devices, and combined into artistic forms, and finally arranged on a larger piece manufactured in New York. I purchased two of these in London from a package of Chinese silks, and two others in the bazaar of Damascus. These pieces I could easily and always carry with me, and use them in the most sacred and crowded places without attracting attention, as I could not have done with the large inscribed banner. Afterward I obtained from our Syrian dragoman a most beautiful and valuable possession, a silk American flag, 3x4½ feet, which had twice made the tour of Europe, Egypt, and the Holy Land, after once having passed over this continent in the Centennial year. Afterward and in our company, and for the most part in my possession, it was borne from Alexandria to Upper Egypt, through Goshen to Suez and to Mount Sinai, back through the lands and over the seas of the present Eastern struggle, from Port Said to Joppa, and thence through Palestine to Damascus, to Cyprus, Rhodes, and along the coast of Asia Minor to Constantinople, from the Bosphorus to Athens and through Greece; then to Sicily and Naples, and so through Europe, the flag was my inseparable companion. After I had gained the consent of my will to make a present of this precious treasure to to the C. L. S. C., from that time forward, no slave of the ring was ever more true to his master than was I to the fancy of Dr. Vincent. Sometimes with tears, and sometimes with laughter, now in open exultation, and now with carefully observed secresy; frequently with the affected pity of my companions, but always in memory of the doctor's request, often when it was a burden, but far oftener when it was a joy, — I used the flag, until I passed into the hands of Dr. Vincent what was to me the dearest memorial of the long and happy months of my journey. Once more I salute the dear old flag whose presence stirs so many happy feelings and memories, and whose folds now bear the names of so many of the places visited And now I ask you in fancy to form one of the party of travel, with the understanding that you be not asked to go where some part of the banner has not been before you

And now what shall be the order of our journey? It would be easy to give, in chronological order, a list of the places visited ; but this would be only a list of names, and history has not followed the highways of travel or passed through one land before visiting the next With the flag we sought chiefly to visit the places made famous by great deeds or great men, to stand at the fountain-heads of history, and to be associated with that which has marked or measured the world's progress So I shall follow a plan that will bring us in order to the great *countries, races,* and *nations* visited, and shall then speak chiefly of the places seen that are famous in the intellectual history of the race, either as marking the originating or moulding forces in the developments of philosophy, art, literature, reform, and religion, hoping that in this way the banner may become associated in your minds with the noblest things in the history of the world

And first we touch the soil of the three historic continents Starting from Brundusium, once the terminus of the old Appian Way, and then, as now, the great Eastern port of Italy, we leave Europe, and after four days' sail we land in Africa at Alexandria From Egypt we cross over at Suez into Asia, and within a few days have raised the flag over the three great continents of the Old World At the same time we have associated with the three great divisions of the Caucasian race that sprang from the family of Noah The Italians represent the Indo-European or Aryan branch, of which the old Greeks and Romans were the highest development. We trace in every branch the great race characteristics that Dr. Schliemann assured us he has found in the earliest art and civilization of old Mycenæ An industrious, inventive spirit, an effort to realize high ideal forms, a special honor given to woman and religion, mark the descendants of Japheth In the Sinaitic peninsula we meet the children of Shem, in the Bedouin of to-day, a race that reached its highest development in the Hebrew and Assyrian branches of old The Jew, while caring little for philosophy and science, gave us the very highest development of government and religion The Assyrians were fond of science and the industrial arts, and gave us the most varied, massive, and richly ornamented buildings of the world, quarrying and moving masses of stone that would task to the uttermost our modern science and art In old Egypt we find the children of Ham living among the oldest known historic monuments, and in the land of their fathers Thus early has the flag touched the springs of history, at its continental and race origins.

And with the flag in hand we salute the great nations of the past as we walk among the ruins of their cities and civilizations From the summit of the Pyramid we look down upon more than forty centuries of history, on the oldest art and civilization of the world. We wander among the old temples and tombs ; we trace the old inscriptions, we handle the old papyri and the famous Rosetta Stone, that, like a key, unlocked the mysteries of the hieroglyphics, we listen for the music of Memnon's lyre, and fail to catch the secret of the Sphinx; we go to the old quarries and turquoise mines, into the heart of the Pyramid, and among the Apis tombs; and in the museum of Boulak, so rich in old remains, we live over again the old Egyptian life, even of that before the times of Moses.

And now we handle the old Babylonian bricks, and the older remains of the libraries of a people who were the teachers of the Greeks; we wander among the old Assyrian slabs, and the winged human-headed lions; we even handle the records of their old philosophies and astronomical observations, that were the wonder of Alexander the Great. We see copies — impressions in the brick — of the hymns used by the Chaldean priests, and that might have been heard by Abram himself in old Ur; and we see with wonder the story of the fall of man and of the deluge written in these strange dialects, that are far older than the exodus. And now we salute the old Phœnicians, whose masons and builders aided King Solomon, and who left their peculiar marks on the foundation stones of the walls of Jerusalem, eighty feet underground, and lately discovered, after being buried 2,800 years, — a wonderful proof of the genuineness of the Bible record.

Next we visit Greece, the land of art and eloquence, of beauty and song. Here in Mycenæ we salute the heroes of the Iliad, and the first growth of Greek life when the Hebrew and Phœnician were at their best. And, returning from the scene of Dr Schliemann's important discoveries, we pause on the site of the great Greek games, we unfurl the flag and salute the host of great men that were accustomed to gather on these memorable grounds. Here the great poets and historians first gave to the world the works that have made them immortal. Here Euripides, Sophocles, and Thucydides were crowned. Here gathered travellers from all nations, and nowhere else in the Old World were such audiences gathered to do homage to the men of genius.

We pass on to the shores of the Bosphorus, and witness in fancy the crossing over of the Greek army under Alexander the Great, that conquered and Hellenized the Asiatic world, so that the literature and laws of these lands were henceforth in Greek. The conquest of the language was far more important than that of the mere cities and armies, for this great language became one of the most important of the providential preparations for the coming of Christianity, and the rapid spread and triumph of the universal religion of Jesus Christ. We go onward to the Roman Forum, and, amid the ruins, we rest near the site of the golden mile-stone that marked the centre of the Roman world. Here we stand, and see in fancy, from Augustus to Constantine, the departure and return of the legions, the growth of the Roman power, the majesty of the Roman law — until within three hundred years Rome has become Christian, and the standards of the army give higher honor to the cross than to the eagles of victory.

With Constantine we pass over to Byzantium, the famous capital of the Eastern empire that remained so long after the break-up of Rome. And now the great nations crowd thick and fast; the map changes like a grand kaleidoscope; and we can but salute them as we pass from one part of Europe to another, and recognize the great debt of gratitude we owe them for their part in history But in passing we may say, that, looking over the Synchronological Chart of Universal History since we have been here on these grounds, we find that we were able, with the flag, to touch some monument or ruin, the writings or work of some prominent man, of nearly every century from the age of the Ptolemies in Egypt to our own time But my limited time forbids even the catalogue of the names, and we pass to the great centres of intellectual activity, the originating points of the great educational forces in the world's history.

We are in Athens now, and stand, with flag in hand, at the prison where they locate the confinement of Socrates, where he reasoned with his friends on duty, the soul, and immortality, and then so calmly drank the hemlock No wonder that the men of his times so hated and caricatured the man who exposed their follies and the fallacies of their false religions and philosophies. No wonder that this strong, brave soul has been the admiration in all ages of those who love the true and beautiful and good We go over to the groves of the Academy where Plato taught his lofty ideal philosophy, that had such a profound influence for ages on religious and speculative thought. And just as we pass here from the Amphitheatre to the Hall of Philosophy, so there we could pass from the Academy to the Lyceum, where Aristotle, the Stagnite, the most logical and systematic of the philosophic thinkers of Greece, taught his methods of deductive reasoning, that for two thousand years guided the investigations of men in every realm of speculation and study.

From Athens we visit Rome, Alexandria, Byzantium, Pisa, Paris, Frankfort, Geneva, Worms, Oxford, the centres of the philosophic systems of later ages, but all using the Aristotelian categories and dialects, until we come to Francis Bacon and the beginning of the seventeenth century, and here we salute the man who led the way to a new method in the study of nature His inductive philosophy, his method of reasoning from facts to laws, really worked a revolution in every branch of human thought and investigation, and was the beginning of our present period of philosophy and science

But let us pass on to notice the outworking of the intellect in art, in its efforts to interpret and fix in beautiful form the thoughts and harmonies of the soul We stand on the Acropolis of Athens, and salute the ruins of the Parthenon and the surrounding temples that give to us the highest expression of Greek art, especially of its great ruling ideas of repose, finish, completeness, and perfect beauty In the galleries of Rome, Florence, Paris, and London, we find the works of this age which must ever be "the despair of the artist and the admiration of the world" In the Vatican we infolded with the flag that old torso that taught Michael Angelo the possibilities of marble, and led the way to that most wonderful period of the Renaissance In St Mark's of Venice, St Peter's of Rome, Milan, Strasbourg, Cologne, Rouen, and in scores of the great cathedrals, we walked with reverence, and laid the flag on many an altar and shrine, realizing how much the world owes to Christianity for its noblest architecture, sculpture, painting, and music. And still more do we feel this truth as we go back to the low, flat, plain basilicas of the first thousand years of the Church But, when the foolish prophecies of men as to the world's destruction had proved false, then, in the first centuries of the second thousand years of Christianity, nearly all the great cathedrals were commenced, the high hopes and aspirations of Christianity break the bud all over Europe, and their broad, high, cruciform plans, their heaven-reaching spires, their combination of perfect beauty and strength, their immense size, all unite to express their magnificent faith in the permanency and universal triumph of Christianity.

At Geneva, Worms, Bonn, Heidelberg, Lyons, Paris, London, Oxford, Eton, and, dearest of all, at Rugby — the Rugby of brave Dr. Arnold — we recalled the work of the masters, and the immense influence of these schools of learning. We laid the flag on the grave of Polycarp at Smyrna, and of Jerome in Bethlehem; and we stood by the reputed burial-places of Athanasius in Alexandria and of Ambrose in Milan, the real Christian fathers of the whole Church. We waved the flag with thankful joy in the Cathedral at Worms, where Luther made his brave defence; and once again on the plaza in its front where one hundred thousand of the noblest and best of all Germany, a few years since, had gathered to the dedication of the great Luther monument raised to him and to all the reformers that had made possible the great Reformation And in Geneva, in remembrance of the catholicity of the C. L. S. C., and with a sort of foreknowledge of the coming "substantial agreement of Calvinism and Arminianism," we saluted with equal deference both Calvin and Arminius. At Stratford we touched with the flag many of the things connected with the early life of Shakspere, and saluted Burns and Scott in the places they have made famous And then, as on sacred shrines, we laid the banner on the graves of John Knox and John Bunyan and John Wesley, the great heroes of religious reformation.

While not failing to recognize the great leaders of thought along the ages, we have yet to name the greatest of all Standing far above the Athenian Academy and Lyceum was the school of the greatest teacher, and on the summit of Mars' Hill, where Paul taught of "the unknown God," and preached "Jesus and the resurrection " His writings have had far larger audiences, and have affected far more profoundly the world's thought, than all its other human teachers He was familiar with the schools and their philosophies, and he brought to the exposition and defence of the gospel all the power of human culture, and on the hill overlooking Damascus, where he was converted, and in Rome, where he died, the flag did honor to his memory.

But the intellect of man has done some of its noblest work in the service of reform, and it was a great pleasure to stand on the spots made memorable by heroic devotion to principle and duty We touched many an early Christian inscription in the Vatican, and laid the flag in a newly opened martyr grave in the catacombs. We sprinkled it with the waters of the spring of the Mamertine prison, where Paul was confined We saluted Cranmer and Huss, where they suffered, and the brave, generous spirit of Joan of Arc, where she was burned in the market-place of Rouen. We unfurled the flag along the region where Constantine had his vision of the cross, and saw the letters of fire, *In hoc signo*, and rested it over the copy of the Magna Charta in the British Museum. The flag infolded, in Jerusalem, the sword of that brave knight of chivalry, Baldwin the king; it rested on the coronation chair, where so many of the English kings have been crowned, and on that anointed stone wrought into its seat that has such a wonderful history; on Pilate's stairway, where the Reformation turned as on a pivot; in the cell of the martyr-monk, Savonarola of Florence; and before the statue of Reuchlin, the scholar of Germany, who made possible the translation of the Bible by Luther; before the statue of Wilberforce in Westminster. We stood with flag in hand to do honor to these great souls, and the movements they so grandly represented.

But in religious aim and work the world has had its noblest manifestations of intellectual activity and power. Chautauqua is Christian; and it will be a pleasure for you to feel that the banner has been associated with the places mentioned in the word of God. We start with the flag at "that hour and place where history was born;" and from Goshen to Suez, where God's people crossed the Red Sea, on the shore where they sang their song of triumph, at Marah and Elim, and up into Mount Sinai, the mount of God, where he gave the law, we follow the steps of Moses. We stand at the Jordan, where the Israelites crossed over, at Shiloh, where the tabernacle rested so long; on Gerizim, where, witnessing the Samaritan passover, the flag was reddened with the blood of the passover lamb that was slain that night; from Dan to Beersheba, in Hebron and Bethlehem, on the rock of the temple and Mount Zion, in Gethsemane and the holy sepulchre, on Calvary and the Mount of Ascension. In every place the flag was used with solemn, prayerful love.

Thence we passed over the places consecrated by the struggles of the early Christians, visiting the sites of several of the first churches, until we stood again in Rome. Here, on the Arch of Titus, we trace the signs of the fulfilment of Christ's prophecy of the destruction of the temple and the holy city; a little way beyond we find the Coliseum that witnessed the heroic martyrdom of so many of the early Christians; and over on the other hill were the gardens of Nero, through which he drove at night by the light of the burning martyrs, whose robes were saturated with oil and pitch; and now, on this very spot, stands the grandest Christian church of all the world. Not far away we bow on the very spot where the kneeling priests received the papal blessing, as they were being sent forth, the first missionaries, by Gregory the Great, to heathen Britain. And here and there in streets in sight of the Vatican we salute half a score of small, unpretentious chapels that represent the great Protestant missionary societies of the world that have come to Rome to stay, and, especially our own St. Paul's, that may yet become the real patron saint of Rome, as Methodism has had a marvellous growth in that and all the great cities of Italy.

Thenceforward we cannot separate Christianity from the history of human thought and progress. It seemed to burst, like the flames, from a score of points at once, and in scores of places we saluted the rising, spreading, conquering spirit of the cross.

Once again we stand on the shores of Alexandria in Egypt, the place that so lately witnessed the massacre of the unoffending Christians, and now, as we hear the sound of England's guns, we ask, may not this be the beginning of the end of the dark, cruel power and rule of Mohammedanism in Egypt and the lands of the Bible ? There, on that very hill-side where the shot and shell were so destructive, once stood the old Serapeum ; and, standing there with the old flag in hand, I recalled that famous night of history when the Roman general, waiting for the imperial orders to destroy that greatest heathen temple of the world, heard, in the midnight, a ringing " Alleluia," that to him was the divine assurance of the final triumph of Christianity over paganism   Would that behind the shouts of men over the victory of the English fleet we might hear the grand ringing " Alleluia" of the spiritual hosts that watch and wait for the final triumph of Christianity that should betoken the speedy destruction of Mohammedanism !

Such, in brief, is the " Story of the Banner" and its associations, which, with such beautiful and varied forms, you have adopted as your own   We do not hold that the banner is either classical or sacred because of its associations. But, with many, its history will give to it a special value, and it may fitly symbolize the great movement it represents   If this C L S C. course of study has not added to your culture as specialists, it has followed the older and better idea of the Greek Academy and Lyceum, that made far more of that broad humanistic culture of the whole man, than of the education that was mainly special and professional. These Halls of the Grove and of Philosophy are doing, in their way, not the work of the colleges, but one that is beyond their reach ; and these " Athenian Watch-fires " are signals to the coming time of the possibility of a true literary education for the men and women who work and are too poor or too busy for the long and special courses of collegiate study   It has already brought joy to thousands who have once drank at the true Pierian spring, and felt the quenchless thirst for knowledge, but knew not how or where to gratify it

Dr. Vincent, I have filled my commission to the best of my ability ; and I now commit the banner to your keeping, which, like Noah's dove, has at last found a resting-place inside of the ark of the C L S C., that bears so much of precious freight and hope for the future of the Church and the Nation.

Printed in the USA
CPSIA information can be obtained
at www.ICGtesting.com
CBHW072237160424
7065CB00014B/204